A PLUME BOOK

THIS IS HOW WE DO IT

"How do working mothers pull it all off? Carol Evans knows. This terrific read highlights the pitfalls to avoid and spells out successful strategies every working mother should steal."
—Soledad O'Brien, coanchor, CNN's *American Morning*

"This book is not just a survival guide for today's working mothers, but an invaluable handbook for today's leading organizations. The challenges of attracting and retaining talent warrant more flexibility and a demand for innovative child-care. A must-read for companies large and small, this book is a secret weapon to winning the talent war."
—Ted Childs, vice president, Global Workforce Diversity, IBM

"Finally, a book for working mothers that is a page-turner. This book counters common wisdom with unique insight and research findings, and is filled with helpful advice. It is jet-propelled by Carol Evans's delightful and honest stories about herself and other mothers, and most of all, by her joy in being a working mother."
—Ellen Galinsky, president, Families and Work Institute, author, *Ask the Children*

CAROL EVANS is the CEO and president of Working Mother Media, which includes *Working Mother* magazine and the National Association for Female Executives, and is the country's foremost expert on working motherhood. A trusted advisor to Fortune 500 companies—including IBM, S. C. Johnson, Procter & Gamble, and American Express—she has appeared on *The Today Show*, *Good Morning America*, *The Early Show*, CNN's *American Morning*, PBS, Marketplace radio, CBS radio, and dozens of regional and local television and radio programs. She also speaks regularly at conferences, women's groups, and companies, addressing audiences nationwide on issues ranging from balancing work and home to corporate support for working families.

After beginning her career at *Working Mother* in 1979, Evans left after ten years to become president of Stagebill, Inc., and COO of Chief Executive Group. She then returned to acquire *Working Mother* magazine in 2001, becoming the first woman and mother to own the publication in twenty-two years. During her tenure as the magazine's publisher, Evans helped develop the celebrated Working Mother 100 Best Companies initiative, which has been published for twenty years. In 2002, she launched the Best Companies for Women of Color, and in 2006, the Working Mother Best Small Companies.

Evans currently serves on the boards of the Advertising Women of New York (AWNY), March of Dimes, Young Playwrights, and IMAG, the independent magazine division of the Magazine Publishers of America. She has received many awards, including the Legacy Award from Families and Work Institute, YWCA Women Achievers, *MIN* magazine's "21 Most Intriguing People" in the media industry, WICA Woman of the Year, and the Women's Venture Fund's Highest Leaf Award, for demonstrating exceptional vision and risk-taking.

A successful working mother herself, Evans lives in Chappaqua, New York, with her husband, Bob Coulombe, and their two teenagers, Robert and Julia Rose.

THIS IS HOW WE DO IT

The Working Mothers' Manifesto

CAROL EVANS

A PLUME BOOK

PLUME
Published by Penguin Group
Penguin Group (USA) Inc., 375 Hudson Street, New York, New York 10014, U.S.A.
• Penguin Group (Canada), 90 Eglinton Avenue East, Suite 700, Toronto, Ontario,
Canada M4P 2Y3 (a division of Pearson Penguin Canada Inc.) • Penguin Books Ltd.,
80 Strand, London WC2R 0RL, England • Penguin Ireland, 25 St. Stephen's Green,
Dublin 2, Ireland (a division of Penguin Books Ltd.) • Penguin Group (Australia), 250
Camberwell Road, Camberwell, Victoria 3124, Australia (a division of Pearson
Australia Group Pty. Ltd.) • Penguin Books India Pvt. Ltd., 11 Community Centre,
Panchsheel Park, New Delhi – 110 017, India • Penguin Group (NZ), 67 Apollo
Drive, Mairangi Bay, Auckland 1311, New Zealand (a division of Pearson New
Zealand Ltd.) • Penguin Books (South Africa) (Pty.) Ltd., 24 Sturdee Avenue,
Rosebank, Johannesburg 2196, South Africa

Penguin Books Ltd., Registered Offices: 80 Strand, London WC2R 0RL, England

Published by Plume, a member of Penguin Group (USA) Inc. Previously published in a
Hudson Street Press edition.

First Plume Printing, May 2007
10 9 8 7 6 5 4 3 2 1

Ⓟ REGISTERED TRADEMARK—MARCA REGISTRADA

The Library of Congress has catalogued the Hudson Street Press edition as follows:

Evans, Carol, 1952–
  This is how we do it : the working mothers' manifesto / Carol Evans.
     p.   cm.
  ISBN 1-59463-030-5 (hc.)
  ISBN 978-0-452-28816-4 (pbk.)
  1. Working mothers.   I. Title.
  HQ759.48.E88   2006
  306.874'3—dc22

                                               2005035732

Printed in the United States of America

This book is dedicated to my beloved mother, Agnes Lange Evans, who was a great mom and a great role model for working mothers. She felt the joy of working motherhood deeply, and shared it with everyone she met.

Acknowledgments

Many people helped to transform this book from a dream into a reality, but no one was more instrumental than Christine Larson. Christine is a renowned journalist who has written extensively for the *Wall Street Journal* and several women's magazines and business journals, and she is the author, with Mary Claire Allvine, of *The Seven Most Important Money Decisions You'll Ever Make*, a book I highly recommend.

Christine did extensive research and writing for this book, including but not limited to: conducting numerous interviews, culling through twenty-six years of *Working Mother* issues for interesting stories, and examining the applications of the 100 Best Companies for examples of excellent support for working moms. In extensive discussions, Christine and I laid out the structure of the book, and throughout the year Christine kept me on track with my weekly writing assignments and to-do lists.

As if this was not enough to contribute, Christine went above and beyond the call of duty by becoming a working mother during the year that we worked together on this book. When we first started to collaborate, Christine was married, but not a mother. Soon after we began our work, Christine became pregnant with twins, and on July 10, 2005, her twin boys, Alexander and Zachary Larson Rojo, were born. They were several weeks early, but they were healthy boys, and in the few weeks that they were in the hospital, Chris made a heroic push to help get the book into final form.

I greatly appreciate Chris's strategic thinking, her organizational skills, her attention to detail, and her tremendous work ethic. Without her collaboration, this book could not have been written.

I also thank Tammy Palazzo, Director of Partnerships at Working Mother Media, who believed in me when I said, "Tammy, I want to write a book about the joy of working motherhood!" Many people would have laughed at the idea of layering this task on top of everything else we need to do to keep Working Mother Media going, but Tammy made it happen by shaping my grand idea into a concrete proposal and bringing us together with our dear friends at Hudson Street Press.

I hired Tammy in 2003 when she was nine months pregnant, which must be a record of some kind. She knows firsthand that company support can make a real difference in women's lives. Tammy's enthusiasm and knowledge of book publishing has been key.

The entire family at Working Mother Media made huge contributions as well. Barbara Rosenthal, my assistant, was tireless in tracking down names and keeping me organized for the book. Susan Lapinski, the editor in chief of *Working Mother* magazine, and her crew contributed their ideas and contacts and can-do attitude at every turn. Each employee gave me encouragement, and Joan Sheridan LaBarge, our publisher, made it possible for me to give attention to the book by doing such great work on the magazine.

Past editors, especially Vivian Cadden, Mary McLaughlin, Andrea Burtman, Susan Seliger, and longtime former editor in chief Judsen Culbreth created the concepts and strategies that are the foundation of this book, through years of dedicated service to *Working Mother*'s readers.

Laureen Rowland, the publisher and founder of Hudson Street Press, was intrigued by the idea for this book, and by Tammy's proposal. She said she was interested, but needed to see a sample chapter or two right away. Since I was leaving with the family for a two-week vacation in Italy, I took her request with me, and wrote the first two chapters on my BlackBerry on gondolas, open-air buses, and high-speed trains in Venice, Florence, and Rome. Somehow, in those BlackBerry installments, Laureen saw the power of what I wanted to say, and she has been our guiding light ever since. I appreciate her patience, as so many life incidents conspired to delay this book, as you'll learn in the following pages. Most of all I appreciate her keen editing, which sharpened the book without causing it to lose its personality.

I want to give very special thanks to Steve Tunney, Bryan Mitchell, Michael Rhodes, Sam Rubenstein, and all the wonderful people at MCG Capital Corporation, the investors behind Working Mother Media. They believed in the magazine, and had the visionary idea that it should be owned and operated by a working mother. They gave me the resources and the support to grow and strengthen our company and our mission, which provide the foundation for this book. Without Steve Tunney's tenacious belief in my work and in our future, _This Is How We Do It_ could not have been written.

The Working Mother 100 Best Companies, and the entire community of work life professionals have been instrumental. Each of the 100 Best Companies has a worklife champion—or two or three—who has helped me more deeply understand what it takes to be one of the best. Thank you for sharing that knowledge. And each has a dedicated person who spends untold hours filling out _Working Mother_'s complex application for the 100 Best, where we get so many of our examples of best practices. Thank you for your stalwart dedication! The work life professionals who advise companies, communities, and government on how to support working families have been very generous with their thoughts, ideas, and research. Thank you!

My mom, Agnes Evans, was beyond excited about this book, and I am heartbroken that she did not live to see it published. She would have loved curling up on her favorite blue couch, book in hand, her trademark smile a mile wide. She would have told all of her many friends, and the Daughters and Sons of Agnes (her former students) all about it many times over. She was one of my biggest fans. To my beloved dad, Willard Evans, and my dear brothers, Scott and Randy, and their wonderful wives, thank you for your strength, especially when we lost Mom. It was a terrible time softened by your love.

To my husband, Bob, and my teenagers, Robert and Julia Rose—thank you for putting up with a full year of the book! As Julia has said, "My mom had work-life balance all figured out . . . until she decided to write a book about it." Yes, the book about work life balance threw off all of my systems for maintaining sanity, as I glued myself to the couch for five or six hours of writing every Saturday and Sunday morning for a year. I even had to give up my usual Saturday morning meetings at Weight Watchers and gained five very unnecessary pounds. The garden had its ugliest year, the house needs major attention, and I'm sure I owe Bob a dinner or two at his favorite restaurant—or maybe a round of golf—to make up for lack of attention this year. But it was fun reading the chapters out loud to my family, and I know I could not have written a word of it if they didn't provide such great material, and such wonderful support.

Finally, I'd like to acknowledge the readers of *Working Mother* magazine. For the last twenty-six years, *Working Mother* has relied on you—our 2.5 million readers—for your ideas, questions, stories, insights, and for your tremendous willingness to share with each other. You write us passionate letters and helpful e-mails, you respond to our surveys, you make our reader panels a rich source of ideas and information. You grace our covers and share your secrets of how *you* do it. I have incorporated your wonderful stories and your wisdom into the pages of this book, and I thank you deeply for your contributions.

If you are not yet a subscriber to *Working Mother* magazine, please join our large extended family by going to www.working mother.com. I look forward to furthering this conversation in the pages of our beloved magazine.

Contents

THIS IS HOW
WE DO IT

"But We *Are* Doing It!"

Fifteen years ago, I was lying in the starkly lit delivery room at New York University Hospital, *supposedly* ready to give birth to my second child. But as push came to shove, I felt about as ready as a kindergartner taking the SATs. It was like a first birth for me because my son, Robert, had arrived three years before in the blur of an emergency C-section, without a single contraction to prepare me for his arrival six weeks early.

This time, my new OB—the well-known and very strict Dr. Livia Wan—had promised she would get me safely to my due date. She had delivered more than three thousand babies throughout her career, and felt I could deliver this one full-term and without surgery. I wanted to believe her, and as my tummy grew to the size of a state fair blue ribbon pumpkin, I grew ever more confident in her judgment.

It was mid-December, and I was two days from my due date— perfect timing—when the contractions started at midnight. We dropped three-year-old Robert off at our friends' house and drove in a light, swirling snowfall to New York City, an hour away from our home in Chappaqua, New York.

At the hospital, I spent seven hours sleeping between contractions, when suddenly a tidal wave of pain hit, causing me to flail my arms, tear an IV from its mooring in my hand, and send the early-morning shift into a whirl of action. I remember hearing a young intern urgently calling Dr. Wan to the scene, warning her that I had achieved full dilation in one Olympian sprint.

The fear that gripped me increased as Dr. Wan entered the delivery room and a hush descended. She was ordering the nurses about in her staccato voice when a brilliant idea suddenly struck me. Instead of struggling with the fear and pain of impending delivery—what if I just went home?!

In that moment of panic and confusion this seemed like an entirely rational request. So I summoned my powers of persuasion, honed by years in sales, to get Dr. Wan to agree to my plan. In between pushes that grew increasingly intense, I used my remaining breath to shout, "I can't do it, Dr. Wan. . . . I want to go home. . . . I really can't do this!" I truly believed I could convince the stern-faced doctor to let me quit pushing and leave the hospital. "Let me go home," I yelled. "I can't do it!!"

Dr. Wan immediately stopped her work and looked directly into my eyes. "But Carol," she said with a big, cheerful grin, "you *are* doing it."

Of course she was right. I *was* doing it. In fact, I *had done* it. "Push!" she barked, and I did. That last effort was no more difficult than the rest of the journey, and Julia Rose, my eight-pound two-ounce black-haired beauty was born moments after my crisis of confidence.

Dr. Wan placed the baby on my chest and said, "See? You *were* doing it."

We *Are* Doing It

Today, as CEO of *Working Mother* magazine, I'm often asked how in the world we working mothers manage to juggle motherhood and career, life and work, self and job. And I always think of Dr. Wan. Because sometimes being a working mother feels overwhelming, and some days we're convinced we just can't do it. We want to yell at someone, "I *can't* do it!! I want to go home!"

And then I see Dr. Wan's smiling face in front of me saying, "But you *are* doing it!" And I realize that *we are*. Twenty-six million mothers—more than 71 percent of all moms in the United States today—work full- or part-time. We raise strong and happy kids. We fuel the economy. We earn money that keeps our families safe and secure. And we get a ton accomplished in a day at work.

Still, most of us draw a blank when friends and family ask us, "How *do* you do it?" Nine times out of ten we laugh (or cry) and say, "I don't know. I just *do*." But in our hearts, we know that response doesn't do justice to the real answer. How *do* we do it? We do it with old-fashioned elbow grease, with humor, with sleepless nights. We do it with the help of family and friends who pitch in, with great babysitters and caregivers, with husbands who learn how to support us (or not!). We do it by cramming more into a weekday and into a weekend than should be humanly possible. We do it by finding confidence in our own choices. And increasingly, we do it with the support of our workplaces.

As I write this, working mothers are about to face a once-in-a-lifetime opportunity to change the way companies work. Employers may not want us to know it . . . but companies are going to face a massive shortage of employees that will last for decades as huge numbers of baby boomers begin to retire. In the next decade, companies will become more and more desperate to find and keep great employees at all levels, so it's a perfect time to tell them exactly what we need. It's time for working moms to step back, take a breath, and ask ourselves, What works for us? What can be done personally and professionally to make our lives easier, our work more productive, and our families happier? What are the most effective ways for our companies and communities to support us?

It Seems Like Yesterday

For more than twenty-five years, I've been passionately engaged with these questions, ever since I helped launch a visionary new magazine, *Working Mother*, which recognized very early on that the model of the American family was changing and changing fast. In 1979, a small but passionate band of editors started telling the stories of the 16 million moms who were then holding down jobs and starting careers at the same time that they were having their babies and raising their kids. From our earliest issues, we explored how working moms pull it off. We published their stories and we championed their lifestyle. And we heard about their needs.

In those first years, we got letter after letter from readers bemoaning companies that offered no maternity leave, bosses who would not give an ounce of flexibility, and communities without quality child-care centers. Moms were desperate for support and *Working Mother* was desperate to speed the rate at which companies were changing their practices and policies. Vivian Cadden, our founding editor, devised a plan to help companies understand what moms need—and to reward companies willing to lead the charge. Using a carrot, rather than a stick, Vivian planned to give an award to those companies that were making their workplaces family-friendly, gaining the attention of the corner office along the way.

"CEOs understand competition," she told me. "Let's ask CEO Jim to compete against CEO Joe to see how well their companies support working mothers."

Thus the first Working Mother Best Companies list was launched, twenty years ago. That first year only thirty companies qualified for the award—but the list soon grew to forty, fifty, seventy-five, and then to the Working Mother 100 Best Companies. We've been measuring companies, holding them accountable, asking them to improve, and giving them guidance on what moms want every year since.

In 2005, on the occasion of the platinum anniversary of the list, Ted Childs, IBM's chief diversity officer and the architect of the world's most progressive family-friendly policies, called the Working Mother 100 Best Companies an "American icon," and said, "Our country cannot prosper without women in the workforce, and our society cannot go forward unless women have children."

His words reminded us of the ultimate reason it is so critical that we get the support we need.

The Working Mothers' Manifesto

In honor of the platinum anniversary of the Working Mother 100 Best, I commissioned a survey to find out exactly what moms want *now* so we can chart the next twenty years of working motherhood. Socratic Technologies, a renowned research firm in California, fielded the <u>What Moms Want</u> survey in 2005 by asking more than five hundred working mothers from all across the country and in all kinds of jobs about the details of their lives: who cares for their kids, how much do they spend on child care, how does having children affect their ambitions and careers? What strategies work? What kind of support do women get from their companies and communities—and what kinds of support do they most desperately crave? The findings of this survey provide a strong foundation for this book.

I also examined twenty years of information from the Working Mother 100 Best Companies, and spoke with work-life experts about what innovative steps companies are taking to truly help working moms, and how moms can persuade *their* companies to hop on the family-friendly bandwagon. And of course I had at my fingertips the remarkable stories, big thinking, and practical tips from the hundreds of writers and dozens of editors who have made *Working Mother* magazine a beacon of support and solutions for twenty-six years.

But let's face it, when it comes to advice, the tidbit someone shares with you while you're shopping for shoes, or the postpartum advice you hear from a mom who's been through it, is the stuff we really need. While our survey, our articles, our Best Companies and our experts reveal the basic principles that working mothers live by, it's the stories of real moms that really show *how* we're doing it. In those stories lie the infinite variety of strategies used every day by moms who combine the love of a family with the rewards of a career.

In response to my "CEO Mom" column in *Working Mother* magazine, I get lots of e-mails from readers who want to share their ideas (carolevans@workingmother.com—e-mail me!). I talk to working mothers in the doctor's office, on the plane, at the Ragamuffin Halloween parade in my town. I get to speak to moms at our reader breakfasts, through online panels, and at dozens of conferences and events that I host or attend. I'm constantly inspired by their deep understanding of the issues and the creative solutions that make their lives more sane . . . and more joyful.

That's why this book needed to be written. Not just to tell *my* stories, funny and crazy, sad and jubilant, but to tell *all* of our stories. To share the secrets of how we do it, to acknowledge our doubts and fears about all that we have taken on our shoulders, to reveal our pride and to trade our personal solutions. To make clear to the world why we do what we do, and to ask our companies and our communities to give us the support we all need.

This Is How We Do It is for all of us who *are* doing it, but want to do it better. It's also for those millions of women who haven't yet added "mother" to their résumés, so they can chart their own courses for the most exciting decades of their lives. As we learn from each other throughout these pages, we find our own ways to be the *best* moms we can be, and be the *best* in our careers as well. Because we *are* doing it . . . and here's *how*.

Chapter One

We Have a Secret: "I'm a Mother First"

I always knew that I wanted to be a mom, from the time I began babysitting at the age of eight right up to the night when my water broke, waking me from a deep sleep—six full weeks before my due date. Two days before my husband, Bob, and I were scheduled to take our first Lamaze class. Five days before our planned excursion to Ben's Baby World on Fourth Street and Avenue A in New York City. Two weeks before we would have passed the safety date when our baby's lungs would be able to inflate properly. And only ten hours after I had said good-bye to the last guests at a luncheon at *Working Mother* magazine. At three o'clock that afternoon, Dorothy Cameron, our number-one salesperson, had said, "Carol, you look tired. Maybe you should go home." So I did. But I didn't have the faintest inkling that my life as a working mother was about to begin.

I had been at *Working Mother* magazine since its very inception in 1978—nine years before I would qualify as a reader! I was a salesperson working in the Chicago office of *McCall's* magazine when word came down that Vivian Cadden, the executive editor of *McCall's*, had convinced the all-male management team that a new demographic had emerged and needed its own magazine. Vivian was a grand woman, a friend of Eleanor Roosevelt and the wife of Joe Cadden, a New York politician and union organizer. Vivian had searched through every women's magazine in 1978 and hadn't found a single article devoted to the needs of America's fastest-growing demographic: mothers who worked outside of the home. She proposed that we test a magazine to serve the then–16 million women who were balancing home and job.

I understood the idea deeply. My own mother had ventured into the workforce when I was twelve years old. She had not worked, except as a tireless church volunteer, since the day she was fired from her job as head dietician at a big Chicago restaurant. She was five months pregnant with my older brother, Scott, and in 1950 any company could fire you just for being pregnant. Fourteen years later, my father was changing jobs and we needed extra money, so they decided she needed to go back to work.

She didn't feel prepared to return to a professional position, so she applied for a job to manage the high school cafeteria. But there was a teacher shortage at the time and the principal of the school persuaded her to *teach* cooking instead of actually cooking. She was qualified—she had a bachelor's degree in restaurant management and a teaching degree—but she was scared.

I didn't know why she was getting a job and I didn't know why she was scared, but as time went by, I noticed that she became stronger and more confident. Having her teach in *my* high school had its drawbacks, of course. My mother was perhaps the world's most gregarious person—she never met a person she didn't like or want to know better. Since she was so friendly, *everyone* in school knew her, and she had embarrassing habits like laughing loudly in the hall, and hugging the janitors to thank them for helping her keep her industrial kitchens sparkling clean. All in all, though, her new career was a happy experience for my two brothers and me. We had more privacy and independence, and we got to stay home alone after school, which we loved. So, when I went out to sell the first ads in the first issue of the fledgling *Working Mother* magazine, it was easy for me to explain the new market of moms who were changing the very structure of the American family—forever.

My first sales call for *Working Mother* was a doozy! Being the new kid on the sales team, I had been assigned the worst account in the country for *McCall's* magazine, our parent publication. Gerber Baby Products had refused to advertise in the magazine ever since *McCall's* had published an article by Ralph Nader about the dangers of salt in baby food. None of Gerber's marketing people would take my calls, even though their nutritionists had agreed with Nader and changed all the recipes to delete salt. So, being young and foolish, I picked up the phone and called the CEO, John Suerth.

"Mr. Suerth," I said, "we're introducing a new magazine that I believe you and your company should know about. Do you realize that thirty-two percent of all mothers with babies are working today?"

As it turned out, Mr. Suerth was so eager to learn about this new audience that he invited me to drive two hundred and fifty miles to Fremont, Michigan ("Baby Food Capital of the World," said the welcome sign) to present the magazine to the entire Gerber sales force—the following day. We didn't even have a sales presentation yet. No matter: I wrote our first sales pitch that night in my hotel room and gave it to four hundred Gerber salespeople at a luncheon the next day. They fell in love with the magazine and became our largest advertiser.

Thus began my love affair with *Working Mother* magazine. Seven years before I had my own first baby, I moved to New York from Chicago to manage this brave new publication for a brave new mother. A seismic shift was taking place in motherhood—one that would grow and endure and become, for many American women, the way to find economic strength and some level of equity with men.

Welcome to Working Motherhood

Despite the fact that I had spent years talking, presenting, and creating a magazine for mothers, I still wasn't prepared for the shock of motherhood when I had my son in 1987. The absolute, unmitigated truth that I know above all else is this: Motherhood changes everything. Forever.

My first preview of the ups and downs of motherhood came in the delivery room right after my emergency C-section. The nurse called out my son's Apgar score to the doctor, "He's a ten!" she said triumphantly. Then she paused. "No, wait. He's a six. No, he's not breathing! Doctor, we have an emergency!"

They whisked him away and I slipped into a drugged slumber. A few hours later, I woke up in a hospital room by myself, instantly panicked about the fate of my son. A volunteer came into the room with a Polaroid that shocked me deeply. "Your baby boy is very sick," she said flatly. I remember, nineteen years later, exactly what she looked like—mean and scary, like a witch who wanted to eat my baby and was disappointed that he was skinny and sick. But, in fact, it was Baby Boy Evans (we'd had no time to name him) who looked scary. He had a huge needle sticking out of his head and one in his foot, a mask over his eyes, and his scrawny arms were strapped down as if they'd been worried he would hurt someone. *Watch out for that little bruiser in the corner incubator!*

I stared at the Polaroid and thought, "He's my baby, my own teeny-weeny, very sick baby, somewhere under all that apparatus." And I fell back to sleep.

Meet Me in Maternity

Back at the office, an emergency of quite a different nature was well under way—one that quickly initiated me to the frenetic juggling act of working motherhood. Good old McCall Publishing Company, which had done absolutely nothing interesting for more than one hundred years (except to launch *Working Mother*), was abruptly sold to an entrepreneur. And not just any entrepreneur, but a fierce competitor: Dale Lang, the owner of rival magazine *Working Woman*. I was devastated. How could it be that just when

I was actually going to experience motherhood, I might lose my now-so-appropriate job?

At the time, I thought it was a horribly unfair coincidence that a personal and a professional crisis would hit at the exact same time. Now, of course, I realize I couldn't have had a more fitting introduction to working motherhood! I was juggling dual emergencies from day one.

Two days after my emergency C-section I called Dale Lang. Unwilling to leave my son's side, I suggested Dale come up to the hospital to meet with me. But Dale, it seemed, wasn't keen on hospitals. In fact, he was so eager to avoid a trip to the maternity ward that we struck a deal: I wouldn't ask him to the hospital again . . . and he offered me a raise and promotion, making me publisher of *Working Mother*.

Three days later, as a brutal January storm descended on New York City, Bob and I left our son, whom we finally named Robert, in the Neonatal Intensive Care Unit and went home without him, a sad and lonely feeling if ever there was one. For the next few weeks, I couldn't worry much about work: I had enough to cope with—hailing taxis in three feet of snow for my daily trek to the hospital with Rose, my mother-in-law; talking to Robert through the opening in his incubator; encouraging him to learn how to nurse, one very weak suck at a time. Gradually, Robert gained strength and overcame his many medical issues, and we were allowed to bundle him into the much-too-large sweater that Rose had knit for the occasion. Handling him like a china doll, we brought him home to start our new life together.

I'm a Mother First

The very first test issue of *Working Mother* included a wonderful feature entitled "I'm a Mother First." Eight years after the article was published, I finally understood its message as I held my fragile new baby in my arms.

Men, it seems, have historically needed (or been content) to put work first, fatherhood second. Women are different. Even the most dedicated female worker goes through an astonishing and shocking identity shift from woman to mother when she gives birth. She falls so deeply in love with her child that even her husband, who was such an important person in her life just weeks before, can seem superfluous at times. Attitudes shift, and the primary force of motherhood asserts itself at every turn. The realization that you would indeed throw yourself in front of an oncoming train to save your baby's life creeps over you, and you stand in awe of motherhood's power.

Although the people in my office would not have known it, I struggled mightily with leaving Robert to go back to work. It's not that I didn't want to work. It's just that the time at home was too short, and the expectation of my ability to perform at the job was unrealistically high. No one's expectations were higher than my own, and I returned to work after just eight weeks off to begin my journey as a working mother in earnest.

As if I needed to understand all the possible challenges of being a working mother, I was given lesson after lesson during Robert's early years. One day, when he was nine months old and seemed to be doing great, I was giving an important presentation to a group of buyers at an ad agency. The receptionist suddenly rushed into the meeting and thrust a note into my hand: "Your babysitter needs to speak to you—*Urgent*."

I used the conference room phone and learned that Robert had had a seizure. Sandy, our babysitter, had rushed him to the doctor. I explained to the group that I had an emergency and left. I was out the door in less than two minutes.

As I anxiously hailed a cab to get to the hospital, it struck me just how completely Robert had become the most important thing in my life. It had stolen over me gradually, without me even noticing. I still loved my job, but it wasn't even a close second to my child. Over the past months, I'd finally been initiated into the secret of working motherhood: No matter how much we love our jobs, we're mothers first.

The 26-Million-Mom Secret

To say that we're mothers first may sound completely obvious. What could be more fundamental than a mother's primary commitment to her child?

But for moms who work, this has often been a silent truth. It's not something we say at the office: an openly "mother-first" attitude can negatively affect our careers at some companies. If bosses or coworkers (even other mothers!) think a woman is too mommy-oriented, they begin to feel she won't be reliable in a crunch, won't want to take on demanding assignments, won't be able to keep up with those who don't have such heavy obligations. So many of us have to keep our secret to ourselves.

One mother, who worked at a large publishing company, said the unspoken rule for mothers at her company was never to mention children.

"A man slips out to see his kid's baseball game, and everyone thinks he's a hero," she recalls. "But if a mother does the same thing, people think she's not committed to her job." Eventually, she left the company to launch her own business.

Ironically, we keep our secret—that we're mothers first—in order to protect our children. Like the earliest Neanderthal moms, we know we have to protect ourselves to keep our children safe. Once that might have meant fighting off tigers. But today, it means safeguarding our economic well-being by protecting our jobs and careers.

Wake Up and Smell the Baby Powder

But with 26 million of us in the workforce, does being a mother first need to remain a secret today? It clearly made sense when working mothers were a rare species around the office. But now it's more common for mothers to work than to stay home. A whopping 71 percent of mothers with children under age eighteen have jobs or careers. And 57 percent of all mothers with babies under age three are in the workforce.[1] It seems we should be able to proudly admit that we're mothers first—and loyal, dedicated workers, too.

Even though working motherhood is the norm, most companies and communities still treat us like we're the anomaly, not the majority. According to the Society for Human Resource Management (SHRM), just 13 percent of companies across the country offer paid maternity leave (beyond short-term disability insurance). Only 20 percent of companies nationwide offer child-care referral services. The vast majority of companies still act like their employees are all men who have stay-at-home wives. That's not even helpful to most men these days, let alone working moms.

But companies are a lot like middle-aged men who won't throw away that ratty, too-tight pair of college sweatpants. Sometimes it's hard to realize that comfortable old styles just don't fit anymore.

The modern company evolved in the early twentieth century, when most workers were, in fact, men with wives at home. Even though only a small minority of the workforce lives that way today, some companies have been slow to wake up and smell the baby powder. But the idea of men working full-time while moms stay home is actually a relatively recent notion.

Rosie Really Riveted

In *The Economics of Women, Men, and Work*, the economist Francine Blau points out that in colonial America, mothers—along with fathers and children—worked hard on the farm and contributed mightily to their families' economic well-being. Work and family fused together naturally for many families.

But when work began to shift off the farm and into factories, work and home life separated, and it became practical for moms to stay home with the children. (Middle-class moms, that is; low-income, minority, and immigrant mothers often continued to work.) The idea of the "traditional family," with a dad who worked and a mom who stayed home, began to evolve. Eventually, many companies adopted the idea that married women couldn't and shouldn't work, and fired women (even teachers) when they got married or pregnant (like my mom).

When World War II came, moms poured into the workforce to take over jobs left vacant when men went to war. My own wonderful mother-in-law was a genuine Rosie the Riveter: her name really was Rose and she riveted canvas roofs for army Jeeps. Her husband, Fuzzy Coulombe, was shipped off to fight in France two months before my future husband, Bob, was born.

Rose went back to work just two weeks after delivering Bob, while her mother (Memere, as the French-Canadian Coulombes called her) watched the baby. But other working moms at that time took advantage of a new development: community and company-sponsored day care. The country was grateful for the important contributions of working mothers, and knew they needed every able person to work, so the federal government provided matching funds to states to encourage child care. But when the men returned, the child-care centers disappeared, and so did many mothers from the workforce. Some stayed: Rose kept her job at that same factory for thirty years.

After the war, the G.I. Bill sent many returning veterans off to college. A college education became much more common. As the standard of living rose through the decades, women began going to college in huge numbers. Once women had college degrees, they started landing more interesting jobs . . . jobs they didn't want to leave when they married and had kids. Periodic labor shortages drove companies to hire more and more women as they struggled to fill their employee ranks. A huge shift was taking place, and by 1975, 34 percent of mothers with children under age three worked. By 2002, some 60 percent did.

But regardless of the wildly changing demographics, much of the corporate world still hasn't changed. And with employer expectations grounded in old traditions, we often keep quiet that we're mothers first—or mothers at all.

Keeping Quiet on the Home Front

Strangely enough, being mothers first also isn't something we have talked about much at home. If we try to explain to our neighbors and friends how we work hard at our career but that we always have our children's interests first—regardless of other commitments and obligations—we suspect that behind the sympathetic head nodding lies a sinister dialogue that would pain us deeply if we listened in. "Oh, *sure*, you're a mother first. Then why is Gretchen in your house ten hours a day taking care of your children . . . wouldn't you be a better mom if you *really* put motherhood first?"

While almost no one actually says this to our faces, we frequently feel a rebuke in the air when we discuss our jobs or careers. Because our communities, too, cling to the idea that a good mother stays home. That may explain why most PTA meetings take place during the day, why mothers' groups meet for afternoon coffee, and why schools still have long summer breaks without corresponding summer care. That may explain why the media constantly rehashes the old debate about whether child care is bad for children, when the overwhelming evidence is that high-quality child care is actually good for them. No wonder half of the moms in our <u>What Moms Want</u> survey said they felt isolated in their own communities.

Why the Heck Do We Do It?

With the lack of support at work and in our communities, and the nonstop battering we receive in the press, why do we do it? Why don't we just throw in the towel and stay home, or "opt out," as the *New York Times* writer Lisa Belkin put it? A few of us already have: the percentage of working mothers with infants dropped from 59 percent in 1998 to 55 percent in 2002, according to the Census Bureau. But the majority of moms do go back to work, despite the stress and guilt and unspoken criticism we receive.

Many of us do it because our families need our income, whether we have high salaries or not. In fact, the most common reason our readers give for working is money. In our <u>What Moms Want</u> survey, 85 percent named money as one of the most important reasons why they work.

Tammy Palazzo, *Working Mother*'s director of partnerships, repeatedly told her young son, Thomas, that she had to go to work to make money. On his first visit to our office, Thomas looked around, baffled, and asked, "Where's all the money, Mommy?"

In my own family, our two-income status let us buy a house in the suburbs, pay for gymnastics, buy toys (lots and lots of toys!), travel modestly for our vacations, host my family at Christmas, and so on. Everything about our lives requires more money than I ever dreamed it would—and more than either Bob or I could make alone. And yet we have never had a fancy lifestyle. I began to out-earn Bob just before Robert was born, making some of my decisions about work even more deeply rooted in money.

Sometimes working mothers are accused of being overly materialistic. We feel the silent reproach—"You could get by on one income if you really tried." In the 1960s, families survived on one income—before plasma TVs, multiple cell phones, and McMansions. But the fact is, for most of us, having two incomes doesn't mean we can buy whatever we want or live in our dream house.

Harvard professor Elizabeth Warren and her daughter Amelia Warren Tyagi studied tens of thousands of families and found that working mothers' incomes usually go toward mortgages, not luxuries—especially toward houses in neighborhoods with good schools. In other words, most of us are working so we can give our children the education and opportunities they'll need to make their way in the world. A mother's income can make the difference between decent and substandard schools, between being able to help our kids with college or saddling them with decades of debt, between saving for retirement or risking our well-being in old age. When mothers work, we provide our families with an economic foundation that allows us to feel comfortable and secure.

I hear from readers at every income level who are proud of and dependent on the income they earn to achieve their lifestyles. They may wish for more, but they are proud to be responsible for what they have. And by staying in the workforce when their kids are young (even when child care eats up most of their income!), they are able to keep up their earning power, making a big difference as their families mature.

The Pride of the Lioness

For several years we ran a feature in *Working Mother* called "Why Do You Work?" We heard a variety of answers, but many contained a common thread: pride.

"My heart is in research . . . it's contributing to something that will make a big impact," Dulce Ponceleon of Palo Alto, California, a researcher at IBM, told us.[2] She knows her pride in her work sets an example for her daughters, Emma, eight, and Sofia, four.

"I'm proud to be a pioneer," says LaShun Lawson of Bowie, Maryland.[3] As the first African-American woman to hold a professional position with the Atlanta Braves and now as an executive with a subsidiary of the NFL Players Association, she's broken barriers . . . and inspired her son, Kendell, age eleven. "My son has told every little boy in his class what I do," LaShun says.

Pride and satisfaction came close behind money in our survey of why moms work: 76 percent said they worked to use their talent and training, 73 percent said they worked for the satisfaction involved, and 62 percent wanted to be a role model for their children.

I don't mean to romanticize working motherhood: not all of us have jobs we love. And even when we do, the joy and pride don't always outweigh the guilt and the challenges of balancing our various work-life responsibilities. But many, many of our readers tell us their work brings them a great deal of satisfaction. In one survey we did of four hundred readers in 2004, 75 percent of working mothers described their lives in positive terms—they said they were fulfilled, productive, organized, challenged, and motivated. "I believe that many of our kids actually do better—they have higher self-esteem and are more independent and social. I also believe that my two boys are growing up learning that women can do anything—I'm hoping that will make them great husbands!" reader Ilyssa DeCasperis, a labor representative from Staten Island, told us.[4]

Packing for the National Guilt Trip

In the summer of 2001, in one of the most satisfying career moves of my life, I acquired *Working Mother* magazine with MCG Capital, an investment group, and formed Working Mother Media. Just weeks after the acquisition, I was invited to go on CNBC to debate whether moms who work outside the home could be good mothers. I couldn't believe that this debate was still going on: twenty years earlier, I had debated the same topic on television.

Rather than continue to debate working motherhood, what if we working mothers instigated a national conversation about how working mothers have positively affected and influenced our society and country? For the past two decades, one president after another has taken credit for the astounding growth in our nation's buying power and productivity. But I believe the true credit belongs to working mothers. Imagine, just for a moment, what would happen if all mothers in the country suddenly decided to stay home. Overnight, more than 26 million jobs would become vacant. The economy of the United States would instantly grind to a standstill. There would not be a financial institution, a hospital, a school, a television station, or a pharmaceutical firm that could continue to function.

Now imagine if families stopped spending the earnings that

working mothers make. According to the Bureau of Labor Statistics, mothers who work full-time contribute $476 billion a year to the household income of our families. And according to Mediamark Research, in 2005, working moms spent a phenomenal $94.8 billion on new cars, $16.5 billion on clothing, and more than $26 billion on vacations. And let's not forget just how many tax dollars we pay on our purchases and our income. Working mothers keep our government in business too.

A few other facts worth noting:[5]

- Nearly half of all working women (49 percent) are mothers.
- 47 percent of women professionals and managers are mothers.
- 49 percent of women business owners or partners are mothers.
- 47 percent of women in top management are mothers.

So you'd think companies, government, and communities would all celebrate the contributions of working mothers. But instead, much of our society chooses to tag along on what I call the National Guilt Trip.

All Aboard!

The National Guilt Trip is what happens when you take 26 million working mothers and put them into offices and communities that cling to the concept that men should work and moms should stay home. It's a deep cultural contradiction that plagues all of us—moms, dads, kids, bosses, companies, and communities. On the one hand, mothers need to work: our families need our income, companies need our labor, and the economy needs our spending power. But on the other hand, deep down, nobody really likes the idea of mothers being away from their children for ten hours a day, five days a week—especially the mothers. The whole country feels guilty about it.

And we're paralyzed by the contradiction. Instead of making

changes, many companies and communities have ignored the paradox and failed to give us the support we need. Most schools still have half-day kindergarten and policies that drive working parents batty; in every state it costs more, on average, to send a four-year-old to child care than to send a student to public college; many companies refuse to consider flexible work options.

The Guilt Department

Nearly every working mother I have ever met has felt plagued by guilt. ("I'm so used to feeling guilty that I blame myself for the weather some days," one young mom told me.) In the very first issue of *Working Mother* we introduced a monthly feature called "The Guilt Department." We interviewed hundreds of readers about guilt, and our editors wrote from their own intense experiences. "The Guilt Department" was our most popular feature for fifteen years.

"When I'm at work I worry that I am not with my baby, and when I'm at home I worry that I am not prepared enough for tomorrow's classes," wrote a teacher to the *Working Mother* editors in 1980.

We didn't foresee that guilt would still be a prime emotion for our readers twenty-six years later.

Not that there aren't guilt-free working moms. A high-level advertising executive I know scoffs at the idea of guilt. "I have a great family, and a great job," says this mother of a three-year-old boy, "and I feel fulfilled in both roles. I love this life. Don't saddle me with baby boomer guilt!" she said to me over lunch.

Based on my discussions with moms around the country, however, she seems to be the exception. More typical is a young media director, Samantha Muchmore, whom I met in San Francisco three years ago. The first time we talked, her daughter, Elsa, was nine months old. Samantha had been back at work for five months. She was deeply surprised at the painful emotions she was feeling about leaving her baby with an au pair.

Samantha was in her early thirties, and had risen to the top of her profession through a killer combination of brains, determination, and style. She had thought that it would be a straightforward transition from executive to executive mom, but instead she found herself weepy and confused. She contemplated quitting her job, but deep inside she felt that if she did, she would regret it and would not be able to regain her position. So she toughed it out.

I recently called Samantha to ask her how she felt now that she had two children, Elsa, now age three and Flynn, age one. Her powerful emotions were still giving her a ride, but she had started using the flex program offered by her company, Foote Cone & Belding, and found that a four-day workweek eased some of the guilt, if not the workload. I was delighted to hear that Samantha's hard work and dedication to being a great mom and a great media director had been noticed: her company had nominated her for the Advertising Working Mother of the Year award, a top honor bestowed on successful working moms by the Advertising Women of New York (AWNY) and *Working Mother* magazine.

Gallery of Guilt

My own personal guilt stories could fill the rest of this book. I still cringe at some of them. When Robert was three, I'd taken a new job at *Stagebill* magazine. Arthur Levitt Jr., my powerful boss, called me at home one Saturday while Robert and I were coloring at the kitchen table. As I started to write down the name of someone Arthur wanted me to call, Robert fell off his chair with a thunk. I screamed and hung up on my boss. When Arthur found out that Robert's little arm was broken from that fall, he must have felt guilty, too: he almost never called me at home again.

Over the last nineteen years of working motherhood, I have personally experienced nearly every type of guilt imaginable. Here are my top-ten personal guilt moments. (Just try to top them!)

1. My son's teacher calls to say he's failing math and asks if there's anything going on at home that might be upsetting him.

2. The school nurse calls to send my daughter home from school and I can't leave the office to get her.

3. I fail to buy the holiday gift my son most longs for because I can't stand in line for two hours.

4. I argue with my daughter about her study habits and she says, "How would you know? You're never home!"

5. I go to parent-teacher night at school and don't know anyone because I've never been to a PTA meeting (they take place at 9:30 a.m. on weekdays).

6. I'm late for my son's important moment—he's finally pitching the game—because my boss asks me a totally inane question as I'm rushing to leave a few minutes early. I could say, "I have to leave!" but I don't. Now I can never make up that loss.

7. I go with my daughter to the dry cleaner on Saturday and the owner says cheerfully, "Oh, so little Julia does have a mother!"

8. The stay-at-home mother I meet says, "I used to have a great job too, but when Timmy was born I just couldn't bear to leave him with a stranger."

9. An old family friend says, "I don't understand why you don't just quit your job. Your children must need you at home."

10. An urgent business trip lands on my son's sixth birthday and I have to go. He's too old for us to pretend it is not his birthday, and too young to understand that this is out of my control.

What, Me Worry?

I doubt if most companies really understand how damaging guilt is to employee performance, and how much they could do to ease that guilt by offering programs like phasing back gradually from maternity leave. Of course, we'll always feel guilty about something. But our guilt volume doesn't have to be cranked up to eleven *all* the time: when companies put the right programs in place, we can turn it down to a four or five. Just imagine how much stronger you'd feel at work and at home if you could dial down your guilt level even a little bit.

For the past twenty years, *Working Mother* has sought out cutting-edge companies that really give working moms the support we need. And we've found programs that could help lessen the guilt in every situation I've listed above:

1. When their kids are having problems at school, employees at the pharmaceutical company GlaxoSmithKline, based in Research Triangle Park, North Carolina, can take advantage of seminars about dealing with tweens and adolescents. And Prudential Financial, headquartered in Newark, New Jersey, offers a free 24/7 counseling hotline to advise parents of teenagers.

2. When kids are sick, the financial services group Ameritas Acacia, headquartered in Lincoln, Nebraska, provides in-home nanny services.

3. To help employees find that most-wanted gift at the best price without leaving the office, American Express provides a free online shopping portal that gives special discounts for employees and makes shopping faster and easier.

4. Your child can't say you're never home if you work for the insurance company Allstate, based in Northbrook, Illinois, or the Wilmington, Delaware–based pharmaceutical firm

AstraZeneca, and use their popular work-from-home option.

5. Parents at First Horizon National Corporation, a financial services group based in Memphis, Tennessee, can stay in closer touch with their kids' progress in school thanks to Lesson Line, an automated phone line with updated assignments and announcements.

Programs like these won't solve all our problems, but they can provide us more tools and fewer reasons to feel guilty. As to that old family friend—just smile and say, "I hear you."

Or you could listen to the words of wisdom that came from Soledad O'Brien, the CNN anchor, who gave a keynote address at our recent WorkLife Congress. A member of the audience asked her how she coped with all the small moments that she missed out on when she was traveling the globe assigned to big news stories. Her response was beautiful: "Remember, they are just that, small moments, and your life with your child will be filled with millions of them. Be happy," she said, "not guilty." And for that small moment, five hundred women in the room felt a weight lift from their shoulders.

Help Us Help Our Families

At companies like those I just mentioned, our secret is out. These firms, and many others that we write about in the magazine, understand that we *are* mothers first, whether we put our family photos on the desk or not.

For twenty years, we've been publishing our most important feature of the year, the Working Mother 100 Best Companies. For a complete list of these wonderful companies, go to www .workingmother.com. Because these companies assume that family needs are an important part of life, they're creating cultures of parenthood, where parents are encouraged to talk about their children.

At S.C. Johnson & Son, a manufacturing company in Racine, Wisconsin, the company's on-site child-care center e-mails pictures of kids to parents' computers throughout the day.

And at Avon, a company where 73 percent of employees and 53 percent of managers are women, you can see what business culture will be like when women run more companies. When a visiting manager from Avon's Europe division nervously asked a colleague how to break the ice at a dinner with Avon CEO Andrea Jung, his colleague replied, "Ask her about her kids."

Okay, I don't expect your average CEO to make small talk about toddlers instead of touchdowns any time soon. But those companies that have invested in a culture of parenthood are finding that the right programs can increase retention, decrease absenteeism, and create a more stable, productive workforce.

For years, we working mothers have kept our secret—that we're mothers first. It's been a beautiful secret, one that has fed us and sustained us. We working moms have made enormous strides by simply knowing that certain things are not negotiable.

But now, the time has come to reveal our secret: We *are* mothers first. *And* we're brilliant, valuable, committed workers. If we admit our secret collectively and ask for the changes we need, using the strategies outlined in this book, our entire society may finally be able to hop off the National Guilt Trip. And all of us—families, companies, and communities—will be the richer for it.

Chapter Two

We Alter the One-Size-Fits-All Career Track

When I was in college I worked as a waitress at the Round Barn in Champaign, Illinois. I'm pretty sure I was the worst waitress in town. My timing was disastrous. I'd forget to ask if you wanted a drink before taking your dinner order. I'd bring you dinner before you had utensils. But I got great tips because I was very happy to hear about your bad day at the office or your granddaughter's piano recital.

I had the same poor timing with my career. Father Time seemed to be enjoying a good laugh at my expense: I always seemed to be in the wrong job at the wrong time. When I started my first ten-year stint at *Working Mother*, I was single. For seven years, I gave presentations about working mothers to thousands of people based on my mother's experiences, research on our readers, and my vivid imagination.

Then, at the very moment I became a mother—just when I could finally talk as an insider about the needs of working moms—*Working Mother* was acquired by our archrival, and suddenly my job was at risk. I had to prove myself all over again to new bosses and new owners, while managing the critical health issues of my premature baby boy.

Father Time wasn't done with his little joke yet. A great new job opportunity came along when I was pregnant with Julia Rose. I had a chance to become head of *Stagebill*, a theater magazine owned by the hugely successful businessman Arthur Levitt Jr., who was the chairman of the American Stock Exchange, and later served as chairman of the United States Securities and Exchange Commission. The job would be a giant step forward: I'd work directly for the owner, one of the most powerful men in the country, and I'd have an ownership stake. It would also mean lots of travel and many nights out at performing arts events. The timing seemed terrible.

From the start, I told Arthur that I was pregnant. He saw the challenge, but offered me the job anyway. We were on the corner of Park Avenue and Fifty-second Street, near his office in the Seagram Building, when we sealed the deal.

"Carol," he said, "I'd be crazy to offer you this job when you're five months pregnant."

"Arthur," I said, "I'd be crazy to accept this job when I'm five months pregnant."

Without another word we shook hands. I started my new job three weeks later. Arthur and I traipsed up and down Manhattan meeting with clients. He was amazed at how often I had to go to the ladies' room, but he waited patiently as his pregnant publisher visited all the best restrooms in town.

Great job, yes. Bad timing, definitely. I thought I would take advantage of *Stagebill*'s rich cultural opportunities as Julia and Robert finally got old enough to go to a few child-friendly shows. What was I thinking? One night at the New York State Theater, Robert stood up in the middle of the New York City Ballet's world-renowned *Nutcracker* and whined at the top of his lungs, "Mommy, this is the l-o-n-g-e-s-t movie I've ever seen!" The entire row of Japanese businessmen sitting in front of us turned to stare.

Three years after this incident, just as the kids started to love the theater, I took a new job as chief operating officer of Chief Executive Group, which publishes a business magazine for CEOs. Can you think of anything *more* boring to kids? Robert and Julia never did understand what a CEO was, and they certainly didn't care that I was lunching with Prime Minister Goh of Singapore or entertaining the CEOs of Intel, Cisco, AT&T, and hundreds more each year. Now I'm back at *Working Mother* again, and my teenagers are on the edge of adulthood. I've got a great business plan for a new teen magazine, but with my luck, I'll be launching it when they turn thirty!

If Only Father Time Were a Mother . . .

I'm not the only working mom flummoxed by Father Time's sense of humor. (No wonder they call him Father Time; Mother Time would have cut us a little more slack.) The traditional career track puts our child-raising and career responsibilities on a head-on collision course. Just when we're becoming really good at our jobs and ready for more responsibility, our child-raising duties emerge—or skyrocket.

The real problem, of course, isn't Father Time. It's the traditional career ladder that trips us up. According to conventional wisdom, first we pay our dues in thankless jobs in our twenties. Then we make a big career push in our thirties, winning promotions and raises and doing whatever it takes to climb onto the fast track for career success. During this midcareer push, we're supposed to work long hours, take part in demanding training programs, and get specific kinds of experience that make us stand-out candidates for future leadership roles.

Depending on your field, that midcareer push might mean pulling all-nighters to please clients, taking the shifts no one else wants, transferring to a new city, volunteering for extra assignments, or going to school at night for an advanced degree or certification. For Debra Relf, an East Chicago, Indiana, special ed teacher and administrator, it meant earning two master's degrees and an education leadership license—while raising her daughter Ariel, now eight, as a single mom. Debra's midcareer push has led to a career she adores that lets her make important contributions: "I love working with students, teachers, parents," she says. "A lot needs to be done in education . . . and I feel I have the skills to make those things happen."[1]

But that push also left Debra—and most working moms on a traditional career path—with simply too much to do at home and at work. We work full days, then come home and give our remaining hours to our kids and families—and still feel like we're not getting everything done.

The One-Size-Fits-All Career Track

I call this collision course between kids and career the One-Size-Fits-All Career Track. And at five feet one, I know personally that "one size fits all" really means "the size that looks awful on everyone." Especially on me!

Moms like Debra Relf have done an absolutely amazing job fitting themselves to the traditional career model. But for every mom like Debra there's a mom like Tricia Robertson of South Bend, Indiana, who wrote to us for our February 2005 issue. "I have a messy house, two dogs, a cat, and one beautiful fourteen-year-old son. When I get home from work, I barely have the energy to feed myself, let alone the rest of the clan."

Moms like Tricia need new ways of working and new career models that can help them keep more energy for themselves and their families—while still being committed workers.

Unfortunately, the One-Size-Fits-All Career Track is littered with creaky old assumptions about what a committed, productive worker looks like. Many employers still assume the most loyal and valuable employees put in fifty hours a week or more at the office; that part-time workers aren't serious or loyal; that the A-team is willing to work around the clock and only the B-team goes home at 5:15 p.m. every night.

The workforce has changed radically, but these assumptions haven't, and they hurt women and families every single day. These assumptions explain why only 17 percent of companies have job-sharing programs[2] (compared with 97 percent of 100 Best Companies), and why many companies don't offer benefits to part-time workers. And they explain why women still feel torn between family and career success.

Fortunately, a new generation of working moms are making alterations to the one-size career model, creating paths that better fit the shapes of their own lives. Again and again, I hear from readers working reduced hours, taking sabbaticals, and following seasonal schedules to creatively reinvent their career paths. Some use many different strategies throughout their careers: Diane Gartner[3] of Atlantic Beach, New York, has kept her career moving ahead in ad sales at ABC Television, but continually changed her work patterns. She worked full-time after her first child was born, then stayed home with her second. After her third, she phased back with a three-month assignment for the company. In January 2005, she returned to full-time again.

Sequencing: It Actually Works

Sometimes academics call this idea of alternating intense periods of work with time off or part-time jobs "sequencing," after the title of a 1986 book by Arlene Cardozo. In the 1980s, sequencing referred to working moms taking a few years out of the workforce, then returning to their careers. But how many of us can actually afford to stay home for several years? Today we think about sequencing as a series of strategies, like working part-time for a while, telecommuting while our babies are little, or taking a sabbatical—as well as time out of the workforce.

For a while, the idea of working mothers alternating periods of less intense and more intense work raised the hackles of baby boomer feminists—including me. We feared that a "mommy track"—jobs that let moms slow down their responsibilities—would mean less respect and advancement for all women. We worried it would give managers permission to stop hiring mothers into key jobs or considering them for promotions. At the time, I found myself frequently asked to debate the issue: I argued that the "mommy track" was simply discrimination of a new and insidious kind.

Back then, I believed that the only way to succeed in a man's world was to play by a man's rules—sticking to the traditional career ladder and never asking for any slack. And for many of us baby boomers, that truly *was* the only way to succeed. We had a lot to prove back then. But now I see things differently.

What changed my mind? I've seen that sequencing actually works. In our <u>What Moms Want</u> survey, we found that more than one in four moms had taken time out of the workforce. Most (58 percent) stayed out less than a year; one-third took between one and three years off; and 10 percent took four or more years off before returning. Nearly all were able to find a job quickly when they wanted to return (71 percent found a job within three months), and a third found returning to work easier than they expected.

Most moms enjoyed the time they took off, although many worried about the lack of income or felt bored. Even moms who didn't take time out of the workforce found ways to make their careers more flexible. About 77 percent of mothers surveyed said they'd made changes in their jobs to better balance work and family. For instance, 27 percent arranged to work from home and 21 percent arranged a reduced schedule.

I'm sure that sequencing works because I've seen more and more inspiring women boldly leap off the traditional career ladder and scale the walls in other ways. For instance, Brenda Barnes, now the CEO of Sara Lee, astonished the world in 1998 when she quit her job as president and CEO of Pepsi-Cola North America to stay home with her three children. Vilified by some camps and glorified by others, Brenda became a lightning rod in the debate about whether moms should work and whether companies can count on moms to keep their grip on the career ladder. We all thought Brenda was fully engaged in her at-home life when we read that she had taken a job as president and COO of Sara Lee. Recently, she was promoted to CEO. Brenda Barnes didn't just bend the rules: she's rewriting them completely.

Another great example of a sequencing mom is Kim Nelson, the president of Snacks Unlimited at General Mills and the mother of Samantha, six, and Taylor, three. As Kim was working her way up the ranks at General Mills, she suffered a death in the family and decided to take time off for herself. An eighteen-month leave gave her space to "recommit to my job, become engaged in my community, and just breathe." Shortly after she returned to work, she learned she was expecting Samantha. "I had just come back and I had to go tell my boss I was pregnant and would be leaving again," she recalls. She feared her time-outs would cost her career progress: instead, she was tapped to manage the Cheerios brand, which led to a promotion to vice president and then to her current position.

While it's true that at some companies, working reduced hours or taking time off still carries a stigma and can slow down your advancement, these trailblazing moms show that change is taking place at progressive companies. These women are proving that full-time work for forty years isn't the only way to succeed, and staying home isn't the only alternative.

And it's not just CEOs and high-powered women who are attracted by the idea of sequencing. Nearly 6 million mothers work part-time today[4]—and many stay-at-home moms wish they had that chance. The staffing firm Aquent studied women college graduates with children and found that among stay-at-home moms, a whopping 70 percent hoped to return part-time or as interim workers. Similarly, in a survey of stay-at-home moms with Harvard Business School degrees, 61 percent said they hoped to work part-time or nontraditional hours. The demand is there—and companies are slowly beginning to meet it: today, 14 percent of professionals and managers work part-time schedules, according to the Bureau of Labor Statistics. But I believe that there is a huge reserve of women who want this part-time professional status, and that this is the next big thing for companies and moms to create together.

Today, many of the strategies that working moms are using to succeed at home and at work are technically "mommy track" solutions. But I call for a new nomenclature. I love the word "mommy"—I still sign my notes to my kids that way—but in the office, it has a condescending tone, and "mommy track" has a condescending reprimand built in. Let's not stratify mothers by whether they want to slow down. Let's not call one set mommies and the other mothers. Let's call it the Flex-Track career instead. The Flex-Track would include a variety of options and career paths, from working reduced hours to taking extended time off. It would also include corporate "on ramps"—programs to make it easier to stay in touch with the office, to keep your training and skills current, even during slower periods of your career. And it would include manager training to help make supervisors and corporate leaders more comfortable with nontraditional options.

All these things are happening already at many of the 100 Best Companies. As a result, the stigma and sacrifice associated with Flex-Track careers are starting to fade, and progressive companies are pushing the envelope on creative career paths for women.

Same Job, Different Hours

At my niece's New Year's Eve party in 2004, I met Connie Ward, a human resources recruiting manager at Avaya, a large telecommunications firm. She had given birth to her daughter Maggie, now one year old, at age forty, and told me that come Monday, she was, regretfully, planning to leave her job . . . unless her company agreed to let her shift from full-time to twenty-five hours a week.

"Maggie is growing up so fast," she said of her not-yet-walking baby. "I just don't want to miss out on these important years."

She told me she wanted to work part-time for a few years, then go back full-time. "I don't want to stay home," she said. "I love my job, my company, and my career. But I want to spend more time with Maggie."

As Connie and I sat on the floor and chatted, Maggie played at our feet, making the cutest faces imaginable. If I were Connie, I'd want to spend more time with Maggie, too.

Connie had done well in her job over the past two years and had just received another solid performance review. She figured that *more*—not less—responsibility might be offered her, but what she really wanted was a few years when she could continue to contribute to the company, stay engaged with her colleagues and the evolution of the business, but have fewer demands on her time by staying in place for a while. She would then be poised to move back into higher gear when Maggie was enrolled in school full-time.

As a boss, I know I would have been disappointed to lose Connie's stellar full-time work for a while . . . but I'd be far more upset to lose her altogether. I predicted her company would give her exactly what she wanted.

Sure enough, Connie asked for a reduced schedule—and was surprised how quickly her supervisors responded. Avaya had a very clear policy stating that they were "committed to helping employees balance career and personal obligations"—and that one way they did that was by "recognizing part-time work arrangements as viable scheduling and staffing strategies." She didn't have to wait long for an answer.

"They came right back to me within two hours and asked what type of part-time plan I was looking for!" she told me. "I felt great!"

But Does Part-time Work for Everybody?

"But that would never work in my profession/job/company."

I hear this all the time from women who feel inspired by trailblazers like Connie—but are sure their companies won't buy it. And it's true, reduced hours are more common in some industries than others: 30 percent of health-care companies offer job sharing (a form of part-time), but only 5 percent of high-tech and 4 percent of manufacturing companies do, according to the Society for Human Resource Management.

Careers in fields where you're on call 24/7 for clients—like law, consulting, and advertising—also seem particularly unfriendly for reduced-schedule workers. But don't assume your company won't go for it. Even industries like law and consulting are feeling the heat—and if they can change, other fields can, too.

When I first met Deborah Epstein Henry, the founder and president of Flex-Time Lawyers LLC in Philadelphia and New York, I was thrilled to learn that someone was paying attention to the needs of attorneys with children. Deborah, the mother of Oliver, nine, Spencer, seven, and Theo, four, started the group when she was working a reduced schedule for a Philadelphia law firm. After she had Spencer, Deborah wanted to spend more time at home, but also keep her fast-paced job in litigation. Deborah wanted some support from other part-time law moms, so one day, she e-mailed a handful of friends whom she knew were part-time attorneys and suggested they get together. She was overwhelmed by the response.

"I e-mailed six lawyers, and a hundred and fifty e-mailed me back," she told me. It turned out many lawyers were already working part-time, but not feeling well supported by their firms. Out of that one e-mail grew Flex-Time Lawyers LLC of Philadelphia, then Flex-Time Lawyers LLC of New York. Deborah's e-mail list now includes more than fifteen hundred people. The groups' monthly meetings, which address work-life balance issues for lawyers, draw up to one hundred attendees and provide networking opportunities and a forum to share information to help effect change in the workplace. Banding together with other part-timers at your work or in your industry gives moms a sense of strength *and* practical ideas they can borrow.

Reduction Therapy

Connie, Deborah, and other moms who work reduced schedules say there's much more to it than waltzing in and asking the boss to lighten up. A few key strategies to landing fewer hours:

Prove Your Worth

"The best way to find a part-time job is to take the existing job you have and build up a part-time arrangement," says Deborah. To do that, she says, you need to prove your value—again and again—before you ask for fewer hours. "It's a question of being talented enough to prove that you're worth it and that it's in your employer's economic interest to retain you."

Be Clear About What You Want

Connie understood her priorities: She didn't want to be promoted or take on more responsibility. She wanted fewer hours and she spelled it out for the company. She also knew what she'd be willing to sacrifice: she didn't mind taking a pay cut in return for shorter hours.

One of the most successful ways to be clear about what you want is to literally spell it out for your employer, by writing a proposal. Explain the changes you want, how the work will get done, and how working part-time will benefit the company (see chapter 10 for more details).

Share and Share Alike

If there's no way to get your job done in less than full time, think about a job share. When Christy Addis, an executive placement manager for Macy's West in San Francisco, told her boss she was thinking of staying home with her child, her boss, Susan Sittig, got creative. Another position in the department had come open: Susan suggested a job share. Susan called Dawn Miller, a former Macy's West logistics manager who had left in 2002 to stay home with her kids, Madeline, now ten, and Maxwell, now seven, and tempted her to take the job share and come back to work. Now, Christy and Dawn both work fifteen to twenty hours per week. The arrangement was made easier by Macy's West's Alternative Work Program, which sets out guidelines for executives who want to work part-time, job share, work from home, or use flextime.

"It's a fabulous program," says Dawn. "My job is very flexible. I work fifteen to twenty hours a week, depending on what's going on in the office and what's going on at home." Although Dawn had always intended to return to Macy's when her kids got older, the job share brought her back to work sooner. "Susan reeled me back in with this opportunity."

No Perfect Solutions

One warning about reduced-schedule work: it won't solve all your work-life dilemmas and it may present some new ones.

"It's proving to have its major positives—seeing Maggie more—and its challenges," says Connie. The big challenge: "Paring down to a workload that truly requires only twenty-five hours a week!"

And sometimes, you may have to accept that a reduced schedule or other flexible options could mean life in the slow lane for a while, unless you're at one of the progressive companies actively working to advance the Flex-Track. As a member of the advisory council for the National Parenting Association, I have been able to track the most progressive work being done in this field. The founder and researcher Sylvia Ann Hewlett, who studies "on ramps" and "off ramps" in women's careers, is dedicated to making sure the collective brain power of senior women is not lost to the world of business.

Sylvia surveyed more than twenty-seven hundred women ages twenty-eight to fifty-five who graduated college with honors or who held graduate degrees. She found that 37 percent had taken time off from their careers (an average of 2.2 years) and that 58 percent had taken "scenic routes," working reduced hours or other flexible arrangements.[5]

Unfortunately, her research showed that it can still be risky to take the Flex-Track. Once you leave the workforce, she found, it can be tough to get back in: while 93 percent of off-ramped women wanted to return to the workforce, only 74 percent had succeeded in doing that. Meanwhile, there's a financial price to pay: on average, women taking time out of their careers lost 18 percent of their earning power.

Despite these risks, many women view the trade-offs and sacrifices as short-term measures that might slow them down, but will allow them to stay on track in the long run.

That's how Melissa Robert, the director of marketing planning for American Greetings in Cleveland, sees her choice. Melissa, who has an MBA from Carnegie Mellon University, had just taken a promotion when she had her first child, Ben, in 2002. Four weeks into her maternity leave, though, she realized she wasn't ready to go back to her sixty-hour workweeks. Her boss couldn't accommodate a shorter schedule, so Melissa canvassed managers around the company until she found a manager willing to create a new position for her. She took a 25 percent pay cut and now works three ten-hour days a week.

"I'm on a plateau as far as career goes," she says. "I won't get a promotion or be considered for big jobs while I'm part-time." American Greetings says they promote based on skill and ability to do the job, regardless of work schedule, but Melissa feels in her particular job, a promotion is unlikely for the time being. For now, she and her husband, John, a project manager for a Web development firm, are comfortable with the sacrifices they're making. They've swapped their Saab for a Pontiac minivan and tightened their belts.

"I used to shop at Nordstrom, and now Target's my favorite store," she says. "My shoes are last season and my heels aren't as trendy. So what? I get to spend more time with my son." Meanwhile, she's confident she'll be able to crank up her career when the time is right. "My boss is always asking me when I'll be ready to go back full-time," she says.

Certainly, there are sometimes trade-offs to make on the Flex-Track—and many working moms like Melissa are actually glad to make them. But the best companies are offering Flex-Track options without requiring moms to sacrifice career goals, even temporarily. Janet Truncale of Ernst & Young, for example, was able to drop her hours and still stay on the fast track. In 1998, she was a manager in the accounting firm's New York office when she had her first child, Gabrielle, now seven. She dropped to part-time and has stayed on that schedule ever since. Meanwhile, she's had two more kids—Noah, five, and Freddy, two. In May 2003—the week she returned from maternity leave with Freddy—she was promoted to partner.

"A year after I went part-time, one of my clients told me, 'I'd rather have you for four days than any other professional on full-time,'" she says. "I'm really proud of the fact that I was promoted to partner in just eleven years." Typically, it might take twelve to fourteen years—or more—to be promoted to partner, even working full-time, according to Ernst & Young.

Shorter Hours for New Moms

One of the most exciting reduced-hour programs, this one specifically aimed at new moms, is "phase back" from maternity leave. Very few companies are currently offering this, but I can tell it's going to catch on: everyone who hears about it wants it! Although there are variations, this is how it generally works: A new mom returns gradually from her maternity leave following the birth or adoption of a child. The first week she comes back just one day to get reoriented. Then she works two days per week for a few weeks, then three days, four days, and finally ramps up to five days at six months. This gradual return to full-time gives the body, mind, and soul—as well as the baby—an appropriate amount of time to get back into the swing of things. Phase back from maternity leave is a tremendous productivity booster. Mom can handle the slower reentry with more confidence and more energy than coming back full-time—but out of steam—right away.

Not all moms will want this—especially those with lots of

responsibility at work—and some will not be able to afford the gradual return to full salary, but it's a lifesaver for many moms. S. C. Johnson, IBM, PricewaterhouseCoopers, and Fannie Mae are among the early proponents of this new idea, but I'm sure many companies will be adding this innovative program to their best practices.

Part-time Hours, Full-time Support

Fortunately, companies are catching on that "part-time" doesn't mean "partly committed." These figures might help you make your own case for a reduced schedule.

- In 1990, 47 percent of the 100 Best Companies offered job sharing. That rose to 86 percent in 1995 and 97 percent in 2004.
- In 1990, just 77 percent of the 100 Best Companies offered part-time work opportunities; by 2004, 100 percent of the 100 Best Companies offered at least some full-time employees the opportunity to drop back to part-time and later return to full-time.
- 71 percent of 100 Best Companies offered benefits to part-timers who worked twenty hours or more in 2004.

While the rest of the corporate world has some catching up to do, these companies are showing that reducing your hours doesn't have to reduce your career expectations. Research supports that idea, too: McGill University professor Mary Dean Lee studied eighty-one part-timers over six years. She found that most received raises and at least one promotion (although some promotions involved a return to full-time work). While she noted that part-time work resulted in slower career growth than full-time work, she concluded that "working on a reduced load basis can be a long-term strategy for achieving career success."[6]

Time Off for Good Behavior

When Julia and Robert were transitioning from adolescence into teenhood, we went through some pretty hard times. In some ways, I felt they needed me more than ever . . . even though they seemed to be pushing me away. Unfortunately, at the time, I worked for a company where I had to fight just to take my vacation, let alone a month or two off.

If I'd been lucky enough to work for one of our 100 Best Companies, I might have had the perfect solution right in front of me: a sabbatical. Originally granted to professors to give them time to recharge and think creatively, sabbaticals aren't confined to the ivory tower anymore: 17 percent of companies offer unpaid sabbaticals and 4 percent offer paid sabbaticals to their employees, according to SHRM.

Kerry Prichard, a mother of three in Tacoma, Washington, took a seven-week sabbatical in 2004 from her job as an account specialist with the financial services company Russell Investment Group, where employees can take paid sabbaticals every ten years as a reward for loyal service. Kerry and her husband rented a house in Florida near her father, and took her three children, ages six, eight, and ten, to a different amusement park every few days. But she also found plenty of time for quiet reflection by the pool.

"The sabbatical gave me an opportunity to look at whether I'm really on balance," she says. "It validated for me that I want to be a working mom. I don't want to stay at home . . . not because I don't love my children, but because I'm a better mother if I work."

Gimme a Break

Sabbaticals and extended time off give working moms an "off ramp" that lets them take the time they need, while promising them an "on ramp" that will help them back to work when they're ready.

A growing number of companies are offering sabbaticals like the one Kerry Prichard took. Intel employees, for example, get eight weeks of paid time off every seven years. Other companies offer paid or unpaid sabbaticals on an as-needed basis. IBM, which has made our Best Companies list for all twenty years, offers unpaid personal leaves of absence for up to three years. The company approves sabbatical time for a long list of reasons, including parenting, education, or "once-in-a-lifetime" experiences, like training for the Olympics.

It's not just large companies that offer sabbaticals. Cheryl Holland, the founder and president of Abacus Planning Group in Columbia, South Carolina, offers her twelve employees a one-month sabbatical every five years. "This seemed like the perfect way to reward loyalty and make sure really good people stay with you," says Holland, who plans to spend her own upcoming sabbatical with her nine-year-old daughter, Hanna.

One of the most progressive time-off policies I've heard of was launched in the summer of 2004, when Deloitte & Touche started its Personal Pursuits program. The program lets moms (and other employees who need a break) take up to five years off unpaid, while making sure they still feel connected to the office.

"I purposely waited to have children so I could focus on my career," says Kathleen Cooper, a special projects manager at Deloitte. "When I found I was expecting in my early thirties, I knew I would face a very hard decision. My family is now the biggest priority for me, but I was apprehensive about leaving the workplace."

But Personal Pursuits opened up a whole new set of options for Kathleen. She's decided to take three years off. During that time, she'll meet at least once a month with a mentor, who will keep her updated on changes at the office. Deloitte will pay to keep any licenses or professional credentials up-to-date and they'll invite her to training sessions. Best of all, she'll have the option to take on short-term projects, for pay, during her leave.

"The thought of cutting all ties with my office was scary for me," she says. "It's a huge adjustment to change my focus from work to family. It's wonderful, but I'm really glad to keep some connection to my professional world."

The program also brings huge benefits to Deloitte. "The program probably costs us twenty-five hundred to three thousand dollars per employee who participates," says Cathy Benko, a principal at Deloitte and the company's national managing director of retention and advancement of women. Compare that to the cost of recruiting and training a new employee, which typically costs at least twice the employee's salary. This is a winning situation for everyone.

If your company doesn't have a sabbatical or extended-time-off policy in the employee manual, you may still be able to negotiate one for yourself. The key is to approach the issue from your employer's point of view.

"Think about the business needs and how it could help the company," says Mary Lou Quinlan, the author of *Time Off for Good Behavior*, who took a five-week sabbatical from her former job as CEO of the ad agency NW Ayer. "Maybe you're willing to take the time unpaid or without benefits. Maybe there's someone else in your department who would really benefit from the training opportunity. You're smart to think it through as a business proposition."

Training for the Short Haul

Years ago at *Working Mother*, we had a talented marketing manager named Susan Goldberg. When Susan and her husband, Bob, adopted a black Labrador retriever named Teddy, she began having trouble with her hour-long commute into the city. The problem became even worse when she had her first baby. So she stepped off the traditional career ladder using an increasingly popular strategy . . . working short stints on a freelance basis. She started taking writing assignments so she could work from home, choosing her own projects and setting her own hours. Coincidentally, twenty years later, she and I ended up living in the same town, and she wrote a profile of me for our hometown magazine, *Inside Chappaqua*. Her last question for me: "How do you stand the commute?"

Many talented professionals like Susan are finding they can use their professional skills, but have more control over their lives, by moving to project-based consulting or professional temp work. Dina Silver of Chicago, for example, used to work full-time as the director of marketing for a men's clothing company. But after her son Ryan was born in 2002, she signed up with Aquent Marketing Staffing, a service that provides Fortune 500 companies with experienced—but temporary—marketing professionals. Now Dina works short stints—usually a month or less, for about twenty hours a week—as a copywriter. It's like being self-employed, without the headaches of finding new business and marketing herself.

"Aquent has people out there finding the jobs. For me, that's huge. And I don't have to invoice people and chase after checks," Dina says. "And you get paid every week. That's a big benefit."

When you think "temping," you probably think about some awful postcollege job you held while looking for a career. But today, agencies like Aquent and OfficeTeam aren't just for administrative assistants: they're for professionals in information technology, public relations, law, accounting and finance, health care, marketing, and nearly any other job where talent is scarce.

Such short-term work seems to be growing in popularity. Aquent's CEO, Sean Bisceglia, says demand for their services nearly doubled between 2004 and 2005. A 2004 survey found that 46 percent of Fortune 500 companies would consider hiring sequencing moms for short stints (up to six months) and 45 percent were willing to consider these mothers at twenty hours a week.

The idea of dipping in and out of the workforce works well for moms who need more time with their kids at certain times of year—the summer, say—but can work more at other times. From January through April, Eileen Brewer of Leawood, Kansas, puts in forty hours a week or more as a master tax advisor for H&R

Block. But at other times of year, she works as little as twenty-five hours teaching classes about tax preparation for the company. And four times a year, Lydia Daly, of Asheville, North Carolina, spends three weeks working as a nurse in California, where there's a nursing shortage. The rest of the year she spends with her five kids, ranging from infants to age thirteen. "The money's so much better that I don't have to work when I'm home. It's nice just hanging around with the kids," she says.

Our Way or the Highway

When I talk with any of these trailblazer moms, I feel proud of the changes they've made in the workforce. It wasn't companies that made these new career paths possible—it was working moms themselves. The danger—and sometimes the reality—of losing these talented women has forced one industry after another to change. Over time, voting with our feet has proven to be the best strategy of all in forging the new Flex-Track.

I personally witnessed how the exodus of top talent forced the consulting industry to change. One day about twelve years ago, I got a call from Mary, a brilliant marketing director at a huge consulting firm, with whom I loved working.

"I'm leaving," she said. "I just can't take it anymore."

I couldn't believe that her firm would let such an incredibly talented woman walk out the door. But she told me there was a serious disconnect between her needs and what the company *thought* her needs were. She repeatedly asked her employer to make changes, but they just didn't get it. I watched how the company lost out due to Mary's departure.

And Mary wasn't the only valuable woman fleeing the field. At that time, firms like Mary's were stuck in a vicious and expensive cycle. They recruited the best and the brightest from the top schools, hiring half men and half women. They trained the new recruits over five years and moved the best onto the partner track, where these recruits traveled constantly and served clients 24/7. When women like Mary tried to fit family into the picture, many firms just didn't listen to their needs or concerns. After exhausting every avenue to get the help they needed, many of these women finally left consulting—often setting up their own businesses or working on a project basis for companies who were previously their clients.

After a significant number of women walked out their doors, several of the big consulting firms decided to take action to stem this female brain drain. They weren't being altruistic: more and more of the executives at the big companies who decided which consulting firm to hire were now turning out to be women—and mothers—and they were very unhappy when all-male teams came to pitch their business. To keep these clients, the consulting firms studied where women were going—and found they weren't leaving consulting to stay home with kids. Most were moving to professions that allowed more flexibility. The best consulting and professional services firms took measures to address the problems, adding flexibility programs, networking groups, mentoring, and more. Now some of the most ambitious and progressive efforts to retain women—like Deloitte & Touche's Personal Pursuits program—are taking place at these previously rigid firms.

So Many Paths

What I love about all these solutions is that they seem to say, "Hey, we're not men, and that's okay!" We can have very successful career paths on our own terms, whether we define success as becoming a CEO, teaching a child to read, or getting home on time. The more companies realize that not all career tracks need to follow the same path, length, or speed, the more working mothers will be able to pursue both their careers and families with confidence. We can slow down if we want—or we can continue to steam full speed ahead, fighting for our place on the next rung of the ladder and tackling the most challenging assignments. The choice is ours.

In the future, I hope we'll see even more creative solutions to the one-size-fits-all career problem. Academics and companies are busy working on prototype programs to help working moms. Kathleen Christensen, the director of the Program on the Workplace, Workforce and Working Families at the Alfred P. Sloan Foundation in New York City, recommends a two-thousand-hour work year. We'd work the same number of hours as we do now, but we'd space those hours out throughout the year, so that a mom could work more hours during the school year and fewer in the summer, when her kids are home. Even the notoriously challenging workplace of our universities are starting to make their ruthless seven-year tenure tracks—where young professors are expected to work around the clock teaching, researching, and publishing—more flexible.

Ultimately, we trailblazing working mothers are creating entirely new career paths that fit the workforce of today . . . not twenty-five years ago. We want to create a workplace where parenthood is seen as such an important component of life that companies and our society will create as many different models of success as necessary in order for moms—and dads too—to be both good parents and good workers.

Chapter Three

We Recruit for the Home Team

When Robert finally came home from the hospital after the scary ordeal of his premature birth, he slept for a long time—and so did I. But after a few days, he decided that sleep just wasn't going to be an important part of his life. By his fourth day home he did not want to be put down in his bassinet for a minute. Like many new moms, I became totally sleep-deprived. We tried everything to get him to sleep. At night I tied a bungee cord to my wrist and attached it to his bassinet so I could rock him by swinging my arm back and forth over the side of the bed. That worked for about twenty minutes. Bob wore a path in the wood floor walking up and down with Robert on his shoulder so I could get an hour's sleep. After my mother-in-law went home in exhaustion, my mother came out from Chicago to stay with us. She gladly took the midnight–to–three a.m. shift for a week or so, then flew home, completely worn out.

After a few weeks of this, I knew I had to find someone special to take care of our insomniac bundle of joy—someone with stamina and patience and lots of love to share. Meanwhile, the acquisition of *Working Mother* by Dale Lang's company was rolling forward and a new course for the company was about to be charted—I needed to be back at work. Getting a support team in place now was essential for all of us—especially for Robert.

When we signed up with a nanny-finding service, the first person who came to see us was a tall, green-eyed young woman with a soft voice and shy manner. She stepped softly into the room where Robert was lying quietly in his bassinet (what a good actor!) and peeked in at him.

"Oh, good, he's a boy," she said with a loving smile.

Curious, I asked why that mattered.

"I have three boys back in Jamaica. I don't know much about girl babies, but boys, I know boys." The love in her heart seemed ready to burst forward into that bassinet and I knew that we would hire this quiet woman and that Robert would be in good hands (and arms) when I went back to work.

Of course we made a lot of inquiries and had long talks with Sandy about our needs and her unique family situation. She had come to the United States to support her three boys, who were back home with her mother. We only interviewed one other person for the job. Sandy easily won out over the straightlaced school-marmish lady who looked a bit like Mrs. Doubtfire, but who clearly lacked Robin Williams's warmth and spirit.

I have hired dozens of people over the course of my career. This hire was the most important one of my life, I believe, and trusting my gut instinct held me in very good stead. Sandy stayed with us for nine years, and I cried pitifully when she left to become a secretary to a lawyer. Knowing Sandy was a privilege; keeping her in this country was a challenge; living through her Herculean efforts to take care of her own children was like reading a nail-biting suspense novel. Helping her to achieve her own goals was a proud part of my life. Sandy made it possible for me to do my best work in the office and know that my children were happy, safe, and loved. What more could any working mother wish for?

"Everybody, Forward!"

One of the most important things we do as working moms is build an all-star home team to stand in for us when we're at work. My team featured Sandy as the star player, but over the years it also included three different child-care centers in town; Bob, who gradually cut back his work hours to spend more time at home; and a helpful backup team of teachers, doctors, neighbors, and friends.

Our Home Teams are a lot like the teams we build in our businesses. Most of the players are really good at their assigned positions, but less skilled at other roles. Some carry the team every day, others come in and out as needed. Some are naturally good at working as a team, while others need a lot of effort and attention before they work well with the rest of the group.

As mothers, we're not only key players, but team managers, too. Kurt Andersen, the former editor of *New York* magazine, once said, "It's tough to make seventy-five people all move in the same direction every day." So, too, for working moms: it can be exhausting to get your Home Team moving in the same direction every day for the eighteen or so years of your child's life. But that is what we do.

Fighting Our Fear

Before we even begin to build our teams, though, working mothers have to grapple with two daunting emotional issues: fear and guilt.

The fear comes from the fact that we have to rely on the intelligence, reflexes, foresight, and care of our team to keep our children safe when we're not there. Even when we know rationally that we have the best possible care, leaving our children can be terrifying, especially when we hear horror stories about the rare cases when things go wrong. When my children were small, I was scared to death by stories about the McMartin Preschool, where a mother and son in southern California were accused of molesting children in their care. The McMartins were never convicted, but the story shook parents to the core. More recent stories—four children dying in a preschool van crash in Memphis, a toddler who drowned in a hot tub at a family-care home in California—continue to terrify us.

What is safe? we ask ourselves. How can we protect against such dangers? Fear for our children's safety strikes mothers of all economic levels and in every community. One way to fight the fear factor is to remind ourselves that these stories are the rare exceptions, not the norm—and the odds are overwhelmingly against such catastrophes. And we can focus on the very practical step of building a solid, trustworthy team by following guidelines for finding safe care such as those available on the Web at Zero to Three (www.zerotothree.org) and Child Care Aware (www.childcare aware.org).

When tragedy does strike, some working moms rally together to make sure it never happens again. Linda Ginzel, one of our Raising a Ruckus Award winners for 2005, lost her son when a portable crib collapsed at her licensed day-care provider while she was at work.[1] After she discovered that Danny was the fifth child to die in a Playskool Travel-Lite crib, which had been recalled in 1993, she started Kids in Danger, a nonprofit that lobbies for safer children's products. "I can't rest until I'm sure what happened to me won't happen to any other parent anywhere," she told us. By supporting groups like Kids in Danger, moms make child care safer for all of our kids.

Grappling with Guilt

Robert was always perfectly happy to hang out with Sandy. But Julia was much less casual about being left with anyone but Mommy. I felt sad and guilty when she threw her arms around my legs as I left for the airport, or clutched my black tights with her sticky fingers and demanded I stay home from work.

I eased my guilt and her anxiety by developing creative ways to stay connected with her during the day—I wrote notes that I left on her pillow, I phoned at prearranged times, and later I sent e-mails. Julia developed her own funny strategies for staying connected with me, too, as I wrote in my journal when she was four:

August 22, 1996
Julia hung my black Ecco shoes on the hooks behind her door so she could remember me when I was out of town Tuesday.

August 23, 1996
Julia has made a ritual out of the shoes: "Every morning I kiss those shoes when I wake up because I miss you when you're at work," she says.

August 26, 1996
Today Julia said, "I kissed your shoes too early today! You were still home when I woke up!"

August 30, 1996
Yesterday, Julia told me that since I had packed my black shoes to go to Atlanta, she had to kiss my beige shoe instead. She could only find one, so she kissed it twice.

These "missing mommy" moments were funny, but they were painful too.

The guilt and sadness we feel at leaving our kids affects almost all working moms, and when I write about moments like these in my monthly column, I always get a flood of letters from other mothers battling their guilt.

"I read your CEO Note in the March issue on the train, in the morning, just after my little daughter (two years old) had grabbed my leg and asked me not to go to work," wrote Connie Capone of Chicago. Reading about Julia Rose, she said, "made me feel much better about my own experience. Thanks!"

Sharing these moments with our friends or coworkers helps

ease our guilt. But the best strategy for coping with guilty moments is finding caregivers we're crazy about—the ones who make our children happy and help them grow.

Loving Our Caregivers

Here's a refreshing truth that no one ever talks about in the media: *Many* working moms love their day-care providers! In the <u>What Moms Want</u> survey, a whopping 89 percent of mothers were happy with their day-care choice: 56 percent were "very satisfied" with their child-care solutions, and 33 percent were "somewhat satisfied." Once we find a really good child-care solution that fits our child's personality and our family's needs, working moms really appreciate the benefits that high-quality child care brings. Many of us are better able to shake off some of our guilt and doubt when we see how great caregivers help our children thrive. "I'm so happy with my day care," says Lilly Kimmelshue, a nonprofit development officer in Redding, California. Her children, ages four and one, are in day care full-time down the street from her office. "They do so much more than I could ever do as far as art and singing and outdoor games. The instructors are really well trained and they're teaching my daughter so much more than I'd be able to at home."

Many moms feel like Lilly. I certainly did. Sandy became an important part of our family over the years and single-handedly relieved much of my anxiety for Julia and Robert's well-being. Even when Julia was sad when I left, I knew she was in good hands, and that she adored Sandy. When we find caregivers we love, it takes away the fear and eases those tough mornings.

"I think a lot of people don't realize that when you stay home, no matter how much you love your child, it's hard to be 'on' all day," Michelle from Nashville wrote me recently. "But when you spend many hours at work, you get butterflies in your stomach when it's time to pick up your baby, and you're actively involved in everything from the minute you get home until the minute he goes to bed." Michelle told us she believes that working makes her a more well-rounded mother and makes her time with her son "high-quality time, all the time."

I know exactly how she feels. From the time Robert and Julia were little, I couldn't wait to get home from work and see them. When we went to parties on the weekends, my friends would tease me because I'd spend the whole time in the playroom running around with all the kids. "Carol," they'd call down to the basement playroom, "come on up! It's time for *adult* dinner!"

Another great strategy for easing our guilt and building confidence in our teams is reminding ourselves that the research backs up what we feel in our hearts: high-quality child care can be good for kids. Just consider:

- Kids in accredited day care were more than twice as likely to be rated school-ready when they started kindergarten compared to kids who hadn't been in day care, according to a 2005 study by the state of Minnesota.
- Kids who spent a lot of time in child care before age one showed *no difference* from children who stayed home with mom in terms of attachment and bonding to their mother, according to a 1997 report from a long-running study by the National Institute of Child Health and Human Development.
- In 2002, the same ongoing study showed that children in child care had better cognitive and linguistic abilities than those who weren't in day care.
- As far back as 1995, a study of 401 child-care centers showed children in day care had better cognitive and social development.

A study released in England in October 2005 did not agree with these findings, stating that mother care was best for babies under eighteen months, while group care was best for children three and over. While rating group care as the least successful choice for babies under eighteen months, the study also concluded that if mothers are unhappy about being home with the baby, group care is, in fact, better.

This last finding reminds me of a common theme that we wrote about in the early years of *Working Mother* magazine: if the mother isn't happy staying home with a baby, that unhappiness will have an impact. In order to make our best choices, we must consider everyone's needs in the equation.

Research will be ongoing on this topic. But we, the moms who make the choices, can agree that high-quality child care is a necessity, and that giving women choices about how long they want to stay home with their newborns is highly desirable.

Finding Our Star Players

Putting together an all-star Home Team isn't a one-time task. Our kids have different needs as they age; our jobs change; the school day starts and ends at a different time nearly every year; and babysitters come and go. As Sophie Oberstein, who is responsible for training and development for the seven hundred employees of Redwood City, California, told us, "When Lily was born, I put 'figure out child care' on my to-do list, thinking I could figure that out and cross it off once and for all." During her seven years as a mom, she's tried all kinds of different arrangements, but she still hasn't crossed "figure out child care" off her list.

Every working mother's Home Team is different—but most contain a mix of some of these ingredients: child-care center, licensed family-care home, babysitter or nanny, and family and friends pitching in. In our <u>What Moms Want</u> survey, here were the most commonly used solutions:

For "star players":
- 45 percent used a child-care center
- 17 percent used a family child-care home

- 12 percent had a nanny or babysitter
- 12 percent relied on relatives, not including Dad
- 6 percent relied on Dad, or a domestic partner
- 3 percent worked at home and cared for their child at the same time.

To supplement the star player:
- 44 percent used relatives, not including Dad
- 21 percent relied on Dad, or a domestic partner
- 19 percent worked at home while caring for their child
- 12 percent used a child-care center
- 10 percent had a nanny or babysitter
- 5 percent used a family child-care home.

The figures hint at the degree of ingenuity that moms use in putting together their teams—but the real stories about how moms pull it off are a testament to the endless creativity and problem-solving prowess of working moms.

For instance, Sophie Oberstein and her husband, Jeff, a management consultant, leave for work before Evan, five, and Lily, eight, get up. So they depend on Fresia, their morning babysitter, to get the kids ready and take them to preschool and kindergarten, where Fresia hands them off to the next players—the teachers at Lily and Evan's schools. Sophie starts work at 7:30 a.m. so she can get off at 2:30, in time to pick up the kids—but when she has afternoon meetings, she recruits her in-laws, who live nearby, to watch Evan and Lily after school.

Home Teams are even more complex for single moms who don't have a partner pitching in. Single mom Kimberly Dewitt, a procurement executive for an entertainment company in Florida, has several key players on her Home Team: the kindergarten teachers who help her daughter, Maddie, during the day; the bus driver from her community after-school care program who picks Maddie up at kindergarten; Kimberly's mother, who flies in from Alabama when Kimberly has to travel; and a single mom girlfriend who takes care of Maddie twice a month so that Kimberly can have some much-needed time to herself. (Kimberly returns the favor and cares for her friend's daughter twice a month, too.) Kimberly also has a pinch hitter: a woman in the neighborhood runs a small, licensed family-care home and takes care of Maddie when she's too sick for school. Obviously, building a team that works for your family takes creativity!

Whether we use child-care centers, nannies, relatives, or other solutions, we all battle the practical challenges of finding and paying for quality child care, and scrambling for backup care when our star players are on the bench.

What Would You Pay for This Babysitter?

At a barbecue recently, I spoke with a newspaper editor with two teenagers. Her older daughter was applying to colleges, and she was worrying about her bank account. "I don't know how we'll pay for it," she told me. "But then again, we paid for day care, so I guess we can manage anything!"

She didn't know how true her words were. In fact, day care for a four-year-old costs more than tuition at a state college in every single state in the United States, according to a study by the Children's Defense Fund in 2000. In some areas it actually costs twice as much: in Albuquerque, for instance, the average annual cost for day care for a four-year-old was $4,801 in 2000; state college tuition was only $2,180.

Our <u>What Moms Want</u> survey found that working mothers spent an average of $700 a month on child care; 54 percent of moms with one or two children spent $500 to $2,500 or more per month. That means more than half of these working mothers are spending at least $6,000 a year on child care—and many are spending $12,000 or more. For the cost of two years of child care, you could buy a new car or put a down payment on a house.

The cost of child care is especially rough on lower-income

moms, who typically spend more than 18 percent of their income on day care. Even middle-income families are struggling. Many families make painful choices between paying for child care and other priorities, like saving for retirement, staying out of debt, or going on vacation.

No wonder some moms question whether it's worth it to work. But from a financial point of view, the answer is almost always yes. Even if child care eats up your whole paycheck for a few years, the seniority, experience, and raises you get by staying in the workplace usually mean you'll earn a higher salary later on, and for many more years. Plus, you're eligible for benefits, retirement savings, and other perks that really add up.

I was shoe shopping at Heller's in Mt. Kisco, New York, recently when the very helpful salesperson, Tara Dzubak, confessed that it was her first day back at work after giving birth to her second child only four weeks earlier. The two children, Christina, three, and Michael, the baby, were being taken care of in two separate family-care centers, because she couldn't find two slots in one center. "Thank goodness they're on the same street so when I drop off one it's just a few blocks to the other," she said.

I asked her how she decided when to return to work.

"I know it's early to be back at work," she told me. "But I want to keep this job—I just can't stand not having my own income."

She knew her earnings would barely cover child care for now—but she also realized this was a short-term problem. In five years, the children would be in school, and she'd have contributed five more years of income to the family, and kept her feeling of independence. Meanwhile, she could use federal tax breaks to ease the money crunch. (The federal Dependent Care Deduction lets you deduct $3,000 for one child, $6,000 for two. Or, if your employer offers a Flexible Spending Account for Dependent Care, you can set pretax money aside.)

Some states and communities are easing the cost of child care while better preparing kids for school through universal pre-K initiatives. In 2002, Florida voters demanded universal prekindergarten for four-year-olds; the law was signed in January 2005. Those extra three hours a day, paid for by the state, will make a dent in the child-care costs of 150,000 parents while better preparing their children for school.

Calling All Moms: Cutting Costs by Teaming Up

While federal and state help for the cost of child care moves along slowly, moms are finding their own strategies to cope—and some of the best solutions come from teaming up with other moms. No one else will understand what you need as much as another mother—especially one with a job.

Jane Hyun, the author of *Breaking the Bamboo Ceiling*, turned to her own mother for help, asking her to be the star player on her Home Team. "I was worried that it might not work out," Jane told me. "But it's been great!" Far more important than the financial benefit of getting free child care is the way the arrangement has tightened family bonds.

"My mother and I have grown closer," Jane told me. "We have so much to talk about now. And taking care of the baby reminds my mother of when I was young, so I'm getting all these great stories about when I was a kid that I've never heard before. It's such a joy!"

Having Grandma or other family members provide care can be the lowest-cost solution out there, but it's a relatively rare option for the five hundred women in our survey: only about 12 percent relied on grandmas or other extended family members as their star player (although 44 percent used relatives to support the star). Many of us live too far away from our extended families to make this practical. My high-energy, fun-loving mom would have been a great caregiver, but she lived eight hundred miles away in Chicago, so I never enjoyed the benefits of Grandma Day Care.

But even when family members are available to star on our Home Teams, that's not always best for us or our kids. One young woman approached me nearly in tears after I spoke about child care at a Credit Suisse First Boston parents' network event in 2003.

"Carol," she said, "my mother-in-law is taking care of my children two days a week and I just can't stand it because she constantly criticizes the way I raise the kids. I hear all the time that I'm not doing the right things. I'm too lenient. I shouldn't be working. What should I do?"

In this case, I suggested that she find an alternative form of child care, especially since Credit Suisse has great child-care benefits. I told her that letting her mother-in-law be just a grandma, not a caregiver, might make her focus less on their differences in parenting styles.

But it doesn't have to be your own mom or other family members to whom you turn for extra help in controlling day-care costs. Other working moms may be willing to share a babysitter or nanny with you.

Susan Davis of New York City, a public relations director, shared a nanny with a friend from the time their daughters were two. Her nanny took care of both little girls every day. "As a single mom, I couldn't ask for a better way to take care of Zoe," she told us. The share cost her less than a child-care center would have, plus it was a lot more convenient. And Zoe and her friend grew up together—a huge benefit since neither had siblings.

Kathleen Quinn,[2] a mother of two in Evanston, Illinois, also found a sharing solution. After she lost her dot-com job, she wanted to keep her fantastic sitter but couldn't pay her full-time salary anymore. So she sent out an e-mail to friends, searching for someone to share. A friend of a friend signed on to use the sitter two days a week, while Kathleen kept her three days.

Some moms take the sharing idea even further, teaming up to create informal co-ops for the summer—or longer. Linda Himelstein, a journalist in Hillsborough, California, teamed up with five friends to hire a preschool teacher one summer to run a mini day camp, rotating homes every week. "There aren't many options for kids under five in the summer," she says. "This worked perfectly.

The kids had a terrific time and it was very flexible." The camp was such a hit that they repeated it the following summer with fifteen families and several teachers.

Of course, larger or more permanent co-ops may require state licensing and other formalities. If you're looking for a small, homey setting but don't have the time or flexibility to organize your own co-op, licensed family care might be the right solution for you.

The Sitter Jitters

You'd think once we found good care providers we can afford, our child-care problems would be solved. But many of us still battle that knot of jealousy that someone else gets to spend so much time with our babies.

"I would halfheartedly joke that the first time he called someone else 'Mommy,' I would quit my job to stay home with him," White House reporter Kathy Gambrell told me.

Bridget Wolf, a sales assistant in Lisle, Illinois, dealt with her own jealousy by asking her sons' caregivers not to tell her when Mike, now thirteen, and Matt, now ten, achieved a "first" when she wasn't home. If one of them took his first step with the babysitter, Bridget didn't know it. That way, she still had the exciting experience of seeing her sons take a step for the first time after work—and she never did ask if it really was the very first! Software engineer Janet Chamberlain managed to talk herself out of her sitter jealousy, reminding herself that learning to love other people was an important step in her children's development.[3]

"Even if a child does lavish love on her caregiver, that doesn't mean there's less affection for Mommy," said the late psychologist Harriet Braiker. "A healthy child with a secure attachment has almost limitless amounts of love."

Although I loved Sandy, I was often jealous of her time with my kids, and I even went so far as to be jealous of her parenting skills.

When Robert was two I noticed that he had developed an odd habit of running around the house as soon as I walked in the door. He would run over to touch the telephone, then run over to the bookshelf and pick up a knickknack, and then run to the new couch and sit on it. "What is he doing?" I asked Sandy. "Oh," she said, "those are all the things I won't let him touch when you're not home."

I had to make adjustments to my reentry time as well. When I got home from work on a beautiful summer evening, I wanted to play with the kids right away, but sometimes Sandy wanted to talk and hang out—after all, she'd been around little kids all day and needed some adult conversation. I had been around adults all day and needed some kid time. But I always learned a lot when I took the time to relax and chat with Sandy—a lot about my kids, my house, and my neighbors!

I'm not the only mom to make small compromises to keep the peace with a babysitter we love. Diane Gardin, an administrative coordinator in Flint, Michigan, tried to wean her son James off pacifiers, but found her sitter was sneaking them to him during the day. Diane relented "because he was in a loving, safe environment. Sometimes it's okay to lose the little battles," she told us.[4] Still, managing our caregivers, and training them on how we want our children to be raised, is part of the equation. It can be tough to be the boss, but it's essential.

We Make Changes When We Need To

In our <u>What Moms Want</u> survey, hardly anyone said they were dissatisfied with their child-care solution: just 3 percent said they were somewhat dissatisfied, and 1 percent said very dissatisfied. Personally, I believe that's because our top priority as working moms is to make changes to our Home Team when something's not working.

I had to make several adjustments in my Home Team over the

years. Robert was three when Julia was born, and since that's a perfect age to start socializing kids, we decided to let Sandy attend to Julia alone every morning while Robert ventured out to Country Day School, a child-care center run out of an old Victorian house just a mile from our home. Robert loved it, and went back each year until he was ready for kindergarten.

But Julia was an entirely different animal when it came to day care. When she was three, we wanted her to spend time with other kids. And Sandy needed to work fewer hours because she had finally succeeded at bringing her three children from Jamaica to live with her. We signed Julia up for Country Day School and expected she'd love it as much as Robert had.

No such luck. Julia had been at Country Day for two months when she started to get stomachaches all the time. Finally, she told us she didn't want to go anymore. So we moved her to the center at the Temple Beth El. After three months she said, "Mommy, I'm so bored there. Can I stay home?" Next we tried World Cup Gym, where the kids had access to gymnastic equipment and training. This too left her cold. We finally let her stay home, with Sandy and Bob sharing in her care.

Robert and Julia were raised in the same house in the same family by the same people, but their reactions to child care were completely opposite. Such differences in temperament is one reason why it's so important to find a child-care solution that fits your child's personality.

Kimberly Dewitt also found she needed to adjust her Home Team when she took a new job as a procurement officer in Florida. The job offered on-site child care, but it just didn't work out for four-year-old Maddie. "The first day, no one came over to greet her and help her. I should have pulled her out then," says Kimberly. "One day, she was crying when I left. I looked in the window at ten a.m. and she was still crying. And when I came by at lunch, she was sitting by herself—crying." That was enough. Kimberly moved her to a center in her neighborhood, where Maddie was much happier.

Similarly, in the last four years, Sophie Oberstein went through three morning sitters before settling on her fourth. The kids just loved their first sitter, Meghan, but she left the job to get married; language problems undermined the second arrangement, and Lily didn't get along with the third sitter, although Sophie really liked her.

"I told the kids that if they weren't happy I'd do something about any child care they were ever in," she says. "So when they told me they hated their sitter I was in a quandary. She was so great from my perspective. But I wasn't the one who had to spend time with her. Lily would leave notes for me to find when I got home from work. 'How do you spell hate? How do you spell babysitter?' "

Sophie had no choice but to make a change—quickly. The kids love their new morning sitter, Fresia, even though no one will take the place of their original sitter, who invited Lily to be a flower girl in her wedding!

The real secret to our success in team building is that, like Kimberly and Sophie, we'll make any change necessary to ensure our children are safe, happy, and well cared for. At a recent GE executive women's conference, Stacey Snyder, the highest-ranking woman at Universal Pictures, summed it all up: "As long as my solutions are working, I can keep doing this," she said. "If it stops working, I'll make new choices if I need to."

Let's Bring the Kids to Work!

Most companies in America don't offer much help to working mothers when it comes to building our Home Teams. In a national survey of more than four hundred companies, the Society for Human Resource Management found that just 4 percent offered on-site child care, 4 percent offered subsidies for child care, 9 percent offered emergency or sick child care, and 19 percent offered child-care resource and referral.

But our Working Mother 100 Best Companies do much better: all of them offer resource and referral services, while nearly one-third offer on-site or near-site child care—and these centers are setting the quality standard for child care across the country.

"The reality is, the best quality child care is corporate child care," says Kathie Lingle, the director of the Alliance for Work-Life Progress (AWLP), a not-for-profit organization for professionals in the work-life field. "In general, it exceeds the quality of anything offered privately, because corporations don't want problems and complaints from employees, so if they're going to get involved, it has to be stellar." To make sure the quality of care meets high standards, most corporations hire well-regarded companies, like Bright Horizons or KinderCare, to build and manage their centers.

Since corporate day care is higher quality than many day-care centers in the community, you'd expect it to cost more, right? Actually, it usually costs less. On average, employees who sent their kids to an on-site day-care center at our 100 Best Companies paid about $111 a week (or $444 a month), although costs ranged as low as $54 a week and as high as $330 per week. The average cost is significantly less than the average monthly cost of $700 paid by the mothers in our <u>What Moms Want</u> survey.

Great corporate child care takes many forms:

- Johnson & Johnson, one of only two companies to have been a Working Mother Best Company for all twenty years, opened a child-care center in their New Brunswick, New Jersey, headquarters in 1989 that set off a competition for employees among New Jersey's many corporate headquarters. That's the kind of competition working mothers love to see.
- IBM, also on the Best Companies list for all twenty years, partners with communities, providing start-up funds to build child-care centers, which it then turns over to the community to operate. IBM has funded the start-up, expansion, or major renovation of thirty-nine extraordinary child-care sites, and

has funded improvements at an additional twenty-six child-care sites in the United States. In 2004, they served 969 IBM children, in addition to thousands of community children. The company also provides start-up or enhancement funds for twenty-six centers in its international locations.

- In 2003, Bristol-Myers Squibb proudly opened its fourth child-care center in Hopewell, New Jersey. The centers serve 1,731 children, and parents pay on a sliding scale according to income.

- Abbott, the health care company, cares for more than 700 kids at its Abbott Park, Illinois, on-site center. Opened in June 2001, the $10 million center, operated by Bright Horizons, awards scholarships to employees based on income. One of the largest child-care centers in the country, the facility boasts ten acres of land, lots of outdoor play space, and a shrubbery maze.

At Working Mother's 2004 WorkLife Congress, Miles White, the CEO of Abbott, said, "It's loss of talent that's expensive, not work-life programs." The company made a huge investment in child care—and the payoff in worker productivity, retention, and recruitment was clear.

I've visited many of these on-site centers, and they often make me wish I'd joined the corporate world instead of becoming an entrepreneur. At IBM's Tom Watson Child Care Center in Yorktown Heights, New York, I found a gleaming Taj Mahal of little bitty science modules designed to inspire experimentation. At GlaxoSmithKline's headquarters in Research Triangle Park, North Carolina, I visited their beautiful center, which features a large outdoor facility that is completely handicap accessible. As we walked around the facility I noticed that several different groups of kids were playing without disturbing each other because of the clever design of shrubbery and play areas.

The consumer products company S. C. Johnson also has a fabulous day-care center at its Racine, Wisconsin, headquarters. "The center was really wonderful," says Kimberly Dewitt, who worked for S. C. Johnson for many years before recently moving to Florida. She desperately misses the center, as does her daughter, Maddie.

"The teachers would ask us to come in from time to time to participate, and the parents all knew each other. We had a parent rep for each room," she says. The child-care center also e-mails pictures of the kids to their parents throughout the day. "I didn't really appreciate how important all that was until I left."

Child-care centers, of course, don't have to be corporate-sponsored to encourage parent involvement—but it's much easier to share a PB&J during your child's lunch break if the center's just steps away.

The Baby in the Briefcase

You don't have to work for a Fortune 500 company to benefit from on-site child care. Small companies are often more creative than large ones—and it can be much easier to get them to change. When orthodontist Jenny Abraham told her boss she was pregnant, the office started preparing for parenthood right along with Jenny. "My employer generously set up an area upstairs from our office to use as a nursery. I hired a babysitter and was able to see my daughter, Isabella, throughout the day. This also facilitated nursing, which I was able to continue to do until she was a year old," Jenny wrote me. "Now Isabella is twenty months old and has truly become part of our office. She is loved and cared for by all of the office staff."

At New Age Transportation, a logistics provider in Lake Zurich, Illinois, new moms are encouraged to bring their babies to the office until they're three months old, while at Zutano, a Vermont children's clothing manufacturer, babies are welcome for a full year.[5] What great places to work!

Teaching Your Company the ABCs of Child Care

Companies like these are proving that, contrary to popular myth, child care isn't too expensive or too much hassle compared to the benefit of making working moms happy, less stressed, and more committed. If I wanted to talk my employer into providing on-site child care, I'd use this ammunition:

- A 2005 study by Bright Horizons, the leading operator of corporate day-care centers, found that companies with on-site day care had much higher retention rates. Overall, workers who used the center were 50 percent less likely to leave their companies than those who didn't.[6]
- A 2003 Bristol-Myers Squibb employee survey showed that employees who used the on-site child-care center felt more supported, more committed, and experienced less stress and burnout than other employees.
- The National Security Agency, which provides intelligence services for the federal government, saves an estimated $4.05 for every $1.00 it spent on its on-site child-care center.[7]
- Dorrit Bern, the CEO of Charming Shoppes, told me that their on-site child care was *the* most effective retention program the company had ever instituted, "bar none!," for her 1,000-employee company.

Calling for Backup

Many mothers tell me that while on-site child care would be wonderful, what they most desperately need is backup child care. As working mothers, we can handle the typical day-to-day child-care demands once we have our Home Teams in place. The real scramble comes when our usual plans fall through—our sitters get sick, the child-care center bursts a pipe, or school closes because of snow. So backup child care is hugely helpful to parents . . . and it's one of the cheapest child-care supports companies can offer.

In my own family, backup arrangements bordered on the hilarious. When Robert was nine and Julia was six, Bob started working more flexible hours at his own business and became the starring player on our Home Team. But as captain of the Chappaqua Volunteer Ambulance Corps, he sometimes had to rush out on calls. The kids would jump in the car with the blue light flashing and he'd race across town to drop them at Penny Auntie, a local toy store right on the way to the ambulance headquarters. The store's owner, Barbara Marks, a former captain of the corps, was happy to watch the kids for the hour or so that Bob was on a call. Julia, in particular, loved it whenever the emergency beeper went off: she'd get to race through town with her father and spend an hour "helping out" at the toy store!

Of course, not everyone can call on a friendly shop owner to provide backup child care. Bonnie St. John, a motivational speaker and gold-medal skier in the Paralympics, shared her backup child-care plan as we flew home from a conference together last year. Bonnie travels around the country giving speeches, and she brings her daughter, Darcy, eleven, with her wherever she goes. She learned that every good hotel maintains a list of highly qualified sitters who work for an hourly fee (usually $15–20 per hour). These sitters are the best in town; the hotels make sure of that because they don't want complaints or legal problems from their customers. Bonnie hired these sitters when she traveled—and then she realized that she could use the same system at home for backup care. She asks the concierge at the best hotels in New York City, her hometown, for suggestions for sitters when she needs someone for a few days or a few hours. She's always been satisfied with the results.

But parents don't have to seek help from the concierge of a swanky hotel if they work for a company that provides backup child care: 32 percent of the 100 Best Companies offer backup or sick child care, ranging from Discovery Communication's emergency in-home child-care service, which pays for a babysitter to come to your house, to American Express, which reimburses for emergency backup care six times a year—even if it's a family member who provides that care—to JPMorgan Chase, which purchases backup slots at child-care centers so there's always space for employees' children when needed.

"We use the backup child care offered by PNC at least once or twice a month," says Maureen Seskey, a vice president of supply chain management for the Philadelphia financial services firm. The company's on-site child-care center provides backup for parents in the lurch. "My husband and I split child-care duties, but sometimes our schedules overlap and we're forced to work the same hours." Without backup care, Maureen or her husband would have to take a vacation day whenever their schedules conflicted.

Measures like these make life easier—while saving a lot of money for companies. Bristol-Myers Squibb contracts with a backup service called Just in Time. In 2003, the company estimated the service saved its employees 1,433 missed workdays, adding up to $528,777. An emergency backup program at KPMG paid for itself in six months. By the time it had been in place for a few years, it was saving an estimated $5.20 for every $1.00 invested.

"Backup child care is the fastest-growing area in corporate child care," says Kathie Lingle of the AWLP. And no wonder: companies can spend just $150–200 per backup day—and most parents only need six to nine days a year. While backup care is just a first step toward the kind of support we need, it's a relatively easy one for companies to take—and for moms to request.

Numbers Aren't Enough

Whether you're arguing for backup child care or a full-time on-site center, you'll have to prove the need and give some compelling stories to make your case. You should poll the other parents at your company about their needs (use the women's or parents' networks if there is one). Take your data to your employer with a plan. For instance, if you want emergency backup care, estimate how many days parents miss every year staying home with sick kids.

You also need to collect stories of how the lack of support is negatively affecting productivity. At her previous job in the Montvale, New Jersey, office of the accounting firm KPMG, Kathie Lingle had struck out when she tried to persuade management to add emergency child care—until she got a call from a highly placed partner in Atlanta. "She said, 'I just had a baby and I've had to miss client meetings three times in the last month. Could I come talk to the partners about the need for emergency backup care?'" A week later, the company signed a contract with a backup center.

"She needed care—and management needed her," Lingle says. "Find out who needs what and who matters to leadership—and tell their story."

Telling our stories so that our companies and communities understand our goals—that we want to be great mothers *and* great employees—is the best way to start getting the help that we need. When companies and communities help us build solid Home Teams by making it easier to find high-quality, affordable care, everyone wins—our companies, working moms, and most important, our kids. For working moms, having a solid child-care team in place isn't a luxury. It's the very foundation of our lives.

Chapter Four

We Know Ambition Is Not a Dirty Word

I never really fit the classic profile of an ambitious young woman climbing her way up the corporate ladder. When I was in my early twenties, I was an intellectual hippie of sorts. I protested the Vietnam War and went to women's self-help and consciousness-raising groups. I loved Mother Nature and backpacked down the Grand Canyon and up Long's Peak in the Colorado Rockies. And I *certainly* did not ever intend to go into business. In fact, I had a downright disdain for it: I remember worrying that if I ever had a son he might become a banker—how awful!

After my escapades as a waitress and my incompetence as a summer intern at a bank (where I used Wite-Out to correct typos on a batch of checks), I grew to believe that work was a terrible imposition on life. I made plans to beat the system. I'd work for a few years and save up all my money so I could live on the savings and do what I really wanted: travel, backpack, canoe, paint, write, sew. Anything but work.

My plan was a very good one . . . except for the fact that I had no idea about *anything*. I had no idea how expensive it was to live in the world. I had no idea that backpacking and canoeing might get tiring after a while. I had no idea that you couldn't get out of an apartment rental agreement just because you wanted to. And I had no idea that you could fall in love with your work.

I tumbled into business through the rabbit hole of literature.

After college, a friend and I decided to publish collections of short stories by previously uncollected authors. I drew the logo—a moose reading a book—on a napkin and we founded Story Press. Our first release was a collection of short stories by the wonderful Chicago writer Norbert Blei. I went door-to-door selling *The Hour of the Sunshine Now* to bookstores in Chicago, walking into one after another asking them to take a few hundred copies. Finally, a big book distributor noticed how many copies I'd sold on my own and offered to take on the book. Story Press's first book was a smash hit, selling thirty thousand copies and getting rave reviews in local publications.

Despite this early success, it didn't take long to run out of money to fund the next book, so I decided to find a job. Publishing seemed like the logical choice, with my BA in literature and my experience with Story Press, so I went through the phone book and made a list of all the magazine offices in Chicago. The first office I found was in the ornate Wrigley Building on Michigan Avenue. The plaque on the door read "Playgirl, Inc." I knew it was a magazine, but that's all I knew. No one was in the reception area when I opened the door, so I called out a friendly "Helloo!" like my mother would have done. A man's voice answered "Who's there?" from the next room, and I walked through as if I knew exactly what I was doing. A friendly-looking middle-aged man with a receding hairline and a slight build was sitting behind a huge desk, looking at me quizzically.

"Hi!" I said in my perky, smiley way. "I'm Carol Evans, and I'm looking for a job with a magazine."

I was twenty-four, but I looked all of fifteen at the time, and I guess Bob Sherman, the man behind the desk, thought this opening gambit was hilarious. He certainly looked amused as he invited me to sit down. He listened with interest as I told him about my book publishing adventures.

When I finished, he said, "We don't have an editorial office here. They do all that out in California." I was crestfallen, but he continued. "What we do here is much more interesting than editorial. We sell advertising space."

Selling advertising space was a totally new idea for me. I didn't even know what advertising space was . . . but I kept talking.

"Oh, I could do that," I said. "I sold the most Campfire Girl candy when I was a kid. And in high school, I got a lot of wealthy dads to give us everything we needed to do a big Hunger Walk. We raised fifty thousand dollars! I'm sure I could sell advertising space for you."

"Well, this magazine might not be to your liking," he said with a paternalistic look. "Have you ever seen *Playgirl?*" I hadn't, although the name of the magazine kind of gave away its secret. He silently picked up an issue and opened it to the centerfold, which showed a smiling man lying across the pages with nothing on and almost everything showing. I felt embarrassed for a brief moment, but quickly refocused on my goal and said, "Oh, I could sell that. I'm all for the equality of the sexes. If men can look at naked women, why can't women look at naked men?"

Bob Sherman laughed, and told me that he actually might need a junior salesperson. A few days later, he arranged for me to interview with the big boss from California at the Ritz-Carlton hotel bar—the fanciest place I'd ever been. I had to borrow a nice coat from a girlfriend because it was raining on the day of the interview, and all I had was a bright orange poncho. The coat was too big, so I put a sweater on under it. At the hotel, the big boss saw me struggling to get off first the coat and then the sweater. I must have looked like I was wrestling with a straitjacket. I'm sure that coat almost cost me the job.

Still, something must have clicked, because he gave Bob the green light and I was thrilled to accept the enormous salary of $11,000 a year. I calculated that I could keep Story Press going for at least five years!

Once in the business of selling ads, my understanding of the world of work slowly emerged. At first, I didn't really understand why I couldn't leave the office at 4:30 if I had something more interesting to do than work. But gradually the pieces started to fit together, and I learned, with the help of my boss and his secretary, what the exact requirements for success were.

That first job lasted only three months, and I sold only one ad. But selling that ad felt great, and lit up my sense of ambition. I learned a lot from Bob and his secretary, who knew as much as Bob about selling ads, and was happy to teach me as long as I bought her a Black Russian after work. In fact, I learned enough to get my next job at the highly respectable *American Home* magazine, where I did really well until six months later, when the magazine went out of business—after ninety years of publishing! After a stop at *Ms*. magazine, where I loved the publication but didn't like my boss, I landed a job selling ads for *McCall's*, one of the largest and most successful magazines in the country. With my whopping salary of $22,000, I figured I'd only need to work for a few years, and then I could quit and devote myself to what I really wanted to do (travel, canoe, backpack) . . . although that picture was starting to get a little fuzzy.

But the *McCall's* job changed my life. I had a boss who thought I was great, who took the time to teach me things, and who helped me to sell more and more ads with each issue of the magazine. And then the big bosses from New York announced that they were going to launch a brand-new magazine—*Working Mother*. As the new kid on the block I surprised everyone by selling more ad pages into this new magazine than anyone else in the country. That got the big bosses' attention, and a few months later I was promoted to New York to run advertising sales for the new publication. We made *Working Mother* magazine a huge success, growing ad revenue from $100,000 to $14 million in just ten years. And somewhere along the way, I realized I would rather write a sales presentation than read a short story. I forgot about saving my pennies to go backpacking and found my adult identity in the work that I did. Business had become a creative outlet for me (so creative that I left Story Press behind when I moved to New York). Selling had become a skill and a passion. My ambitions became clear and focused: I wanted to reach the highest level of success that I could.

Ambition Is Good for Our Health

At every point in my career when I could have just stayed steady, I felt driven to move ahead. Having a baby changed everything, but my sense of ambition, once enflamed, never diminished. I don't mean to imply that I was not conflicted, but when those telltale moments of choice came up, I always chose the path that would bring me more responsibility, more learning, closer to the inner circle of management.

I was, apparently, not alone in embracing ambition. In our What Moms Want survey, we found that most of our readers also embrace their ambition:

- A whopping 63 percent agreed or strongly agreed with the statement "I am very ambitious when it comes to my career."
- 63 percent agreed that getting promoted is important to them.
- 57 percent agreed that making a lot of money is important to them.

More important, the happiest working moms—those who described themselves as "fulfilled"—were also the most ambitious! Kim Nelson, the president of a division of General Mills, made this clear when she spoke at our Best Companies for Women of Color Multicultural Conference in July 2004. "Working gives me a sense of achievement and makes me a role model for my daughters," she told us.

We hear the same thing again and again from our readers: their ambition is to succeed at work *and* at home—and when they succeed at work, they often feel even more successful at home. Perhaps this is because success gives us a feeling of being in control. I was fascinated to read an editorial in the *New York Times* that challenged the belief that higher-level executives experience more stress than lower-level employees. In February 2005, Michael

Marmot, a professor of epidemiology and public health at University College London, explained that positions of greater control and higher status can reduce the negative effects of stress and lead to better health.

He cited studies of British civil service workers, which indicated higher-level workers with more power had better health than those lower on the totem pole.

"Higher control is associated with lower risk of heart disease, back pain, mental illness, and ailments that make people stay home from work," he wrote.[1] The reason for the better health of the higher-level employees? "The higher your status in the social hierarchy the better your health and the longer you live." He went on to cite example after example of how high achievement correlates with better health: "Americans with more income or education have better health than Americans with less; a Swedish Ph.D. graduate has longer life expectancy than a Swede with a master's degree; a British civil servant at the top of the employment hierarchy has greater longevity than one not quite at the top." My personal favorite example that Marmot cited in the article, however, is that Academy Award recipients live about four years longer than actors who don't win an Oscar.

No wonder working mothers want to succeed: it's good for our health!

Go, Girls, Go!

Ambition takes different forms for each working mom. Some aspire to the next promotion, while others want to start their own businesses. But however they define their goals, highly ambitious working mothers exude a sense of exhilaration: they are ready to go for it, seeking action, charged up by their heavy load, proud of what they have accomplished, and looking for more. It's not that they don't feel conflicted; they often do, especially when their jam-packed schedules clash with their children's important moments, but they plow ahead with a longer view and a more distant goal ahead of them. What I admire most is their passion. These high-powered women are not taking life in small bites: they are chewing off huge amounts at a time and going back for more.

One ambitious mom who really inspires me is Colleen Arnold, our cover mom for the October 2004 100 Best Companies issue. The highest-level woman executive of IBM in North America, responsible for marketing a $20 billion business, Colleen is a very well-organized executive and mother, who takes her international travel and high-pressure deadlines in stride, right along with the needs of her children, Christie, ten, and Jack, fourteen. Three months after her cover story appeared, I learned of Colleen's promotion to General Manager of northeast Europe, making her one of the highest-level executives in IBM's entire global workforce of 300,000. Mark Loughridge, the CFO of IBM, told me that Colleen earned her promotion by "knocking the ball out of the park on every assignment." Clearly a working mother with high ambition, Colleen has support systems most of us can only dream of, like a corporate jet at her disposal so she can get home to her kids as quickly as possible after meeting with colleagues around the world. But she only has these support systems because she's earned them by performing at a remarkable level.

Ambitious women like Colleen are unambiguous about their drive to succeed at home *and* at the job. They take the time needed to arrange things on both fronts. Colleen, for example, works hard to make sure everyone on her team—her kids, her husband, Jack, her assistant, and her caregiver—all know where she'll be at all times, even when she's jetting around the world. She keeps a color-coded At-a-Glance schedule in the kitchen: her activities are in green, her husband's are in yellow, Christie's are in pink, and Jack's are in blue. She schedules ahead in ninety-day blocks, adjusting week by week as things change.

"When I'm with a client, I'm listening intensely," she says. "And after I walk through the front door, I'm here—really here—with my husband and kids."

Colleen is the kind of mom we often think of when we hear the word "ambitious." But not all ambitious women are running companies or divisions. One of the most ambitious women I know is my own wonderful administrative assistant, Barbara Rosenthal. Her ambition is not to climb higher in job status, but to get everything done as efficiently and effectively as possible so that our company can be successful. Barbara has been the primary financial support for her family for years, because of her husband Gary's debilitating chronic illness. Early on, they decided he would stay at home and care for the kids while she became the breadwinner. Their kids, Eric, twenty-three, Gail, twenty-one, and Glen, eighteen, are all off to college now.

"I didn't plan to be the breadwinner, but it's worked out well," she told me. To achieve her goals—to be there for her kids and to be efficient and effective on the job—she has shifted her work schedule several times. When the kids were younger and Barbara worked for me at *Stagebill*, she came in early and left early to be able to help her kids with their homework. Now that they're grown, we're often together at seven at night, wrapping things up and telling each other to go home. Barbara's dedication to both her family and our company knows no bounds, and her ambition to succeed at home and at work has been part of her—and our—success.

I could fill the rest of this book with profiles of the ambitious working mothers I admire: many of them are our readers. I get reader mail from hotel workers, teachers, entrepreneurs, union members—all expressing their desire to move up, to get a raise, to achieve a promotion.

At a reader breakfast in 2005, I asked twelve readers if they felt ambitious about their work; they all raised their hands. But they all defined ambition in their own way.

One young woman had twins at home. "I feel very ambitious, but I want to be able to work at home and start my own business," she said.

Another reader, Lorena Michel, is a young Latina who had been a teenage mom. She had worked her way up to associate branch manager at a bank. Lorena said she had a strong ambition to get ahead—so strong she was thinking of switching to another industry because she was afraid she had reached the highest level she would get to in banking. One source of her ambition: she knew her twelve-year-old daughter Sasha looked at her as a role model, and she wanted to set a great example for her. I checked in with Lorena a few months later. She had indeed decided to change fields and had become associate director of admissions at a private preschool in Manhattan—a position she thought would offer more long-term growth and challenges.

All around the table at that breakfast, the twelve women had different interpretations of what being ambitious meant to them. What they all had in common, though, was the drive to meet their goals both at home and at work. And they all knew that wouldn't happen by accident.

Seven Strategies for Ambitious Working Mothers

Ambitious working moms, or moms who feel they might embrace their inner ambition sometime down the road, need to take advantage of all the tricks, ideas, and strategies they can find. Several strategies can make all the difference in achieving our ambitions—regardless of whether you are trying to become a senior executive, an entrepreneur, or a well-adjusted multitasker.

I've talked to dozens of working moms to find their most effective strategies. And I've collected data on companies that excel at encouraging women to move up the ranks. Every year, Working Mother Media's networking group, the National Association for Female Executives (NAFE), publishes a list of the Top 30 Companies for Executive Women, honoring companies that have women on their boards, women in their highest-paying positions, and large percentages of women in their executive ranks.

By looking at what successful working moms and companies

are doing, I've found seven strategies that will help working moms achieve their career (and personal) ambitions:

1. Mentoring (an old idea . . . with some new twists)

2. Skill building

3. Gaining confidence through conferences

4. Tooting your own horn

5. Tackling big jobs

6. Finding companies with women at the top

7. Managing profit and loss.

I spoke with moms and companies alike about the best ways to use these strategies to succeed at work and at home. Here's what they told me.

Ladies: Find Your Mentors!

I love mentors, and I think people create barriers to finding one by having lofty expectations about what a mentor really is. A mentor is someone who takes the time to give you consistent advice over some period of time, who learns enough about you to really be helpful, and who puts his or her own needs aside to focus on yours. I found my most important mentor when I was at Chief Executive Group, and I believe her perceptive guidance, her insight into my psyche, and her solid advice made the critical difference in my getting to the CEO level. But more on her later. . . .

Lots of women I speak to cite their mothers as their first mentors. I certainly include Agnes Evans on my list of mentors. Agnes could befriend anyone instantly: no one felt alone in the world when she was nearby. She taught me how to feel comfortable with a thousand people in the room or just one-on-one with someone I'd never met before—what great mentoring for someone who would build a career grounded in sales.

My first work mentor was Jerry Greco, the hotshot Italian-stallion kind of sales manager who hired me at *McCall's* and taught me how to walk into an office and make a memorable connection with the potential customer. Vivian Cadden, the founding editor of *Working Mother*, was another important mentor, and taught me to respect my readers by treating them as if they were in the room with us as we made our decisions. Arthur Levitt Jr., my boss at *Stagebill*, taught me how to handle very powerful people and find consensus where there seemed to be none.

My network of mentors helped me move along in my career, and I call upon the lessons they taught me every day. But I also know how hard it can be for busy working mothers to find the time to seek out and cultivate mentors. That's why I'm excited about the creative new forms of mentoring emerging at companies around the country, new twists on mentoring that often work wonders for working moms.

Working Mom Sponsors

My first work mentor, Jerry Greco, wasn't just a mentor, he was actually a sponsor (at the time I only thought of him as my boss). At first he suggested that I invite the big New York bosses on a business trip to my sales territories. There they saw me in action with my clients, and learned how I handled a wide variety of situations. He then went beyond mentoring by talking me up to them, smoothing the way for my promotion to national sales manager of *Working Mother* in New York, from which everything else in my career flowed.

Today, we call this kind of mentoring "sponsorship." A sponsor identifies you not as a person who needs mentoring, but as a person who should be considered for higher-level positions. A sponsor goes out of his or her way to make sure you are known to those who can do you the most good.

This kind of relationship—where someone up the ladder from you serves as your champion—can make it much easier to achieve your ambitions.

"Research shows that the ways people advance in an organization is through mentorship and sponsorship, not through hard work alone," says Dr. Mary Trigg, Ph.D., a director of leadership programs and research at the Institute for Women's Leadership and the Center for Women and Work at Rutgers University in New Jersey. "You've got to be good and do your work well, but you also need to be known. Your name needs to come up in those meetings where decisions are made about who will be advancing to leadership positions." A mentor familiar with your work can be the sponsor you need to move up.

That's what Elvia Novak of the consulting firm Deloitte & Touche found out when she joined the company's Parsippany, New Jersey, office. The mother of Isabelle, three, and Daniel, four months, sought out another working mother at a higher level, Lucia Capozzoli, to be her mentor. Lucia ended up serving as a sponsor for Elvia, pushing her up the ladder.

"Lucia was the first female partner I met, and it felt natural to ask her to be my mentor," Elvia told us.[2] Their mentoring relationship began when Elvia was pregnant with Isabelle in 2001. Lucia, the mother of Michael, eighteen, Joseph, ten, and Angelo, six, understood the challenges Elvia would face. "She's a mother who'd come in as a consultant, like me," Elvia said. "And she didn't work in my group, so I knew I could talk openly and I'd get an unbiased opinion. She told me that having this job and kids was doable if I had family support and could stay flexible. She said I would find a balance between work and family, but not always on a daily basis."

Lucia and Elvia connected on a work and family level, but also on a cultural level. Both were born outside the United States—Lucia in Italy, Elvia in Mexico—and were the first in their families to go to college. Lucia offered practical, as well as moral, support.

She helped Elvia advance her career, advising her to apply for a project manager position, overseeing some three hundred people around the world.

"She told me, 'You can do it. No problem.' Then she convinced the partners that I was up to it," Elvia told us. "Now I have more visibility with a new group of partners and I'm set to move up to the next level, as a partner or a director."

Finding a sponsor to push you up the ladder means trying to connect with as many higher-level people as possible until you find someone you really click with. Fortunately, a variety of new mentoring programs are making that easier at many companies, especially within the 100 Best, where almost 90 percent offer a formal mentoring program.

The More, the Merrier: Group Mentoring

We usually think of mentoring as a one-on-one relationship. But it doesn't have to be. Often, working moms find it difficult to connect with a like-minded mentor simply because there aren't enough high-level women mentors to go around. Group mentoring, like IBM's "subnet" program, helps solve that problem. In IBM's program, networks of six to nine women, including at least one manager, who serves as mentor, meet together for twelve to eighteen months. Then they split up to form two new subnets with new members, which brings new people into the learning experience.

Federated Department Stores, which owns Macy's and Bloomingdale's, uses mentoring "circles," where several women and one mentor meet regularly. "Participants get the benefit of forging relationships and working through organizational and developmental issues with a variety of more senior people in the organization," says Sue Allen, vice president of business relationships and risk management at FACS Group, a subsidiary of Federated. These groups also allow one mentor to work with several people—especially useful when there's a shortage of women role models at the top.

If your company doesn't have mentoring groups, it's easy to start one up by asking a higher-level mom you admire to speak with a group of your peers. Approach her by saying, "A lot of us really respect what you've done and it would be valuable to hear how you did it." Hardly anyone will refuse a flattering invitation like that. Start with a one-time event, then ask if she'd be willing to speak to the group periodically in a group mentoring situation. This kind of group will also help you connect with other women at your own level.

Mentoring Up

Mentoring is never a one-way relationship: you may have valuable insight to offer to upper management. That's why some companies, including Procter & Gamble, are adding "mentor up" programs, where senior managers are paired with women of color and younger employees to help management understand a different point of view.

Elia Lopez, a supply chain leader in P&G's North American diapers division, mentored Jane Wildman, the vice president of global baby and toddler care, for more than a year. Elia helped Jane understand how important it is for senior managers to understand the variety of styles and backgrounds people bring to work. Elia's in-the-trenches point of view helped Jane become a better manager, at the same time that Jane helped Elia relate more comfortably to other senior managers.

"Elia's philosophy is that people bring much more to work than you see. What you see is just the tip of the whole person," says Jane. "Based on Elia's feedback, we created decision-making training where we really looked at the whole person and how each individual makes decisions. People shared in great detail how they approach decisions, and we all learned more about where people fit."

Being Jane's mentor also brought huge advantages to Elia. "Jane helped me connect with other higher-level women in my function so I could work through issues I was struggling with," she says. "That's given me courage to give other leaders feedback and tell them what I think. It makes me feel empowered to know I can provide my ideas and feedback without fear."

Walk Off Your Wait: Making Mentoring Moments

Finding time to create a mentoring relationship is tough when you already have your family and work relationships taking up every free moment. That's why I love Gerry Laybourne's idea. As the CEO of the women's cable channel Oxygen, she realized she didn't have enough time for mentoring—whether it was mentoring up or mentoring down. She also never seemed to have enough time to exercise. So Gerry put these two needs together by offering anyone in her company a mentoring hour if they would walk with her in the park. It worked: many mentees got the attention they needed and Gerry gained an hour of exercise several times a week. So many people loved her idea that Gerry held a Mentoring Walk in Central Park last April, inviting other mentors to walk with their mentees to give visibility to the need for women to actively engage in mentoring . . . and exercise. Gerry also told me that she believes peer-to-peer mentoring is very powerful for women. She learned more from other women at her level on the way up than from the male bosses above her.

You can use this strategy yourself by simply inviting a mentor, or a peer you admire, for a walking date to discuss how she manages her own career.

Outside Advice

For twenty years, I've belonged to Advertising Women of New York (AWNY), an industry networking group. And for the past few years, I've taken part in AWNY's mentoring program, which pairs up experienced women from different companies with less experienced members. I've been surprised at how much I enjoyed this formal cross-company mentoring. My mentees found it very helpful to be mentored by someone who didn't work in their companies—the level of honest exchange was very high as we assessed career risks and rewards on a regular basis. And I gained a lot of insight into how other companies managed their people.

Research supports what I observed—that outside mentoring can give you a leg up on your career.

"One study shows that fast-track women had two kinds of ties that regular-track women didn't," says Connie Gersick, a faculty codirector and founding faculty director of the University of California at Los Angeles Women's Leadership Institute. "One was close ties with strategic partners inside—a trusting relationship with someone powerful in the organization. The other was a strong *outside* network or relationship where they could talk through situations and get advice."

To help form those external relationships, Compuware—one of NAFE's Top 30 Companies from 2003—chooses women with high leadership potential to attend Menttium, a one-year external mentoring program. Menttium, which runs programs in cities across the country, pairs a class of a hundred women, all from different companies, with outside mentors. Many of our 100 Best Companies participate in this revolutionary program.

"The most important thing I took away was the need to keep evolving and stay up-to-date. Staying in touch with other industries can help keep me fresh and give me new ideas to apply here at my own job," says Theresa Mayfield, an administrative services manager at Compuware. Theresa was teamed up with a senior manager at General Motors who helped her gain a broader perspective on business.

Build a New and Improved You: Skill Building

No matter how good you get at your job, one of the most important things you can do to advance is learn new skills. That makes you a more and more valuable employee, which makes your employer want to keep you even more—a powerful bargaining tool when you're asking for family-friendly programs.

I learned the importance of adding to my skills at *Stagebill* when the advertising industry went into a deep slump. Suddenly, advertisers weren't buying as many ads in the program guides, and I had to keep my promise to our owners to maintain the profit level of the company consistently from year to year. So we had to find something else that we could do to generate funds instead of just selling ads in *Stagebill*. I knew how to sell ads . . . but now, I had to develop a whole new set of skills.

Carnegie Hall was celebrating its centennial in 1991 and asked us if we could publish a special magazine for the occasion. Working closely with their marketing team, we created a new kind of publication that celebrated 150 years of Carnegie Hall, and asked all our advertisers to sponsor it. Carnegie Hall didn't have to pay a penny for the beautiful publication that they wanted, and we kept the profits from the program. I had invented a new kind of business for *Stagebill*—a business that went on to generate $2 million every year for our company.

From then on, I wasn't just an advertising specialist: I was an expert in creating and selling all types of marketing programs, and integrating them together. And I learned that I could make companies profitable as circumstances changed. Those new skills transformed my professional identity and put me on the path to becoming CEO of my own company.

The great thing about skill building is that it usually doesn't cost you anything. Often you can learn on the job. And companies are eager to train their employees in valuable new skills: a whopping 96 percent of our 100 Best Companies offer tuition reimbursement for classes and training. If your company offers tuition reimbursement, you're passing up free money—and a chance to reach your ambitions—if you don't take advantage of it. True, we working moms can hardly squeeze in a shower some days, let alone a class, but companies are making it easier by offering on-site college and graduate courses.

That's how Kathy Fabyan of Allstate managed to finish her MBA while working and raising her son.

"I started my MBA program the year before my son was born. Once he was born, I felt I had to put the idea of further schooling to the side. I was certain my advanced learning would have to wait until much, much later," she told us.

But Allstate offers an on-site MBA program, with classes right there in the Northbrook, Illinois, office where Kathy worked, so she was able to complete her master's degree . . . and network with lots of other Allstate employees in her classes, too.

If your company doesn't offer the on-site classes and training you need, try to carve out time to build the skills you think are most important. Online classes are a great solution for working mothers, although they don't offer the extra networking benefits that come with real-time classes. Most classes are short-term commitments, so the time bind won't last forever, and it could give you the skills necessary to transform you into a higher-level worker.

Having a college degree can make a huge difference in lifelong income, but many women who don't finish college find it impossible to fit school into their schedule once they start their families. I was really impressed with a program I learned of when I was speaking at the Connecticut Women's Expo in Hartford last year. Diane Rinaldi, Dean of Continuing Education at Bay Path College in Longmeadow, Massachusetts, came to hear my speech about work-life balance, and stopped by afterward to tell me about a wonderful program they began five years ago that working mothers just love. It's called One-Day-A-Week Saturday College, and as the name reveals, this is a program that allows you to get your bachelor's degree by taking all of your classes on Saturdays throughout the year.

Over seven hundred adult women (Bay Path is a women's college) are enrolled in this program. Most of them are working moms, including many single head-of-household moms. This creative thinking is just what working mothers need from communities, schools, and companies. Diane told me they had no idea when they started the program five years ago that it would be such a success, but the response has been overwhelming. Many of the graduating moms know they would not have been able to earn their degrees without this smart program.

Moms who need this kind of schedule should ask admissions personnel at colleges in their area if they offer such a program. The college that I graduated from—Empire State College—has programs specifically designed to meet the needs of adult students, including working moms, and they have campuses all across New York State. I didn't have my kids yet when I graduated, but I felt I needed a special program since I was paying my own way through school and had to work full-time. The "school without walls" program that I took advantage of at Empire State gave me the flexibility to work on my degree without being tied to the campus, which was eighty miles away from where I lived.

Leaders Are Trained, Not Born

One day, when I was working at the Chief Executive Group, the career coach Mary Lynn Heldmann called me from out of the blue to ask if I needed some consulting on how to be a better leader. She caught me just at the right moment, as I'd been wondering about how I might make a move to the next level. We had lunch, and I told her about my deep desire to be more than I was, to accomplish more, and to create more. She advised me not to be satisfied with taking small incremental steps ahead, but instead to look for the big leaps forward—and that was just the advice I needed at that time. Since those days I have had regular sessions with Mary Lynn and her talented son and business partner, Mark Cunningham, receiving advice on both the large overarching issues of leadership and the smaller details of managing my business. Mary Lynn calls herself a coach, but to me she has done double duty as a leadership trainer and my most important mentor. The fact that I pay her for her services allows me to access her as much as I need to—or can afford.

Leadership training, whether it's one-on-one coaching like I do with Mary Lynn or group coaching, can be a very important step for ambitious working moms. Managing people is never easy, but learning to inspire our teams and produce the results we want is one of the most important skills we can build.

If you're already a manager, don't assume you won't benefit from leadership training. Even the highest-level leaders regularly engage in this kind of skill building. For instance, Susan Trainer, a mother of six and the president of Trainer Communications in Danville, California, found her life transformed after she took a leadership seminar with Rayona Sharpnack, the founder of the Institute for Women's Leadership in Redwood City, California. Rayona has coached women executives at some of the world's most powerful companies, including Apple Computer, Levi Strauss & Co., Wells Fargo, and Hewlett-Packard.

"For seven years, my schedule looked like this," Susan told us. "I went to work around eight thirty a.m. and never stopped working until six thirty p.m. I'd come home and spend several hours with my kids. After they went to bed, I'd be up working until two a.m."[3]

After working with Rayona, Susan realized she was acting like she had to audition for the job she already had. "I realized that after seven years of being a CEO, I was still trying to prove myself—to my staff, to the venture capitalists I work with, to myself. It was ridiculous. What's more, the strategy that had helped me grow the business to its current level wouldn't work going forward if I insisted on being so hands-on."

Thanks to her leadership training, Susan started delegating. She stopped leading every client meeting and every new customer pitch. At home, she got more sleep, took up tennis again, and spent more time with her husband and kids.

Leadership training isn't just for CEOs. Any mom in a management position—or who hopes to move into management—can benefit. The best leadership seminars don't just give you management tips, they help you get to know yourself better as a person and as a manager, and figure out how to make it all work together. Most of our 100 Best Companies and Top 30 Companies offer leadership workshops, seminars, online instruction, and leadership retreats, and many are especially tailored for women.

For Diane Fox, a vice president of specialty realty and general merchandise manager for Liz Claiborne, a four-day women-only leadership retreat made a major difference in her work and home life. She loves her job at Liz Claiborne, which is consistently one of NAFE's Top 30 Companies for Executive Women, and loves being mom to her two children, ages four and seven. But between pressures at work and guilt about not being home to help her first-grade son with his homework, she felt out of balance.

"I was really spinning, trying to figure out how to manage work and life," she says. "I felt like I couldn't do them both well, and if something had to give, it wasn't going to be my personal life."

Then, as a perk, her boss sent her to a leadership seminar offered by the Center for Creative Leadership, held in North Carolina.

"I've taken a lot of courses, but this one was definitely the best. Because it was all women, we all had similar issues. I've been in seminars with men, but they don't have the same challenges," she says.

The four-day course focused on self-evaluation. Diane and her twenty-five or so classmates took personality tests and received feedback from a survey of their supervisors, peers, and direct reports about their management style. They spent lots of time discussing their challenges at work and at home and offering each other advice. In a one-on-one session with a career coach, Diane discussed her concerns about supervising her son's homework. The coach helped her view the problem in a new way, suggesting that now and then she stop at home in the late afternoon, help her son with homework, then go out to visit the stores in her territory at night, since the stores were open until 9:30 p.m.

"It sounds so simple, but she created awareness for me," Diane says. "She made me realize if I strategically plan it out and prioritize it, I can really do both."

When she got back, she told her boss about her new plan. He agreed immediately. Once she started doing it, she realized her son was sailing through his assignments without her help. Now, she does homework with him once a month, but she has the peace of mind of knowing that she can be there for him if he does start struggling.

"Just having that option lowers my stress level," she says. "But the lesson I learned was much bigger than that. It was that no one else is going to plan your work for you. Your boss is not going to tell you, 'Why don't you go home from five to six and work with your son.' But if you come up with a strategy and a game plan, you just might not have a problem. It's a matter of stopping and thinking about what you really want that makes the difference."

If your company doesn't offer leadership training for women, sometimes it's worth seeking it out on your own, through a career coach, as I did with Mary Lynn Heldmann. Or encourage your company to do what I did for employees of Working Mother Media. I hired Mary Lynn and her company, Future 1st, to work with anyone at Working Mother who needed a job coach or leadership development, and it has made the difference between success and failure for many of my key employees. This kind of solution—having a coach available to a company or division—is a relatively low-cost way for small companies to compete by providing leadership training and coaching.

Confidence Through Conferences

I go to a lot of conferences. Many of them are conferences that I run, and often emcee, as part of the work we do at Working Mother Media. We welcome 500 human resource professionals every year at our WorkLife Congress, 700 executive women at our Multicultural Women's Conference, and 450 NAFE members at our annual NAFE Conference. I'm so happy that I'm in the conference business, because otherwise I might never have found out about the remarkable power of conferences to move your career ahead, solve problems, and make professional and personal connections. I think I might have done what many moms do: kept my nose to the grindstone and wondered what goes on at all these seemingly glamorous events.

Well, I can tell you what goes on: inspiration found, friendships formed, secrets shared, obstacles explored, spirits lifted, and skills built. Over and over at my own conferences women come up to me and say, "Carol, I wasn't going to come to the conference because I have so much work on my desk—but I am so glad I did! What a difference this will make in my life. Thank you!"

No one is more tempted to pass by the opportunity to go to a conference than a working mother who doesn't want to spend even one more night away from her family. But the ironic thing is that she's probably the one who needs it the most. I have found that I can not only learn and build my skills (at my own conferences and many others), but I can almost always make a big leap forward in some area of my business at a conference. So don't think you're too busy to go to a conference . . . think that it might be the most important step you take all year in support of your own career *and* your family.

In 2006 we are launching Working Mother Media's newest series of events: the Balance Seekers Town Halls solutions and inspiration to last the whole year. For a schedule, go to our Web site, workingmother.com.

Tooting Your Own Horn

Peggy Klaus, the author of *Brag! The Art of Tooting Your Own Horn Without Blowing It*, told her own story to our NAFE members at a breakfast last year. A human resource director once said to her bluntly, "Peggy, no one in this company gets up in the morning and asks, 'What can I do for Peggy Klaus today?'" And Peggy realized the truth in that statement. "While there may be people along the way who help you, you have to be the one steering your own career," she says.[4]

Most of us working moms are happy to brag about our kids, but we're not always so eager to talk about our own accomplishments. As practice for tooting your own horn, Peggy recommends writing down the ten most interesting things you've done, or that have happened to you. Then she recommends that you practice talking about those "brag points" in a very excited way. That way, you'll be prepared the next time you have a networking opportunity and want to promote yourself: you'll sound enthusiastic without sounding arrogant. And you won't waste that elevator ride when a senior executive asks casually, "How's it going?" You'll have a killer answer ready—one that will get noticed.

Let's face it: we women have a bad habit of working hard and thinking somebody will notice. Nose to the grindstone, we assume that the time and effort we put into our jobs will be rewarded with well-deserved raises and promotions. But this is often not the case. Instead, it's the squeaky wheel that gets the grease—and men are notoriously better squeakers than women, always asking for more oil and making lots of noise. But to satisfy our ambitions, we need to make sure that people understand just how talented we really are. There's no better way to do this than letting your managers—or their managers—see what you do accomplish on a day-to-day basis.

Several of the most progressive companies have actually designed programs to let talented employees interact with top management. For instance, Dona D. Young, the chairman, president, and CEO of the financial services group the Phoenix Companies, Inc.—a company frequently on the Working Mother 100 Best list—conceived the CEO Think Tank program to develop high performers at her company. CEO Think Tank participants meet once a week for eight weeks with a senior advisor, exploring one of the company's top strategic priorities and presenting a recommendation to the senior management team.

Avon chair and CEO Andrea Jung, who has a six-year-old son and a fourteen-year-old daughter, convenes a CEO Advisory Council every year. The ten-member council, plus Jung and president/COO Susan Kropf, spend two or three days together every quarter. The sessions include briefings about various parts of the company and working sessions with Jung and Kropf, focusing on specific strategic areas.

"It's very valuable to see how senior management gathers information and makes decisions," says Renee Johansen, Avon's vice president of investor relations, who took part in a CEO Advisory Council. "You can leverage that knowledge in the future. If you're asked to present to them, you have a better understanding of what they want."

However you do it—whether it's through preplanned bragging or formal company programs—make sure that managers above you know about your accomplishments and understand your worth so you'll be top of mind when the next big opportunities that you desire come along.

Tackling the Big Jobs

At that reader breakfast last year that I mentioned earlier, a New York City research librarian, Jennifer Krueger, told me she was struggling to reconcile her ambitions for her job and for her family. She'd been offered a very prestigious job at the research library at Los Alamos National Labs in New Mexico, where she'd have the chance to work closely with world-famous scientists. It was her dream job—a once-in-a-lifetime opportunity. But she was worried about uprooting the kids, moving away from family and friends, and, most of all, she was concerned about the impact the job would have on her family's work-life balance.

"If I took the job, it would mean a totally different balance in our family," she told me. She would be the primary breadwinner, while her husband, Mitchell, an attorney, would spend much more time at home with their children, Zoe, nine, and Eliot, five. They'd be leaving their friends and family behind and uprooting the kids from school and Zoe from her ballet studio, where she was a serious student. She and Mitchell had made long pro-and-con lists, run the numbers, talked endlessly, but she still wasn't sure what to do.

As working mothers, we often face tough decisions when we're offered a promotion. Taking the big jobs also means taking trade-offs . . . in the amount of time we spend at home, in where we live, or in how much time we spend on the road. Sometimes moms don't even consider taking bigger jobs if they require the family to make big adjustments. But many moms do want the big assignments—and feel frustrated when supervisors *assume* they're not interested just because they're mothers. In fact, many moms do take challenging assignments. And by weighing both our own needs and those of our families, and helping our children adapt, we sometimes discover new things about ourselves and our kids.

That's what Anne Altman, a sales executive at IBM in Washington, D.C., discovered when she was offered a dream job with the company in Somers, New York. The one-year assignment would put her on track for important promotions, but it didn't make sense to move her husband and two children—Zachary, five, and Stephanie, nine—for a year, so Anne would have to commute on a weekly basis between New York and D.C.

Anne and her husband, Xavier, debated the pros and cons of her taking the job, and Anne wrestled with her own fears. "Being a great parent is very important to me," she says. "I was leaving my babies. Would they hate me? Would they forget me? Would they decide life was easier when Mom's not around? Would they grow up thinking, 'She left me'?"[5]

Her husband encouraged her to try the job. "She had the potential to go high in her career and New York would launch her on that path. In the end, we'd all benefit," he says.

To make the new arrangement work, Xavier switched to shorter hours so he could take over many of the home duties that Anne had covered. Anne would fly to New York on Sunday nights and come home Friday. The kids took awhile to adjust—for a few weeks, Zachary refused to talk to her on the phone—but after those painful early days, the new job turned out great for Anne and for the whole family. For the first time, Anne was able to devote every second of her weekend to the kids, instead of trying to get extra work done. "The year away created an opportunity for balance that I never had," she says. "I became fun. We became closer—and that sustained us. It still does." The stint paid off career-wise, too: after a year, Anne returned to Washington and later became head of IBM's business with the federal government.

Anne was successful thanks to great support from her husband—and her own belief that in the long run, her choices would help the whole family.

But sometimes, of course, achieving our ambitions for our career and family means turning down big jobs if the time isn't right. Jennifer Krueger, the research librarian, ultimately decided it would be too big a sacrifice for her family to relocate to New Mexico. "We kept running the numbers and it just didn't seem to make sense, plus we'd be thousands of miles away from our family. And yet, if I'd been single, I would have been on the plane in two seconds." Jennifer believes she made the right decision, but it wasn't an easy choice, and she still feels the regret of the lost opportunity.

How you make these decisions depends on the kind of decision maker you are in general. With me, big life choices always come down to a gut feeling—an urgent need to say yes, or terrible dread of saying yes. When I heard that *Working Mother* was for sale, I didn't have to think about the decision to go for it: I was writing the business plan before I even knew if the opportunity was real. Nothing was likely to stop me—except not getting the funding I needed.

Look for Women on Top

In this day and age, when women have been joining the workforce for more than three decades, it's shocking to see how few big companies are run by women. Year after year, the Fortune 500 list contains only a handful of women CEOs. As I write this, there are only nine in the Fortune 500—and only nineteen in the Fortune 1000. But many of these women-run companies appear in the 100 Best list or the NAFE Top 30 Companies for Executive Women list, including Avon, Xerox, and Phoenix. As we've studied great companies for executive women, we've often noticed that companies with more women at the top (not just the CEO job, but on the board of directors, senior managers, and department heads) tend to have more women-friendly programs and a better track record for promoting women. You might move up the ladder more quickly if you work for a company that already has lots of women—and moms—at the top.

Some of the most progressive companies keep an active lookout for women and minorities they can promote. In addition to offering mentoring, women's networks, and leadership training, these companies think hard about women and minorities when planning their future generation of leaders. Often, they identify these future leaders through a process called succession planning, where high-level executives make an annual plan to replace themselves and their direct reports. At Procter & Gamble, for example, top managers are required to identify three potential replacements for each person they manage: an "emergency" candidate who could step in at a moment's notice; a "planned" candidate, who could be ready in several months or years with the right training and career experiences; and a "diversity" candidate, a woman or minority who will also be groomed for the position.

"We started this several years back because we found we weren't readily identifying women and minorities who could step into these jobs," says working mom Deb Henretta, the president of global baby and adult care at P&G. "We felt if we could identify them early in the succession-planning process, we might think about them differently and focus on their training and development, and the types of assignments they get."

Succession planning programs like this one often go hand in hand with "high-potential identification" programs at lower levels, where companies identify up-and-comers. These high-potential programs are great, because they provide special training and attention for ambitious employees. If your company has one, try to learn more about it and how people are selected for this elite group.

Follow the Money: Managing P&L

One surefire way to get noticed is to earn—or save—a lot of money for your company. If I hadn't been a strong seller who produced a lot of revenue, my managers would probably never have noticed my talent. But when I built sales so quickly at *Working Mother*, I was pulled into discussions about the company's bottom line—its profit-and-loss status, often called P&L, for short.

If your ambition is to reach a high-level position in your company, focus on what's most important to the company and the company's shareholders—P&L. Usually that means learning to run a business unit, whether it's a store or a division—anything that can make or lose money for the company. Unfortunately, women hold only 9 percent of all corporate P&L jobs, according to Catalyst, a nonprofit organization promoting the advancement of women in business. Why? Women often aren't groomed for these key positions; they may not have access to the informal networks that help lead men into these roles; and these roles often require relocation or extensive travel, so managers sometimes assume working moms won't be interested.

Betty Spence, the president of NAFE, believes that women will not attain pay or promotion equity with men until they get profit-and-loss experience.

"Being responsible for the bottom line is the quickest way up the ladder," she says. "Not understanding the role that profit and loss plays in the business world is keeping the gender gap going."

Even if you don't aspire to a top slot in your company, you're more likely to rise when you understand how your job and your division affect profit and loss. That starts with managing budgets, but also includes truly understanding how your budget, and your bosses' budgets, play into your company's bottom line.

Some of our Top 30 Companies actually provide training for high-potential employees on managing the bottom line. Ellen Meiner, a vice president for talent management at Liz Claiborne Apparel, doesn't have P&L responsibility. Yet. But a two-day business simulation taught her what it feels like to run an apparel business.

"In my real job, I manage a support function, so it was really good for me to better understand how my actions affect the decisions of the people I work for who do have P&L responsibility," she says. During Ellen's simulation, the five members of her team received a packet describing their make-believe apparel company and the competition. Each team member chose an executive role (Ellen played a marketing director), and they worked together to make decisions about research, pricing, promotion, and other strategic issues. Each team included a real financial analyst to help interpret profit-and-loss documents showing the results of decisions their team made.

"I brought back a higher appreciation of how specific decisions can have a meaningful impact on profit and loss," she says.

All of these strategies, from finding a mentor to understanding the bottom line, can help you advance in your company and your career. You don't need corporate-sponsored programs to start using most of these strategies. But that doesn't mean you shouldn't ask for them! Programs that help women advance in business can make your company—whether it's a huge global organization or a ten-person business—more competitive. At the very least, companies end up with happier, more productive employees who understand a more diverse range of customers and clients. And in the best case, companies discover untold treasures of talent and dedication in their working mother employees who truly want to contribute as much as they can to their enterprises.

Ambitious Women Helping Ambitious Women

Sometimes the most ambitious women are also the ones who support other women the most. This was certainly the case with my dear friend Barbara Bella. Barbara became my right-hand person when *Working Mother* magazine was only a few years old and I began looking for a dynamic person to open a California office for advertising sales. I knew Barbara would be an important person in my life when the plane got me in four hours late for our interview and she cheerfully offered to meet me for dinner at midnight! It was an unusual time to interview a candidate, but Barbara was, and is, an unusual woman. We talked and talked until 3:00 in the morning, and I hired her on the spot.

That hire was one of those life-changing decisions that we don't recognize at first: Barbara became not only my West Coast sales director and then my ad director when I promoted her to New York, but also my best strategist, confidante, and friend. I could always count on Barbara—whether it was for day-to-day excellence or those crisis moments when you can't even stop to ask for help. Barbara worked endless hours as she stood in for me at the helm of *Working Mother* when Robert was born six weeks early, and again when he had surgery before his first birthday. But she actually helped me the most by bringing in an unprecedented amount of advertising from California, and making us the number one magazine in our field year after year after year.

Eighteen years after that early-morning dinner, Barbara was the first person I called for advice and support when I acquired *Working Mother* from its third male owner. Barbara gave whatever time I needed, answering my urgent calls at all hours and thinking the most difficult problems through with me—and there were plenty! Even when Barbara eventually decided to branch out on her own, after having her daughter, Bree, she remained a loyal ally: She started a magazine rep firm in California that took on *Working Mother* as its first client!

A remarkably ambitious woman, Barbara wants to be the best at everything she does, and she wanted our magazine to be the best. Her ambition drove her to get every single piece of business for *Working Mother* that she possibly could, and her insistence on excellence has helped make *Working Mother* a better magazine. But her unselfish support of women in business is a lesson to all of us that we can and must to turn to those strong, ambitious, highly successful businesswomen when our own need is greatest.

Chapter Five

We Teach Our Schools a Lesson

Ever since she started school, Julia has been very opinionated about her teachers. She has a passionate love for the good ones. The great ones (Mrs. Bernstein, Miss Linn, Miss Burke, Miss Higgins, and Miss Nehaw) get homemade gifts and cards with poems. At home, we hear lots of animated reporting about what they said and did in class. The not-so-good ones get acerbic evaluations that could play on Comedy Central. "She's so easy to sidetrack that we had a twenty-minute discussion about *lentils* instead of our chemistry lesson!" she said of one teacher recently.

But whether they're connecting deeply with our children or just teaching them the basics, teachers are a key part of our Home Team.

As part of the team, teachers have lots of time to observe our children in a setting to which we have only limited access. They see things about our children that we don't. Bob and I always knew that Julia had a vivid imagination, but we didn't realize that this could be a problem until a parent-teacher conference in the third grade.

We were all sitting in those tiny chairs around a low, small table—four of her teachers, Bob, and me—when her writing teacher enthusiastically described how good Julia was at observing and writing details.

"The detailed description that Julia wrote of your mother's

farm in Illinois is amazing," she marveled. "I can just see the horse barn with the twisted oak tree, and the old spotty cow that Julia describes so lovingly. It must be wonderful for Julia to be able to spend so much time there with your parents."

The only thing was, my mother didn't have a farm. She lived in a modest Craftsman house on a thirty-five-foot-wide lot just twenty-five minutes outside of Chicago. The only thing farmlike in my mother's house was a poster that read "Hogs Are Beautiful," which had hung in the basement since I was sixteen. The teachers were a bit embarrassed to learn that they had each been duped by Julia into crediting her observation skills instead of her imagination. This episode, however, proved very useful to us later on when we learned that Julia, in seventh grade, was using her imagination in a way that might be harmful to her.

Up to that time, Julia had never shown much interest in the Internet. Then she suddenly realized it was a great way to get attention from her friends—especially boys. I found her e-mailing extremely tall tales about untold numbers of people in our family dying of horrible causes, and stories of a neighbor stalking her—all designed to solicit tender feelings or protective ardor from the newly discovered male gender. The completely realistic details of these fictional accounts reminded me of that day in third grade, and it didn't take me long to set her straight on the dangers of misusing her talents.

I know other working moms share my gratitude for the part that teachers play on our Home Teams. Susan Lapinski, the editor in chief of *Working Mother*, decided to start the Working Mother's Awesome Teachers Awards because she remembered crying tears of gratitude over the support she got from her two daughters' teachers as she struggled with her career during their younger years.

When we called for readers to send us nominations for the Awesome Awards, we were inundated with hundreds of nominations from all across the country—many with art projects demonstrating their appreciation. All this from busy working moms! Our readers recognize that school is not just about education, it's about the mentoring and molding of the spirit of the child—and teachers play a critical role in this process.

School Craze

Not only am I a big fan of teachers, but I'm a staunch advocate of the public school system: I went to Cossitt Avenue Grade School, Lyons Township High School, Eastern Illinois University, and Empire State College—all public schools—and was well served at each. My kids have gone to public school, with the important exception of three years that Robert spent at the Windward School in White Plains, a marvelous school for kids with reading disabilities. But for all my enthusiasm for public education, even I have to admit that sometimes school feels like part of the problem.

It often starts in kindergarten, which presents a crazy-quilt set of problems for working mothers. First, in many school systems, like Chappaqua's, kindergarten is only half a day. And then to make the whole thing more complicated, many schools switch the children from morning to afternoon sessions halfway through the year. So after you've set up a Home Team to meet the peculiar needs of a half day of kindergarten that starts at 9:00 a.m. and ends at noon, you then have to solve the same problem for a 1:00 p.m. start time. No matter how much we've complained here in Chappaqua, the system is still the same. Working mothers are frequently ignored by the community. Why schools ignore the needs of 26 million customers is just plain hard to imagine.

And it's not just kindergarten. All the way through high school, the thinking in schools seems to be stuck in an era when all moms stayed home. That not only means they're way behind the times— but it means they have *never* understood the needs of moms at the lower end of the economic spectrum, who have always been part of the workforce, and always suffered from the lack of sensible scheduling. Even teachers who are working mothers—and many are—

have difficulty with school schedules. My mom often had to attend "teachers' institutes," or meet with her department head on days that we kids had off from school, and the summer was not very long for her as she worked after our school year ended in the summer and before it began in the fall. Teachers' easy hours are a myth.

Here are some of the things about schools that drive working moms crazy:

1. PTA meetings at 9:30 a.m.

2. Parent-teacher conferences scheduled only during work hours

3. School volunteer programs that don't accommodate the schedules of working mothers

4. School start times that vary by the age of the children, so one year's solution won't work the next year

5. School days that start and end very early, with a seven-hour day that doesn't match anyone's work schedule.

If you look hard enough, there are creative solutions that we can use as role models in solving the urgent problems of before- and after-school care, volunteering, and school schedules.

The 3:00 p.m. Shuffle

Robert was nine and Julia was six when our babysitter Sandy landed a great job as an administrative assistant to a lawyer. Since the children were both in school, they didn't need her full-time attention anymore. But they did need supervision when they got home.

At first, we hired housekeepers, who served as an adult presence after school. But we soon found a much better (and cheaper!) solution. As the kids got older, Bob gradually changed his work schedule, eventually launching his own financial planning business at home. He loved working out of the house, and we realized we saved a lot of money by having him take on more child-care duties. He has always been a very involved dad, but being truly responsible for the kids brought him to a whole new level of engagement. He became our after-school solution and a key player on the Home Team—and he still is.

Like Julia and Robert, about 43 percent of all kids in K–12 are supervised after school by a parent or relative, without any other after-school backup.[1] Many moms use the most popular of all work-life benefits—flextime—so their day starts and ends at about the same time school does. (Sophie Oberstein starts her workday at 7:30 a.m. and goes home at 2:30 p.m. most days so she can pick up Lily and Evan at school.) But millions of families don't have that luxury. On average, there's a gap of twenty to twenty-five hours per week between the time school lets out and the time parents get home, which can be a harrowing period for anyone who doesn't have a reliable after-school care solution.

"I look at my watch and sit at my desk until my daughter calls," Karen Bellemore of Lowell, Massachusetts, told us. "If I don't get the call at the exact time, I'm a wreck. I'm distracted from my work, and my coworkers know better than to schedule a meeting at that time. Once she's home safely, I'll call again later to check up on her: Is she doing her homework? Is she eating ice cream instead of an apple? Is she on the Internet?"[2] Millions of parents can't find affordable after-school programs in their area, so they leave their older kids to supervise themselves. In fact, 14 million school-age kids are unsupervised after school, according to a 2003 survey by the Afterschool Alliance, a nonprofit that advocates for quality after-school care.[3] We started to let Robert and Julia stay home alone occasionally as they got older and found it was a big step toward independence. But it's okay only if the kids are ready for it . . . and unfortunately, the lack of after-school care means some kids supervise themselves at a very early age, long before they're ready (over a million kids in K–5th grade supervise themselves). Working parents aren't happy about this: 31 percent of working parents who lack after-school care say they'd enroll their kids in a program if one were available.[4]

In some states, school districts themselves are coming to the rescue. In 2001, we reported that about 40 percent of school districts in the United States offer before- or after-school care.[5] And some communities offer very strong, affordable programs through YMCAs, Boys and Girls Clubs, or religious organizations. Moms told us how much peace of mind these programs give them. "I'm a single mother, so the fact that my son's school has always offered before- and after-school care is an enormous relief to me," says Kim Breakey, who runs a consulting company specializing in historic preservation. "The programming is terrific, engaging, and geared to his school day. Before school, he's given a nutritious breakfast. Afterward, there are extracurricular activities that he could not take advantage of otherwise."[6]

From Tutors to Tai Kwan Do

In the many, many communities across the country where there just isn't enough affordable after-school care, some working moms are taking it upon themselves to start programs. Some of those moms lobby their city officials to fund new efforts . . . and some working moms, like Donna Perham and Tricia Carella of Walnut Creek, California, roll up their sleeves and put together programs themselves.

Donna, a nurse, and Tricia, a preschool director, were both usually home in the afternoons when their kids got home. Once the kids reached sixth grade, they usually had friends in tow . . . because the district only provided after-school care through fifth grade.

"So many kids hung out at our houses, it showed us how big the need was," says Donna, the mother of three kids, ages fifteen through nineteen. She'd started a drug awareness program at the local middle school and was bothered by the level of stress and depression she saw in students. "This is a time when kids really need someone there for them, and there are no options." She and Tricia, who has three kids, ages fourteen through nineteen, would talk over the problem while jogging. Finally, they decided to start their own after-school center for tweens.

They started by creating a not-for-profit organization and approaching their school district and the city of Walnut Creek for support. The city offered a $20,000 matching grant, and a local middle school agreed to rent them land for the center for just $1 a year.

The center, built mostly through private donations of $100 to $200 per family, opened in September 2005 with a wide variety of activities. High school students tutor middle school students in the computer room, kids play pool or board games in the game room, fix snacks in the kitchen, or play basketball outside. And talk about affordable—parents pay the center just $5.50 an hour.

Obviously, not every working parent is about to quit her job and start a new career running an after-school center. But the need is so pressing that some groups of working moms are actually teaming up, volunteering their time, and creating their own after-school programs. For instance, when a survey of parents' needs showed an overwhelming demand for after-school care at her kids' elementary school, Christine Gingerella of Westerly, Rhode Island, volunteered to pull together an after-school program. An editorial cartoonist, Christine had only limited time to work on the project. But by recruiting about thirty community volunteers, she managed to create a fun, free program that ran three days a week, offering kids ten different activities to choose from.

"A grandmother taught needlepoint, an executive chef taught children how to decorate foods, an architect used LEGOs to introduce students to basic design and construction," she says. The program was such a success that it eventually became a funded part of the school system.

I find moms like Christine, Donna, and Tricia truly inspiring.

They see a need and find a way to meet it. And although there's no way most working moms have the time to organize their own after-school program, these moms show that you really can make a difference. "You don't have to do it all on your own," says Donna, a cofounder of the Walnut Creek program. "Mothers can get the idea going, put together the model, and present it to the city, town, or civic organization."

Jen Rinehart, an interim director of the advocacy group After-school Alliance, agrees. "Parents can be a strong voice in helping us convince policy makers and corporations to provide and sponsor after-school programs," Rinehart told us. To get a program started, study what other districts, cities, and parents have done, then go to your school board or city council to rally support. Contact the Afterschool Alliance at www.afterschoolalliance.org for more ideas.

Kids on Campus

At *Working Mother*, I've been excited to see that many of our 100 Best Companies are catching on to the need for after-school care, especially for tweens. When Abbott, for example, conducted its first employee work-life survey in 1999, one thing came back "loud and clear," according to Sharon Larkin, a divisional vice president for human resources and diversity. Parents needed help with kids in that "in-between stage . . . too old for day care but not old enough to stay home."[7]

The most progressive are helping moms to meet that need by providing before- or after-school programs for employees' kids. Almost half of the 2004 class of the Working Mother 100 Best Companies sponsored after-school care. S. C. Johnson, which makes Ziploc, Shout, Drano, and other household products, runs the most magnificent program of them all at Armstrong Park, a gigantic 110-acre facility that houses swimming pools, basketball courts, a yoga center, and tennis and squash courts for use by employees and their families. There's an after-school program for employees' children *or* grandchildren that keeps kids focused on physical fitness after school. The company will pick your kids up from any school in the greater Racine, Wisconsin, area to join in the fun at Armstrong Park, even if she is the only child eligible at that school. Privately owned, S. C. Johnson created this private park for employees decades ago, and has adapted its use as the needs of its employees change.

Other companies reimburse parents for the cost of after-school care. Bank of America, for example, reimburses its employees up to $152 a month for child care for school-age children. Still other companies put money into community programs, rather than sponsoring their own after-school care. MBNA built Camden Skate Park in Camden, Maine, to provide a fun resource for kids after school.

Then there's a much more radical approach that some of the most creative companies are adopting: they're bringing schools to work. When I visited the child-care center at Abbott's headquarters, I was surprised to see a full class of adults there too! They were Abbott employees, learning about the new all-day kindergarten that launched on the Abbott campus in 2003. The program is a huge hit with parents, many of whom had their children in the Abbott child-care center since infancy.

JFK Medical Center in Atlantis, Florida, takes the idea of kids at work even further: it opened a charter school in 2002. About four hundred children attend the hospital's public K–5th grade school right there on the campus. JFK maintains the facilities, subsidizes utilities, and pays for a professional management company. Because many of JFK's two thousand employees work twelve-hour shifts, the school also provides before- and after-school care for a fee.

The on-site school made a huge difference for Patricia Hajduk-Condon, whose son Patrick transferred there in third grade. Before transferring, Patrick was struggling with a learning disability. Patricia worked closely with the charter school's teachers, administrators, and after-school caregivers to help bring Patrick up to grade level. By fourth grade, he was among the top five students in his class, thanks to the great teamwork—made easier by the fact that the school and the after-school care program were right there at Patricia's job. "[Patrick] feels good about himself and he's more confident," Patricia told the *Nursing Times*. "This changes my entire world as a single mother to see my son become a happy and independent child."[8]

I know how she feels. When Robert failed to learn to read after going through first grade twice, I thought we would never solve this problem. We were lucky enough to find Windward, a school for kids with reading disabilities, and Robert learned to read in just three months after he started. Our journey would have been far more affordable if we'd been able to turn to a school with specialized resources right there at work, like Patricia did.

Of course, only a few companies are prepared to go as far as Abbott and JFK Medical Center have. But that doesn't mean they can't find creative options. In Des Moines, where many employees commute into the city's downtown from distant suburbs, a group of companies joined forces to create a school right there in the downtown area for commuters' kids.[9] The 160 students at the Downtown School enjoy small classes—just 16 students per class—and often commute to school from the suburbs with their parents. Before or after school, the kids can stay at one of several child-care centers that have partnered with the school. During the day, parents are encouraged to drop in and attend parent-child activities scheduled at lunchtime. Parent-teacher conferences happen anywhere, anytime: mornings at the parent's workplace, afternoons at school, evenings at the child's home, and any other combination that works for teachers and parents.

Home Alone

If your kids are mature enough, letting them supervise themselves after school can be a great experience for everyone. As Julia and Robert got older, Bob started leaving them alone at home when he had to go out on an ambulance call. They soon learned all the latchkey kid best practices: Know where the phone numbers are and who to call in an emergency. Know where the fire extinguisher is (under the sink) and how to use it (pull the red tab and then pull the trigger). Know what to say when someone calls (never say the adults aren't home), and know what to do when someone comes to the door (don't answer it).

The kids did a great job. My uncle Paul and aunt Lois, who were in their seventies and looked pretty harmless, decided to stop by unexpectedly as they drove from Florida to their home in North Dakota. Robert, who had never met them, wouldn't let them come in the house. Even though it was kind of embarrassing, Uncle Paul and Aunt Lois were impressed with his authoritative decision. Another time, Bob was returning from an ambulance call when he heard the fire pager go off and the dispatcher say, "Fire emergency call from a child." At our address! You can imagine how fast Bob drove that ambulance to our house! Julia's computer had caught on fire (maybe from spinning all those tall tales on e-mail!), and Robert was not the least bit intimidated by the four-foot flames. He put the fire out with the extinguisher (which was under the sink) while Julia called 911.

Some companies are giving parents a hand in preparing kids to stay home alone. Eli Lilly offers a half-day workshop for parents and older kids, called Children in Self-Care, which helps families decide if their kids are ready to stay by themselves and trains kids in latchkey safety. Many of our other 100 Best Companies offer a range of parenting workshops, lectures, and brown-bag lunches. If your company doesn't offer sessions like these, it's a very easy and inexpensive place to ask for support. Ask your human resources director to set up a brown-bag lunch for parents about preparing kids to stay home—you might even want to suggest a speaker yourself. Local public safety agencies like the police department have great resources for events like this.

The Volunteer Army

After-school supervision isn't the only problem working mothers struggle with when it comes to school-age kids. Many, many working mothers want to volunteer at our schools: we know it improves our children's grades, and it gives us the chance to get to know their classmates, friends, and, most important, their teachers. I especially like the chance to see what the other kids are wearing so that I can tell if my daughter is telling the truth when she says everyone wears those low-rise jeans.

But getting involved with schools can be incredibly frustrating for working moms. Even after all these years, many PTA meetings and volunteer schedules don't fit into a working day. In the <u>What Moms Want</u> survey, 66 percent said they would like to volunteer more at their schools than they do. When we asked what was stopping those who wanted to volunteer more, two out of three said that their schools' volunteer activities didn't fit their work schedules, and one out of five said PTA meetings took place during their workday. Many also blamed their own schedule: 41 percent said they just didn't have the time.

The lack of volunteer opportunities for working mothers is heartbreaking for some moms, like Marcy Holmblad, a financial analyst in Brunswick, Maine. When her daughter started first grade, Marcy couldn't wait to volunteer—and she figured she'd have plenty of time to do it, since she only worked Wednesday through Friday. But at first-grade orientation, she learned that even her part-time schedule wasn't flexible enough. "We were told that if we couldn't come in on Wednesday or Thursday mornings, then we weren't needed," Holmblad told us. "When I explained my schedule to my daughter's teacher, she suggested that I chaperone a field trip or two on my days off."[10] For Marcy, field trips were a disappointing compromise: she wanted to be in the classroom on a regular basis.

I always want to volunteer more than I am able to, so I look for assignments that I think I can handle. For several years I signed up for the Halloween Fun Fair run by our PTA. I volunteered to work the booths, and was struck by a wave of envy when I walked into the gym that first year. I was amazed by the elaborate crafts that other moms had created for each of the booths. One mom made intricate dolls that the kids could dress up. Another made green gloves that kids could decorate with gruesome stuff to make them into monster hands. Flower pots were ready for little hands to glue their names on with letters cut out ahead of time by a mom. Where did they find the time to do this? How did they manage? Each booth seemed more fanciful than the next, and at the end of the gym the school stage had been transformed into a Broadway-quality fun house. I felt like *I* had walked into a fun house myself—into a time warp and energy field that I couldn't relate to. How could I compete with these moms who dedicated so much time and talent to making the Fun Fair so perfect?

Help from the Goddess

There have been many times when I've felt almost sick at the difference between myself and the stay-at-home moms in my town. For years I lived next door to a neighbor who was the Goddess of Suburban Perfection. She knew everything that was going on at school—down to what they were serving in the cafeteria that day. I never had to turn on the radio to find out if there was a snow day. I just called the Goddess. She knew. She knew which teachers she hoped her children would get, when every school club met, and all the schedules for all the sports activities. I wanted to be like her but I wasn't. I wasn't even close. I felt hopelessly out of touch whenever we talked about our school, like I lived in a different town rather than right next door.

These are the kinds of feelings that fuel the mommy wars, where stay-at-home and working moms feel judged and judgmental. The envy that working moms feel for the time and energy stay-at-home moms devote to kids and community is perhaps only matched by the envy that stay-at-home moms feel over the arc and passions of our careers. The jealousy is real, because the grass often really does look greener from the other side.

But the mommy wars are as pointless as most wars. Each side gains very little from engagement, but there is much to lose. "Why can't we all just be friends?" might sound a bit Pollyannaish, but it's the attitude that will help both camps the most. The moms who put on the Fun Fair still needed as much help as they could get to make the fair work. And the Goddess didn't seem to mind telling me that it wasn't a snow day, just a two-hour delay. Many other stay-at-home moms have stepped up to the plate since the Goddess moved away, and I have learned not to engage in even a skirmish in the mommy wars. If I do, I will lose some of my best supporters, just when I need them the most, as we confront those dreaded late teen years.

Better Together

The fact is, when working moms and stay-at-home moms team up, we come up with some of the very best solutions for everyone. Danielle Davis, a public relations executive in Baltimore, couldn't say no when her third-grade son asked her to volunteer as class mom. With her busy schedule, she feared a stay-at-home mom would have a better shot at the job, so she applied an idea from the business world: job sharing. She suggested to the teacher that she share the job of class mom with a stay-at-home mother—and the teacher loved the idea. So Danielle took the lead on out-of-class tasks, like phone calls, volunteer scheduling, party planning, and field trips, while her stay-at-home partner spent more time in the classroom. The arrangement worked out well for everyone.[11]

In another terrific working mom/stay-at-home mom partnership, Gloria Flarsheim, a parent volunteer coordinator at Virginia Heights Elementary School in Roanoke, Virginia, came up with a great new system. Her traditional in-class volunteers—many of them stay-at-home moms—collect assignments for the at-home volunteers, and send them home with the kids. At-home volunteers—mostly working moms—complete the projects. They might cut flash cards into puzzle pieces or make signs and posters, for example. Then they send the projects back to class with their kids. "At-home volunteering has been a godsend to teachers," Flarsheim told us. "They're really grateful they can get things done that are very time-consuming." Moms like it too: the school's volunteer army grew by more than 70 percent.[12]

Sometimes our job skills can benefit our communities. Joan Sheridan LaBarge, the publisher of *Working Mother*, volunteered to be both an assistant soccer coach and an assistant class mom—and found that her ability to put everyone's needs into an Excel spreadsheet was appreciated far more than anything else she contributed. Then she got in a bit deeper when she decided to start an all-girls soccer league in response to her daughter Katie's question, "Mommy, when will the girls be allowed to score a goal?" The all-girls soccer league of Forest Hills is a smash hit, and Joan enjoyed the ultimate reward when she saw Katie score her first goal this season.

Perturbed by the PTA

Unfortunately, in many school districts, it's hard for working parents to volunteer because they simply can't make it to PTA meetings. Moms often tell me how frustrated they are with PTA meetings that happen during the school day. While some PTAs, including Chappaqua's, are alternating meetings at night with those in the morning, it doesn't completely solve the problem . . . because many stay-at-home moms won't come to evening meetings. It also doesn't solve the problem of volunteer projects. Many school volunteer projects are still developed around the model of a handful of parents giving eighty hours a month, rather than dozens of parents giving one or two hours a month.

"We're trying to get PTAs to realize what a powerful thing it would be if all parents just gave fifteen minutes a month," says Linda Hodge, the president of the National PTA, a Chicago-based organization that supports PTAs around the country. To encourage PTAs to include a broader range of parents—working moms, fathers, and minority parents—the organization encourages PTAs to hold meetings at more accessible times and places. "Some of our PTAs are holding meetings at seven a.m. or after five p.m. And we're seeing PTA meetings take place at soccer fields and workplace lunchrooms and places of worship."

Meanwhile, Hodge says, the best way to transform your PTA is to take the bull by the horns. "If you really want to be involved, don't just check off your interests on a piece of paper," she says. "Find out what needs to be done and work creatively to do it. Tell them, 'These are my interests, these are my talents, this is the time I have available, and this is what I'd like to do.'"

Summertime Blues

When lots of Americans worked on family farms, it made sense for the school day to start early—so kids would still have daylight hours to do chores after school—and for schools to shut down in the summer, so children could help during prime growing season. But those schedules don't make sense anymore, now that our kids aren't working the harvest, and now that most parents work full-time.

Don't get me wrong. I love the fact that kids have a lot of time off. Julia in particular is a huge advocate of summers off. "We need the long summer vacation because it's the only time we don't have to worry about school," she says. "During winter and spring breaks and other holidays, we still have a lot of pressure on us."

But working moms are severely tested by the generous time off that students in this country are given. Our kids spend about half as much time in school as children in other industrialized nations![13] Christmas, winter, and spring breaks create their own challenges, and then there's summer. Two months off for kids, but not for moms.

My own best practice for handling my children's school vacations is to join them whenever possible. I believe in vacations, and I believe that every mother and father in America should take *every day* of vacation their company allows *every year*. Whether taking vacation is encouraged or frowned upon at your company, you earn your vacation just like you earn your paycheck: you wouldn't think of turning a paycheck back to your employer, would you? And yet in 2001, 36 percent of employees surveyed by Ellen Galinsky's group, Families and Work Institute, said they did not intend to take their full vacation that year.[14]

Here's the best way to be sure to take your vacation time: plan ahead. I have four weeks of vacation time and I plan it to correspond to Robert and Julia's time off. I take a week at Christmas, a week for spring break, and two weeks in August. Because some of the days during Christmas are holidays anyway, I have two or three days left over that I can take when I need them. This schedule works for me, my employees, and my family. I plan the time at least six months in advance, and tell everyone I'll be gone then. And I never back down from my vacation weeks. To make it all work, I pick the weeks when I think things will be the slowest at work anyway—and I pick times when my kids will appreciate it the most.

Summer Solutions

No matter how well you plan your vacations, you're going to have to work on the majority of summer days when your kids are off, and during many holidays. After all, how many companies close for Cesar Chavez Day, a school holiday in California?

Progressive companies are helping solve the problem. Some companies, including Working Mother Media, provide flexible schedules, including summer hours, where you have half days every Friday, from Memorial Day through Labor Day, or every other Friday off, usually from July 1 to September 1.

Other companies offer holiday programs for kids. I recently visited a child-care center in midtown Manhattan that serves employees of JPMorgan Chase. During school breaks, the center becomes a school break center for older kids. These big teens look kind of hilarious playing in the day-care center, but they seem to be enjoying all the activities designed especially for them—from karaoke contests to babysitting and CPR courses. The kids get to know each other over time, and look forward to seeing each other again.

Intel solves the tweens-in-day-care problem by providing the older kids with their own rooms at its eight child-care centers in Oregon, Arizona, and California, so the tweens don't feel "babysat." Abbott keeps tweens busy on school holidays with computer classes, tai kwan do, poetry writing workshops, and more. And three times a year (on Martin Luther King Day, Presidents' Day, and during fall break), the pharmaceutical company Eli Lilly, based in Indianapolis, offers field trips for the school-age kids of Lilly employees. Recent trips have included visits to Conner Prairie, a living-history museum north of Indianapolis, the local Children's Museum, and Apple Works, an apple and pumpkin farm.

The age-old solution of sending kids off to overnight camp for eight weeks (which preceded the working mother revolution) is very popular all across the country, but it was not a solution that I ever tried. Many of my friends swear by summer camp, and I can fully understand why. The kids build friendships, learn new skills, get experience at being away from home, and are usually excited to go back year after year. I just could not bear to be away from my kids for eight weeks, so I never signed them up for a sleepaway camp. I employed other methods, though, including all kinds of day camps.

Most moms I know create a patchwork of day camps, babysitters, vacation time, and other activities. So it's really helpful when companies speed up the process for us by holding summer camp fairs at lunchtime, like Allstate does at its Northbrook, Illinois, headquarters.

"They brought in summer camps from all over the area at lunch hour one day," says Melinda Tunner, an assistant vice president and the mother of thirteen-year-old Alec. "In one hour, I talked to program directors and counselors from all kinds of local camps. It saved me a lot of time and let me see all the options that are out there."

Coordinating a summer camp fair is a relatively low-cost measure that can help employees be more productive and take less time tracking down summer solutions. It's a great place to start asking your company for help!

Some companies go much further. Eli Lilly sponsors three summer camps at different locations around the country, which hosted 579 kids in 2003. At the company's summer camp in Indianapolis, kids enjoyed a different science-based theme every week: Zoo-apoolza; Weird, Wacky, Wild and Wet Times; and Start the Chemical Commotion, to name a few. Some on-site child-care centers, like the Bright Horizons center at JFK Medical Center in Atlantis, Florida, offer summer camps featuring arts and crafts and swimming lessons. In 2003, IBM developed "gap camps," special camps for the tricky week between the time school lets out and the time traditional summer camps start. IBM teams up with camp providers like YMCA and pays them to develop the camp, setting up a curriculum and activities. Parents still have to pay for attendance, but their children get priority in enrollment, which means less scrambling for parents. IBM is also proud of their EXITE (Exploring Interests in Technology and Engineering) Camps for girls, which allow high-achieving female science students from all over the world to work on math- and science-related projects, from building robots to making ice cream with liquid nitrogen.

When companies don't have the means or the drive to sponsor a full-fledged summer camp (and let's face it, most of them don't), they sometimes team up with other companies in their area to fund programs. Allstate works with several other companies in the Chicago area to fund the Summer of Service day camp especially for tweens (ten to twelve-year olds) who pose special day-care challenges: they don't want to be babysat, but many parents feel they're too young to be left alone all day.

Melinda Tunner ended up enrolling her son Alec, then twelve, in Summer of Service in 2004 after she learned about it at the summer camp fair. "Alec was excited to have something aimed at his age group, and what intrigued me was the community service approach," Melinda told us. During Alec's six weeks at camp, he helped raise money for an animal shelter and planned activities with residents at an assisted living center. Because Allstate is a sponsor of the Summer of Service program, Melinda also got a healthy discount on the cost of camp.

All in the Timing

Of course, moms and companies wouldn't have to scramble in the summer if school schedules made more sense. Some moms love the year-round school movement that's grown rapidly in the past decade, where schools have several substantial breaks during the year instead of one long summer vacation. In 2000, nearly 3,000 schools around the country offered year-round schedules, up from 618 in 1990.

Jill Clark, a registered nurse in Bardstown, Kentucky, told us she's crazy about her school district's full-year schedule. The district sticks to a traditional 180-day school year, with just six weeks of summer vacation in June and July, and longer breaks throughout the year. "After six weeks, my kids are sick of each other and more than ready to return to school," she says.[15] Of course, this raises the new challenge of longer breaks throughout the year . . . but it means parents don't have to fill up two and a half months of downtime all at once.

You don't have to persuade your school to go to a year-round schedule to make academics and work fit together. Schools around the country have come up with creative strategies to make school schedules easier on working parents. E-mail and the Web are making it easier for parents and teachers to connect. Yvonne Jensen of Minneapolis, for instance, can log on to Washburn High's Web site to see her daughter Chelsea's homework assignments. More than once, she's discovered her daughter really did have homework—even when she said she didn't.[16] Yvonne has also participated in parent-teacher conferences online and regularly e-mails her daughter's teachers. In our survey of working mothers, we found that 49 percent e-mail with teachers and 19 percent can log on to a class Web site providing updates on class assignments and their children's progress.

Sometimes, simple awareness of working parents' dilemmas can lead to small, individual solutions that make life easier. My favorite ideas:[17]

- Solomon Schechter Day School in Skokie, Illinois, combines events like science fairs and parent-child lunches so moms can take time off on just one day, not two.
- Maine West High School in Des Plaines, Illinois, started making guidance counselors, school psychologists, and other support staff available to parents in person or by phone several evenings a week.
- West Elementary School in Lancaster, Ohio, holds repeat

performances of school plays, inviting parents to a dress rehearsal during the day or the main performance at night.

Even small adjustments like these let working parents get involved—which helps everyone. Kids do better in school, schools get more support, and working moms can feel more in touch with their kids' lives—while feeling less stress and more peace of mind when they're at work.

Chapter Six

To Find Balance, We Seek Fusion

My mother and father both had careers when I was growing up, but they had very different models of working. My dad, a deeply intellectual man who loves to read about history and ponder economics, was the chief financial officer of the Casper Tin Plate Company, a manufacturing firm on the south side of Chicago. He maintained the traditional separation between work and home with Ozzie and Harriet rigidity. Dad came home every day at the same time, read the paper, and waited for dinner to be served. He rarely talked about his work, never took us to his office, and never brought his work home.

My mother, on the other hand, fused her work and home life completely. She started teaching when I turned twelve and included me in her work from the start—because she needed help, and because I was willing and, surprisingly, able to help her.

My mother was a creative, social, energetic bee buzzing around the hive of the high school that I attended. She created a vocational restaurant program for kids in my school who were unlikely to go on to college. Her students went to school in the mornings and worked in local restaurants in the afternoons. I pitched in, at home in the evenings, by helping her match kids to jobs, and by listening to her problems with administrators, parents, employers, and the students themselves. Of course, when she was at school I mostly tried to ignore her, as teenagers *must* ignore their parents. But a few times a month I stopped by her classroom, an elaborate industrial kitchen, to grab a cookie or have a chat. My biggest project was creating a slide show for her called "Careers in Food Service." (I later discovered that my mother had kept that film in her top drawer along with her favorite jewelry for thirty-eight years!)

I didn't know that I would end up following my mother's model of fusing her work and family life, but I'm sure I was deeply influenced by it, because blending my two worlds has always seemed very natural to me. I put this strategy into place right from the beginning. Just after Robert got home from his long stay at the hospital, I had a business meeting in my apartment. Robert was howling, and as my colleague was a woman (though not a mom) and Robert hadn't yet taken a bottle, the only solution was to nurse him right there. She didn't mind, I didn't mind, and Robert was sound asleep in ten minutes.

That was just the beginning of my practice of work-life fusion. As I returned to work at *Working Mother* magazine after my maternity leave, I was able to combine work and family with great success. We photographed Robert for the Working Mother Bulletin Board poster that went up in every KinderCare center as part of an advertising program for Sears. Our babysitter Sandy came in to care for the kids of employees when we did a holiday photo shoot, and her eight-year-old son, Andre, became part of the shoot. I talked about Robert and Bob on all of my sales calls, using myself and the other young working mothers on my staff as real-life examples of the target audience our advertising clients were looking for. Everyone knew all about Robert and his sleepless nights!

Fusing was easy at *Working Mother*. But I've found ways to marry my work and home life at every place I've worked, including at Chief Executive Group—where working mothers were definitely not in vogue. This blend of work and home has contributed to my success by making me feel good about my choices, and bringing me closer to my business colleagues.

No More Phone Booths!

Fortunately, companies are starting to see the value in fusion—and not just because it makes workers feel more balanced. There's a new idea percolating in the world of work: companies are realizing that they might get a better deal if they allow the whole person who works for them to be present on the job—not just the part of the person who answers phones, or manages sales, or works on the assembly line, but all of the qualities and characteristics that make them who they are. By making room for the whole person, with each individual's unique combination of tastes, talents, personal experience, and background, companies reap the benefits of an employee's individuality. And mothers feel more balanced if they don't have to go through a superhero-in-the-phone-booth change twice a day.

"Why should I leave half of myself in the parking lot when I get to work?" asked a young mother from Verizon Wireless when I gave a talk there recently.

And yet that's exactly what women have been doing for decades. Never mentioning the family at work because it might make them sound less committed. Not putting up their children's artwork in their cubicles because they'd look less serious. Saying they're stepping out for a meeting instead of a teacher conference. Fortunately, at companies that are fostering a family-friendly culture, that's all changing.

"I used to say, 'I'm going to an outside meeting' if I went to a pediatrician. Now I feel zero guilt if I say, 'I'm going to a school play,'" Andrea Jung, the chairman and CEO of Avon and a mother of two, told us.[1] "I think it gives the women with kids who work here freedom—because it starts from the top—to feel like there are moments that family comes first, and that's not only okay, it's important."

When we fuse our work and home lives, we no longer have to hide the 26-million-mom secret—that we're mothers first. Fusion—the freedom to let our home and work lives blend together at certain points in our days and our lives—allows a person to bring her home life to work and her work life home. Fusion allows us to live whole lives, so we don't feel torn and bereft of our families during work hours and panicky about work when we should be fully present at home.

Points of Fusion

Fusion doesn't mean you have to combine 100 percent of your work with your life, so your kids are running in and out of the office and you're always answering your cell phone at soccer games! That sounds like a nightmare to me—I really value my time in the office when I'm focused entirely on my business. And I cherish my time at home, when I'm totally focused on Bob, Robert, and Julia. Instead, "fusion" means selecting certain key points where you want your work and home life to blend. Maybe that's feeling comfortable enough to talk about your child's school play at work; maybe it means having the flexibility to leave during the day to see that play. Maybe it means bringing your work to your home and telecommuting a day or two every week. The points of fusion that work for each parent will be different. But in the end, finding a degree of fusion can help you feel like a whole person and make you happier at work and home—for many moms, fusion is the tool that creates balance.

For Janet Truncale of Summit, New Jersey, who works four days a week, fusion means making sure her clients at Ernst & Young know what she has planned during her days off with Gabrielle, seven, Noah, five, and Freddy, two.

"Because I'm on a flexible schedule, it's very important to me to be responsive and get back to my clients even more quickly than if I were full-time," she says. "I'm very open with my clients, and they know when I'm not in the office and they also know that if anything's important, they can reach me on my BlackBerry. My clients know my children's schedule, so when I'm driving Gabrielle to dance class or taking Noah to the gym, they won't call me."

For Diane Wedderburn, the information technology expert in our office, fusion meant bringing her daughter Alía, ten, into the office in the summer last year. Alía loved coming in almost every day; she even had her own desk next to her mother's, where she could read and play on the computer. She became so much a part of our office life that we threw a company party for her birthday in July.

Of course, there are some mothers who prefer my dad's model of perfect separation between home and work. Denise Favorule, who had her first child while she worked for me at *Stagebill*, is a great example. Years after we both left *Stagebill*, Denise had risen to a powerful job at Rodale, a large magazine publishing company. Her two children, Francesca and Alex, are now nine and thirteen years old. I had drinks with her and she shared her recipe for balance.

"Carol," she said, "what I do is this. I work very hard Monday through Friday and do whatever it takes to get my work done. Dinners out, travel, writing proposals at midnight, early and late meetings with my clients or my boss—whatever it takes. Then on the weekends, I do whatever I need and want to do with my family and for myself with laser focus. I don't mix the two together, but I balance the needs of work and home separately." Denise told me that when the perfect workweek/weekend separation is not possible she just keeps her priorities straight: "The kids come first, and I make sure they know they always have that first-place position in my life. Impacting a child's self-esteem for life is a much higher priority than making a meeting that could probably be rescheduled."

I've spoken with a few other women over the years who maintain strict separation between work and life and wouldn't want more fusion. But many women—especially single moms who don't have anyone else to cover school plays, track meets, teacher meetings, and the like—long for some degree of fusion. And that depends on the participation of companies who are willing to make changes and create a parent-friendly culture—an environment where talking about your kids, leaving work for a doctor's appointment, and seeking flexibility won't hurt the way you're perceived.

That's not an easy change for companies to make because it's the company's culture that we're talking about.

At *Stagebill*, it seemed very natural to help parents feel comfortable in fusing work and family life. It was a small company of about seventy-five employees—many of whom had young children—and we had the freedom to chart our own course. We made our family-friendly culture clear by literally inviting the kids to work now and then.

"It's Easter next week and the kids are out of school," the ad director would say. "Let's have a Kids' Day!" I'd announce it, and on the designated day all the kids would traipse into the office, along with our childless CFO's dog. The kids would play bowling in the halls, race around on office chairs, use the white boards for artistic masterpieces, chase the dog around, and eat lots of junk food. Babies were diapered, videos were watched, older kids amused younger kids, and by the end of the day I'd find an exhausted Julia sucking her thumb, sound asleep on the office couch. The family-friendly atmosphere made us all feel closer . . . and more loyal to the company. Believe it or not, we actually did get work done on Kids' Days, and in between the work and the parenting we felt fusion in its fullest form.

At Working Mother Media, we don't have to declare Kids' Days—they just happen, on any given school holiday, when a dozen kids show up at work with their moms to watch movies in the conference room or play with our impressive stash of toys (working for a magazine that covers toys has its perks).

Not every company can allow this kind of fusion. The chaos that kids create in the office doesn't work at most big corporate workplaces. That's why Take Your Daughter to Work Day was created—to give big companies a framework for bringing our daughters, and later our sons, into the office for a day of fusion.

But you don't have to offer bowling in the hallway and office chair races to create more fusion in your life. Women are fusing their work and home lives through flextime and telecommuting programs, job sharing and compressed workweeks. More new moms are able to fuse their desire to breast-feed with their desire to work thanks to the rapid spread of office lactation programs. And companies are starting to do their part to bring home and work together by offering everything from take-home meals from the company cafeteria to parenting workshops in the office, all designed to acknowledge and support the family side of their employees' lives.

Fusion Through Flextime

In our <u>What Moms Want</u> survey, our moms were loud and clear on the topic of fusion. We listed more than two dozen work-life benefits, from on-site child care to paid maternity leave to fitness centers—and asked them what they longed for most. The number-one answer: flexible hours. Not shorter hours (although that was number three on the list). Flexible hours. They wanted flextime—the ability to name their own start and end times, to take an hour or two off for a doctor's appointment or school event, or to be available for an important meeting with a teacher.

Some of the mothers we surveyed (about 54 percent) already worked for companies with flextime policies on the books. And nearly *all* of those mothers who had flextime (a whopping 94 percent!) said it was the benefit they most valued. For moms whose companies didn't offer flextime, it tied for first place with working from home as the benefit they most wanted.

Unfortunately, flextime is often only as flexible as your immediate supervisor. Just because a company has a flextime policy on the books doesn't mean all managers will comply. (I'll talk more about the problem of managers who aren't on board with flexibility and other family-friendly measures in chapter 10.)

What those managers—and the companies *without* flextime—don't realize is that it's one of the cheaper benefits a company can offer. I know because I've seen it work. My assistant, Barbara Rosenthal, used flextime during a period when her kids needed homework help. She only flexed a little—she worked 8:00 a.m. to 4:00 p.m. instead of 9:00 a.m. to 5:00 p.m. But it helped her integrate her work and family lives—and it didn't cost the company a thing. (Actually, it might even have been more efficient, since she came in early and got a head start on the day before anyone else was there to distract her.)

So if flextime would make so many working mothers happier—and it can be done in a way that costs companies very little—why don't all companies have it? According to the Society for Human Resources Management, 43 percent of companies still don't offer flextime. (Although I'm proud to say that 96 percent of the Working Mother 100 Best Companies do.) There may be industries where flextime just doesn't work—but aside from these exceptions, more companies should be providing this simple benefit that improves their employees' lives considerably without blowing corporate budgets.

Similarly, companies need to work harder to provide flextime to all their workers—not just managers and executives. While conventional wisdom says you can't give flexibility to assembly-line workers or other nonmanagement positions, that's just not true.

Look at Kraft Foods. For years, higher-level workers had long enjoyed the flexibility to take short amounts of time off for doctors' appointments and school events, but factory workers had almost no flex. Some plants required workers to take vacation a week at a time and to schedule it a year in advance—no room for dentist appointments there! But after employees and line supervisors spoke up, things changed. Ginger Kraft (no relation to the company name), an assembly-line worker in Kraft's Mason City, Iowa, plant, used to have to take a whole day off without pay if she wanted to go to her six-year-old son Garret's T-ball game or doctor's appointment. But now she can take as little as an hour or as much as a half day off. "It's wonderful to say, 'I have something going on. I have to leave early,'" she told us.[2] If Kraft can make flex work on an assembly line, why can't other companies?

It goes without saying that there's no one perfect solution for flexibility. The best flexible schedules are, well, flexible. Some even change from one season to the next. The possibilities for fusion go on and on. You might find the best way to fuse work and life is to have a "compressed workweek"—working forty hours in four days—like Kim Small, a senior project coordinator at the financial services company Flect Bank (now part of Bank of America). Kim transitioned to compressed hours after her daughter Abigail was born. The long days can be grueling, she told us, but "it's all worth it for that extra day off on Monday."[3] (Only 20 percent of the women in our survey worked for a company that allowed compressed workweeks.)

Or you might find, like Ginger Kraft, the assembly-line worker at Kraft Foods, that all you really need are a few hours off here and there to make your work and home life blend more easily. When it comes to fusion, there are many models, and only you can determine the right combination that will make your life feel more seamless—and more manageable.

Share and Share Alike

If there's no way to get your job done in less than full-time, think about a job share. One of the most successful job shares I know is Sandy Sullivan and Nancy Schumann, who have been job sharing for eight years at GE. Not only do they share a job together, they get promoted together. In the fall of 2002, they jointly applied for and were jointly promoted to the role of manager, Executive Development at GE's John F. Welch Leadership Center in Ossining, New York.

Nancy and Sandy together work forty-eight hours a week, with one day shared in the office. Their success strategies include an evening phone call after the kids are in bed to debrief, cell phone availability during the day, and flexible child-care arrangements that allow for schedule changes.

Sandy has two kids, twelve and ten, while Nancy has four kids, twelve, ten, five, and thirteen months. Their enthusiasm for job sharing seems boundless. "We know that the work we produce together is greater than either could do separately," they told me recently. "We draw on our complementary skills and experiences while providing coaching and support to each other. We're a seamless team, invested in each other's success. We also have a lot of fun!"

Nancy and Sandy believe they have gone farther as a team than they would have on their own, and to hear them is to believe them.

What's in It for the Company?

Not only do some forms of flexibility cost little to the company, but they can actually boost a company's bottom line. That's what Kay Hirai, the owner of two Seattle-area hair salons, discovered. A mother of two grown children, Kay always tried to help staffers who needed flexibility for their families. But her case-by-case approach caused her major headaches: she couldn't always make exceptions for every working mom who asked, and staff members without children wanted flexibility too.

So finally, she decided to rework her schedules entirely. She surveyed the twenty-eight employees at one of her salons, and also surveyed customers about when they most wanted appointments. She created a wide range of schedules: some workers work short days six days a week; others work four long ones. The new schedule has let the salon stay open longer, and sales jumped 20 percent in the first three months.

"If employees are happy, the customers will be happy," Kay said.[4]

It's not just small companies that find flexibility can help profits. First Tennessee Bank, a large bank with locations in three states, did a controlled experiment to measure the impact of flexibility on its business. At several branches, the company trained managers about flexibility and really pushed to create a culture supporting personal lives. The results were impressive. Employees were much less likely to quit the family-friendly branches—which boasted employee retention rates 50 percent higher than other branches. More important to the bean counters, these branches retained 7 percent more customers. It's very expensive to lose customers and attract new ones, so keeping customers meant big savings for First Tennessee—to the tune of an additional $106 million in profits over two years![5]

Why does flexibility make such a dramatic impact on employees and on customers? Partly, it's because we feel better. Employees with flexible work arrangements are less likely to experience job stress and burnout, according to companies surveyed by Corporate Voices for Working Families, a nonprofit group of large corporations interested in work-life issues. And you're a lot more productive if you're not burnt out.

That's what Sarah Moore and Hilary Hausman found when they agreed to share the job of account director at DDB San Francisco. The two moms each work two and a half days—thirty hours—a week, but share the salary and benefits of one employee. "Any one person who works sixty hours a week would tend to burn out," Sarah told us. But since she and Hilary share the job, the company gets much more for its money.[6]

If you're arguing for more flexibility at your company, you'll find plenty of ammunition to help make your case. Just a few examples:

- When Ikea North America adopted flexible work arrangements, the company's employee turnover dropped by 25 percent.[7]
- IBM surveyed their top performers and found they valued work-life balance as much as compensation when they were deciding whether to stay with the company.
- Some 94 percent of IBM managers say flexible work options improve the company's "ability to retain talented professionals."[8]
- In a study by Corporate Voices for Working Families, one

firm reported that flexibility arrangements reduced turnover enough to save them $41.5 million in 2003 alone.[9]

- The HR consulting firm Watson Wyatt found that firms with high employee satisfaction also have a higher stock value and that, specifically, a flexible workplace can boost a company's market value by 9 percent.[10]

Home Sweet Home Office

When my kids were young, almost no one I knew ever worked from home except my friends Frank and Luci Knight, who were part of a NYNEX experiment in telecommuting way back in the early 1980s. But when I started working on my book, I had to write almost all of it at home, and I realized that I needed a whole setup in my house so that I could be as productive as possible on the weekends. I wrote and edited most of this book with my butt glued to the couch on Saturday and Sunday mornings, or in my backyard using a wireless laptop that can go anywhere with me. Writing in the office would have been impossible, with its nonstop pace, back-to-back meetings, and endless impromptu pop-ins and brainstorming sessions. But working at home isn't a new idea in my family. Bob has been running his financial planning business out of our house for over ten years and has found it to be a terrific arrangement. He saves lots of time every day by not commuting, he's home after school for the kids, and he has lots of flexibility for his volunteer ambulance corps duties.

Working from home falls under the bigger umbrella of tele-commuting, which includes people who work at home, as well as employees who work from different locations in a given month—sometimes at the main office, sometimes at home, sometimes at a customer site, sometimes at another branch office. Companies with great telecommuting programs set employees up with the technology they need—sometimes even sending IT support to workers' homes. The energy company BP America provides work-at-home employees with laptops, access to BP's networks, and "Road War-rior" training for the use of technology at home and on the road. As laptops, wireless Internet, and corporate networks have made it easier to become mobile, telecommuting has become a more and more popular choice for all kinds of workers.

Of course, there are some jobs where working from home just isn't an option. If you're a nurse or elementary school teacher, there is no substitute for your physical presence. And most man-agers need to be on-site most of the time . . . that's just one reason why, with a company full of employees to manage, I can't work from home much myself. If your job requires your physical pres-ence, that doesn't mean you can't find flexibility in your work— just that telecommuting probably isn't the solution for you.

But for the many jobs that are suited to telecommuting, it's a benefit that working mothers crave. It was one of the two most de-sired benefits in our survey of working moms. And IBM found the same thing when it surveyed 98,000 employees around the world in 2004, asking where employees would most like the company to put its work-life efforts. The top answer: "Flexibility in where work gets done."

Amy Ramsey, who works in the benefits department for the fi-nancial services company Wachovia—a 100 Best Company year after year—had long benefited from the company's flexible hours policy. The mother of Ethan, eleven, Kaitlyn, eight, and Jordan, six, Amy started working a three-day schedule after Kaitlyn was born in 1997. But a year later, her husband, Tom, took a new job in Florence, South Carolina—three hours away from Amy's office in Charlotte, North Carolina. Fortunately, the company let her set up a home office and start telecommuting, an arrangement she kept when her youngest son, Jordan, was born.

"This was an incredible arrangement, because he was home with me and a sitter, and I could take a break whenever I needed to feed him. This setup allowed him to stay home for the first cou-ple of years of his life before he was old enough for preschool," she says. Telecommuting has worked out well for Amy, but also for her employer, which was able to hang on to a valuable, experienced employee. "Wachovia's flexibility and work-life options are the main reason I have remained loyal to the organization all these years," Amy says. "They make it possible to have a career and create a good family life where I can be involved with my children." In 2004, some 21 percent of Wachovia employees worked from home.

"I telecommute one day a week now," Maria Barry, a mother of two who worked at Fleet Bank (now part of Bank of America), told us.[11] "I find it to be extremely helpful. I have a chance to think strategically and do a lot more planning. It helps me to be more effective when I'm in the office. Also, since I can work without interruption at home, I have less work to do on the weekend. That gives me more time with my family."

Telecommuting and working from home sound ideal. But from personal experience, I also know the limits of both. You need a place of your own to work, where kids aren't tromping through constantly. If your kids are small, you need child care. You need self-discipline, so you don't succumb to the distractions of unwashed dishes or a garden that desperately needs weeding. Another essential for telecommuting: a firm schedule. Working at home works best if you have clearly defined work hours, so people can find you when they need you. At *Working Mother*, we have several employees who work reduced schedules or work from home, so Barbara made an Excel spreadsheet of everyone's work-at-home schedule to help her with meeting planning. It helps to know where everyone is and when they're available every day.

Another thing you need when you work from home is boundaries, so your work life doesn't completely overflow into your home life—after all, there's such a thing as *too much fusion*!

"Often what happens with flexibility is that work encroaches on home life, because home life is more permeable," says Sue Campbell Clark, a professor at the University of Idaho, who studies work-life flexibility arrangements.[12]

To keep that from happening, make sure you and your supervisor agree about what's expected of you, how many hours you'll put in, and when you'll be available. Then, don't check office e-mail during your off hours.

About 36 percent of employers nationwide allow employees to telecommute from home at least one day a week. If your employer resists the idea of you working from home, point out the very tangible bottom-line benefits. In some cities with serious traffic problems, employers actually receive a tax break if they let employees work from home, because it helps reduce rush-hour traffic. And many workers say telecommuting increases their productivity. At Merrill Lynch, where at least 3,500 employees telecommute, managers found that productivity increased by 15–20 percent when employees worked from home.[13] The International Telecommuting Association and Council in Washington, D.C., found that telecommuting policies increase productivity by 22 percent, and decrease absenteeism by 60 percent.[14]

Don't Put That Breast Milk in Your Coffee!!!

At the same time parents are starting to fuse their work with their home life, the best employers for working mothers are taking giant steps toward welcoming family life into the office.

Of all the programs that gracefully blend work and family life, lactation programs are my favorite. What could be more important than helping a new mom continue breast-feeding after she returns to work? I think every company should help nourish moms and babies by finding a private space for a lactation room in every facility. Although nationwide only 21 percent of companies offer lactation rooms,[15] the Working Mother 100 Best do much better: 99 percent have private rooms used for lactation and other purposes; 80 percent have rooms dedicated strictly to breast-feeding.

When I was pumping at work I was lucky that I had an office that was private—sort of—and that had a lock. I locked my door twice a day, pulled the curtains closed, and used my breast pump to pump milk for Robert and later Julia. It was not the most convenient arrangement—but I had it very easy compared to my assistant, Barbara, who didn't work for me when her babies were born and who pumped her breast milk for all three children without ever having a private space. Barbara still gets red in the face when she recalls being interrupted by a male colleague who burst into the office she was using as a lactation room. And you can imagine that he was probably more embarrassed than she was. Then there's the ad agency executive I know who watched in horror while her male boss poured her breast milk from a bottle in the office refrigerator into his coffee. She just couldn't get the words out in time to stop him—and confessed to me later that she never had the heart to tell him afterward what he had done.

Ross Products, a division of Abbott, has been a leader in lactation rooms and support for the last several years. They came to us and asked if *Working Mother* would partner with them in spreading the news to major companies around the country. Knowing from personal experience how important privacy is for lactating moms, I signed on to support their educational program, Business Backs Breastfeeding. I know the powerful bond that nursing creates between mother and child, and I believe no working mother should have to give that up. Pumping in the office is critical to successful breast-feeding for new working moms. As part of the program, Ross created an exhibit at our WorkLife Congress showing attendees exactly what a lactation room looks like—by building one right there on the conference floor!

At *Working Mother*, we'd built our own lactation room in honor of Shari Arbital Jacoby, our managing editor and a dedicated pumper. But when I saw the lactation room exhibit at our own conference, I was surprised to see how many errors we'd made. (But Shari tells us she's still very grateful that we tried.) Here are the basic components of a good lactation room:

- a hardback chair to sit in (we had a soft chair, thinking that comfort, not support, was needed)
- a mirror so that Mom can put herself back together properly
- a timer to know when to switch breasts (we should have thought of that one!)
- a clock so that she can keep track of time without looking at her watch
- a radio because music helps with let-down
- a sink to wash her hands
- a small refrigerator to store the breast milk
- labels and markers to clearly mark which precious bottle belongs to whom
- a bulletin board so moms can post their schedules and pictures of their babies
- a sturdy table to hold the pump (well, we got that one right).

This sounds like a lot—but it also shows you how preposterously inadequate a broom closet, a borrowed office, or the ladies' room is for the job.

Some of our 100 Best Companies aren't just building lactation rooms. Two-thirds provide pumps, and over half provide access to a lactation consultant. IBM even created an online directory of all its lactation rooms, in hundreds of offices around the United States, so traveling moms would always be able to find one!

The popularity of breast-feeding programs is often underestimated. Maureen Corcoran, a vice president of diversity at Prudential Financial, told me in 2005 that they estimated that three hundred employees would use their lactation program in a given year and were astonished when eight hundred employees took advantage of their progressive policies. One of the reasons for the increased interest was that Prudential offers the program not just to employees, but to spouses, too, so wives of male employees can use the resource and referral service.

The Family in the Office

Lactation programs are just one example of how progressive companies are inviting family life to fuse into the office. Many of the 100 Best Companies continue to welcome the family as children grow, offering all kinds of programs, including parenting classes, workshops for teens, hiking and fitness facilities for families, college coaches, and "concierge services," like on-site dry cleaning, that make life a little easier.

One of my favorite examples is Eli Lilly's "safe sitter" workshop for employees' children,[16] which they offer during school vacations. It's a full-day seminar for kids who want to learn how to babysit.

"It was great," Sandy Sommers, an associate general counsel at Eli Lilly, told us. She didn't have to find backup care for her twelve-year-old daughter Betsy for a whole day during the school break. "I could take her to work and walk in with her—it was that easy." And Betsy learned how to be a better babysitter.

Many companies are starting to realize that the parents of tweens and teens need a little extra help—and are offering parenting classes and online groups to help guide parents through tough times. Citigroup, Ernst & Young, General Motors, Texas Instruments, and many other Best Companies offer classes, support groups, or newsletters for parents. The health-care organization TriHealth, in Cincinnati, Ohio, offers parents a "personal parent coach" during key transition points in their children's growth. When PNC Financial's Heather Buehler, a vice president and manager for work-life strategies in Pittsburgh, decided to test the idea of a seminar called "Parenting Styles That Work with Teens," 150 people signed up for fifty slots. "We realized we really hit a nerve," Heather told us.[17]

While demand for parenting workshops wasn't nearly as high as flexibility in our <u>What Moms Want</u> survey, these inexpensive measures represent an important step for companies in creating a parent-friendly culture.

Here are a few more of my favorite programs helping parents
fuse work and family:

- IBM launched a pilot program with executive women last
  year called Family 360. A leadership coach surveyed women
  participants and their family members (spouse, children, siblings, parents, or anyone else the woman identified) to see
  how well the executives' work-life balance was functioning
  overall. The expert also coached the women on how to have
  a family meeting to explore work-life issues. "The women
  executives who participated described it as a life-altering
  event. Not only did they learn a great deal, but their families
  learned a great deal," says Maria Ferris, the director of IBM's
  global workforce diversity programs. One key lesson almost
  all the participants took away—don't rush into tasks as soon
  as you get home. Slow down, decompress, and just enjoy being at home for a few minutes.
- For $49.95 a month, the travel company Carlson will dis-
  patch a "job squad" to employees' homes to take care of odd
  jobs around the house, like fixing screen doors or regrouting
  the tub. (I could sure use that service myself!) CEO Marilyn
  Carlson Nelson was a working mom herself for many years
  and appreciates how much fusion it takes to keep a household going.
- Timberland has miles of hiking trails and acres of sports
  fields, and encourage employees and their families to use
  them.
- Johnson & Johnson, the Phoenix Companies, Union Pacific,
  Carlson, and several other 100 Best Companies offer take-
  home meals so parents don't have to worry about what's for
  dinner. Employees can stop by the company cafeteria on the
  way home and pick up some chicken parmesan or a chef
  salad. Many of these companies have great cafeterias, and
  some are even subsidized, so the food's delicious and a bargain, too.

The options that progressive companies use to create fusion are endlessly creative—but they all spring from the idea that welcoming the whole employee to work will help both the employee and the company. While the 100 Best Companies are making big strides toward creating parent-friendly cultures, many other companies haven't yet caught on to the fact that flexibility and fusion aren't just nice perks: they're quickly becoming business as usual. Younger workers—Gen Xers and Gen Yers—expect flexibility, ask for it, and in fact require it. Some of us baby boomer working mothers feel shocked at the amount of flexibility that Gen X and Gen Y moms and dads demand! But we should set aside our shock and start congratulating them . . . and supporting them. This way lies sanity.

The Fusion Family

Way back when I was helping my mom grade papers and brainstorm ideas for her school programs, I never imagined I'd be involving my daughter in my work someday too! But from an early age, Julia was involved with my work at every turn. When she was little she would carry my big briefcase around, playing "work." At *Chief Executive* magazine, she came to the office to help stuff goody bags for the big conferences we held.

"Mommy," she complained one year, "that old woman just watched me stuff all those bags and didn't do *any* of the work!" It was true. The woman we had hired to stuff the bags (who wasn't really very old) had found that Julia would do all the work if she just sat back and ordered her around. Lesson learned for Julia!

My favorite moment of fusion was when Julia introduced me to eleven hundred attendees at our annual 100 Best Companies Gala dinner in October 2004. I asked her if she would introduce me, knowing that she had never spoken in front of an audience before—least of all an audience of eleven hundred people dressed in black tie! True to her lawyerly nature, Julia responded with a proposal: "I'll do the speech," she said, "if I can bring Connor and Victoria with me to the dinner." Connor Styles, her boyfriend, and Victoria Migdal, her best friend, were immediately invited.

Julia wrote her own speech, got up in front of that huge sea of adults at the Sheraton Hotel in New York City, and spoke to the crowd as if she did this every day. She stole the show, and got more laughs than all the rest of our speakers combined. Here's part of her speech:

I'm going to give you a very rare thing tonight, the teenager's insight on working women and men. Thinking about tonight, I can see myself about twelve years ago . . . okay, I lied, five years ago . . . grabbing on to my mom's leg, yelling at her not to leave me for the dinners and conferences. And now . . . I'm yelling at her to let me bring my boyfriend.

I think being a working mom is pretty cool. It's got some perks and some downers. Some may see travel as a perk. Some may see it as a downer. Mostly, kids see it as a perk. I mean, of course I miss her when she's traveling, and I don't like it when she's gone too long because there's no one to call when my brother won't drive me somewhere, or Dad won't let me go out past nine. But on the other hand, there's no one to tell me to go to bed or turn the music down, and no one to make sure I'm not on the phone when the lights go out. (She's the only one awake at that time—Dad goes to sleep around eight!)

Another perk is the weekends. What people don't realize is that no matter how much us kids love our moms, it doesn't mean we want to put up with her seven days a week.

If my mom didn't go to work, she'd drive me absolutely insane. I won't lie. So when I do see her on the weekends, it makes me want to be around her more. I'm more patient and I can have more fun.

> *Moms are also very handy on the weekends. My mom and I find quality time in some random places. Like shopping. Shopping can be fun because you get to walk around and talk while doing something you both enjoy. As you have probably heard, my hobby is buying my mom new clothes. Recently she's been made over from wearing black and brown every day of her life to wearing pink florals and even polka dots. And by the way, I'm available for personal shopping Thursday through Sunday. Give me a call.*
>
> *I also love that my mom's a working mother because it gives me a perfect edge on our fights. I can always pull out the innocent yet somewhat evil, "How would you know? You're never home!" Gets her every time.*

Julia's speech was an extreme moment of fusion (and joy), but even the less dramatic fusion points—where work and family seem to blend effortlessly—make me feel more in control and more comfortable with my choices. I feel I'm being a good role model, that my children value what I do when I'm at work, and that they know I value them. I feel I'm bringing my whole self to the office and my whole self back home.

"It's not about work separate from home," Laura Alber, the president of Pottery Barn and Pottery Barn Kids, told us. "It's all one thing for me."[18]

Of course, that fusion won't always be consistent. One week might feel like you're fusing your life with a blowtorch, and the next might feel like you're using a Band-Aid. When the kids are four and eight, your work and home life might feel more integrated than when they're twelve and sixteen—or vice versa.

But the effort on the part of millions of women to build a new, more satisfying lifestyle will go on and on—with experimentation, failure, success, loss, and triumph—until we get to the point where every company offers a culture that accepts and adapts to family life and develops creative solutions for fusion.

Chapter Seven

We Build the
New Girls' Networks

I've been taking the train from Chappaqua into New York City, about an hour away, every workday for sixteen years. For most of those sixteen years, I've felt like I was the only working mother in town, even though I know it isn't true. Occasionally I'll spot someone I know—Roseellen Gonzales, a working mother who's also a law student, or Mara Weissman from Deloitte & Touche—on the train, but on many days, it feels like I'm the only one.

My work-at-home husband, on the other hand, knows so many stay-at-home moms in Chappaqua that he's sometimes invited to lunch with "the girls." When he was captain of the Chappaqua Volunteer Ambulance Corps, he recruited volunteers by showing up at PTA meetings at 9:30 in the morning (the ones that most working mothers can't make). He figured the PTA moms were home during the day and might be available to volunteer for the ambulance corps during the weekdays, when volunteers were in short supply. This idea turned out to be the most successful recruitment campaign of all time for the ambulance corps.

So Bob goes out to lunch with the stay-at-home moms, and what about me? I'm the mom who walked into the dry cleaner with Julia on a Saturday to be greeted with this zinger: "Oh! So little Julia does have a mother!"

I think it's easy for working moms to feel we're on the outside looking in at a tightly knit community of stay-at-home moms. In our <u>What Moms Want</u> survey, we found that almost half (48 percent) of the respondents often feel alone or unsupported within their communities. I hear about that same sense of isolation every month when I sit down with Susan Lapinski, our editor in chief, and a small group of readers.

"I feel like I'm the only mom in my neighborhood who works. I know it's not true, but I hardly ever meet anyone who is doing this," one mother told us. Her words reminded me of the flood of reader letters we got after we published the first issue of *Working Mother* back in 1979.

"Thank you for the support . . . I wondered if I'd have to always fight the battles alone," K. S. Simpson of Alhambra, California, wrote us way back then.

When I came back to the magazine in 2001, after twelve years away, I couldn't believe we were still receiving almost exactly the same letter! "Keep up the good work. Mothers need to know they're not alone," wrote reader Karen Rhodes of Albuquerque, New Mexico.

Why do we keep getting these "alone" letters year after year after year? We know there are 26 million mothers in the United States with paying jobs, according to the Bureau of Labor Statistics. And 47 percent of all women managers and professionals are moms. With so many of us, why is it so hard to find and support each other?

A Club of Our Own: Working Mothers' Groups

When Linda Tulloch of Greenwich, Connecticut, had her son Jack nearly seven years ago, she couldn't wait to join a mothers' group. Her hopes were dashed, though, when she discovered her local moms' group met on weekday mornings—when she was at her job as vice president at Crédit Lyonnais.[1]

But that didn't stop Linda. She set out to find other working moms to form a group of their own. She posted a flyer at the local

YMCA and soon teamed up with three other working moms. They started meeting on Saturday mornings, and before long the group swelled to include twenty-seven working moms, with forty-six kids between them. Now, after nearly seven years, the group is still going strong—and now Linda brings her second child, Claire, four, as well as six-year-old Jack.

"Once a month, I get this shot in the arm that makes me feel really good about what I'm doing," group member Deborah Von Donop, an interior designer, told us. "When you're working seventy hours a week, it's hard to make friends in your community."

Linda and Deborah are both benefiting from one of the most exciting developments working mothers have seen in the last twenty-five years. There's been a movement afoot to connect working mothers through clubs, networks, and online forums. Many of these groups, like Linda's, are based in neighborhoods and communities, finally giving working moms a sense of belonging in their own towns. Others are business networks or online forums based at the office. But they all share Linda's goal—to end the isolation that working mothers can feel in their communities. The women starting these groups don't have a lot of time on their hands, but they're making the effort because they're eager to find and befriend other working moms. And they're finding that meeting regularly with other working mothers reaffirms their commitment to work, gives them new ideas for balancing work and life, and sometimes even leads to new jobs or new clients. Linda offers these tips on starting a working mothers' group like hers:

- **Look for women with breast pumps.** One member of Linda's group spotted a woman on the commuter train carrying a breast pump and immediately invited her to the group. Being personally invited into a group can make all the difference. Less individual methods work too—flyers at YMCAs, local coffee shops, or grocery stores can alert hard-to-find working moms that you're looking for them. Some towns also have newcomers' clubs or free neighborhood papers or newsletters that might mention your group in mailings, and some libraries have "community answer" desks that can share your information.

- **Hold the caviar, bring on the juice boxes.** Linda's group keeps it simple. They don't usually have a formal program or an elaborate meal. Instead, they serve light snacks and juice boxes for the kids.
- **Same time, different house.** Make regularly monthly dates (say, the first Saturday morning of the month) so they're easy to remember. Then take turns hosting the group. About twelve to fifteen moms, with kids in tow, usually show up at Linda's group, rotating houses every month.
- **Appoint an e-mail czar.** Someone needs to send out reminders and keep track of who's hosting. Linda takes on that role for her group, keeping the group apprised by e-mail.

So That's Where All the Moms Were Hiding!

In February 2005, my friend Mara Weissmann—one of the working mothers I sometimes spot on the train from Chappaqua—asked me to speak at a moms' group she'd started called Second Shift. Of course I said yes . . . but I was amazed when 112 people showed up at the Lexington Square Restaurant. I guess I was wrong about being the only working mother in Chappaqua!

Mara, a high-powered lawyer and mother of two, started the group after yet another friend complained about the isolation of working motherhood. "One too many women said to me they felt they were the only ones doing what we were doing, and I was convinced that was not the case," she says. So Mara invited several women to dinner, and they decided to reach out to other moms. For Second Shift's first official meeting, Mara passed out flyers on the train platform inviting moms to get together at a local restaurant. Thirty-three moms came to the first meeting, forty-four to their second, and seventy-one to their third. Now the moms meet quarterly at a restaurant—leaving the kids at home—and most of the meetings feature an expert speaker. They've heard from financial experts, health experts, and even a sex therapist!

"Career moms need outlets like every other person," Mara says. "Second Shift allows women with common interests to come together and be with friends and find each other in the community."

My own informal talk at Second Shift was a blast (although probably not as exciting as the sex therapist). I talked about my crazy experiences looking for investors to save *Working Mother* magazine. Then I asked the audience to tell me about their experiences—and they were off and running. They asked questions, I asked questions. I gave advice, they gave advice. We were all experts and we were all seeking answers. It was invigorating and challenging. We didn't stop talking until eleven o'clock—long after I expected to be home on that Tuesday night.

It's inspiring just how much working mothers can help each other when they team up through groups like this. From just that first meeting at Second Shift, I reconnected with a long-lost friend, sold a $500 ticket to a charity event, and learned that an old friend had left her job and was now a potential client for advertising in *Working Mother*.

Working Moms: Better Together

No two working mother groups are exactly alike. Some welcome kids; others give moms a night out. Some are small and informal; others are large and highly organized. But they all have one thing in common: they help working moms feel more connected.

"I've gone to regular alumni networking events at my business school, and I've picked up ideas for my career here and there, but I never feel like I have that much to offer other people," says Jennifer Krueger, the New York City research librarian and mother of Zoe, nine, and Eliot, five. But for the past two years, she's been meeting for tapas every other month with about a dozen other women, mostly fellow graduates of Columbia Business School, many of whom are working mothers. "Many of the people in the group are having their first child, and suddenly I have all sorts of information to share. Suddenly, I'm the one who knows something useful about how to apply to preschools or find a nanny. Finally, people have questions and I have great answers." The group has also been a useful sounding board for Jennifer and other members when they've been seeking jobs or weighing new opportunities.

Some working mother groups help moms reclaim their creative side, keeping their old interests and activities alive even during the all-consuming vortex of working motherhood. That's why Suzie Riddle, a Dallas librarian and mother of Polly, seven, Daisy, thirteen, and Cecil, twenty, started Frump—a garage band of five working moms she'd met at playdates and at church. The band's regular Saturday night practices are a great release for all five women. "People would never look at me when I'm at work or with my kids and think I'm in a rock band," says Suzie, the band's drummer. "I love breaking that mold."[2]

Likewise, a dozen Philadelphia artists got together to form Women Holler!, a working mothers' group that offers friendship, artistic encouragement—and sometimes babysitting.[3]

Other working mothers' groups get together around a specific activity—like cooking or exercise—to make it more fun. Charla Cooper of Boise, Idaho, for example, created a cooking co-op with three friends. The four moms each make a big dinner once a week and drop off the hot meal to the other three families. "Before I joined the group, the kids would be going berserk while I was trying to get dinner on the table every night after work," she told us. "But now I spend most evenings playing with the kids until dinner arrives."[4]

Some moms, like Marisa Thalberg, are even making a business out of mothers' groups. Marisa was vice president of global advertising at Calvin Klein Cosmetics/Unilever International when she had her daughter Hannah. Tired of feeling isolated, she created Executive Moms, a New York City group that hosts lunches for working mothers. She put together some spectacular panels, and then persuaded companies to sponsor her luncheons, which drew about three hundred working moms.

Other working moms become so passionate about the plight of working mothers that they reach out to help less fortunate women. That's what happened with Mothers Off Duty, a group of African-American working moms in New York and New Jersey. After meeting socially for several years, they decided to start a scholarship and mentoring program for college-bound teenage moms. "Starting MOD was about keeping that vibrant, beautiful woman in all of us alive," cofounder Lori Bryant-Woolridge told us.[5]

At *Working Mother*, we've been so impressed with all these different working mothers' groups that we created a Web site to bring them all together, at www.workingmother.com/momsnetwork. Our database can help you find a group to join . . . or give you advice on starting your own.

The New Park Bench: Parent Groups at Work

When Stephanie Shaw, a tax manager in the Dallas office of PricewaterhouseCoopers, needs parenting advice about her kids, Veronica, eight, and Venson, two, she's just as likely to find it in the office as in her community. That's why she joined PwC's Parents Networking Circles, which hosts luncheon sessions and panel discussions.

"The Working Parents Networking lunch is a great way to learn about everything . . . sick child facilities, local day care, and even birthday party ideas," she says. "There's a real sense of relief knowing that I am not alone."

She's definitely *not* alone. When her office held a panel of partners, managers, and other senior executives talking about their own flexible work arrangements, the session was so packed the company added a second session.

Where moms used to share ideas while chatting on a park

bench, today they also find solutions in the office. Some of those answers come during water cooler chats and lunches with friends and colleagues, but others come from office-sponsored parenting groups, seminars, and forums. The consulting group Accenture, for instance, has ten working parent groups across the United States, but it also offers a Working Parents Discussion database, where parents swap ideas. PNC Financial includes parents around the country in its "Ask the Expert" conference calls, which let more than a hundred parents participate. And Texas Instrument's online support groups include a parents' network, a new moms' network, and an adoptive parents' network.

Groups like these can be a powerful force for change at companies. For instance, the Intel Parents' Network (IPN) told management that new mothers needed more help. The result: Intel agreed to start offering a ninety-minute workshop for all expecting and new parents to help them understand and navigate all of Intel's parenting resources, maternity leave options, and flexible work arrangements. The company also launched a pilot program providing more lactation support, including a subsidy for breast pumps.

With support like this, it's no wonder working moms in the <u>What Moms Want</u> survey didn't feel nearly as isolated at work as they did in their communities: only 35 percent said they felt isolated at work, versus nearly 50 percent who felt isolated in their neighborhood.

The benefit of these groups, though, isn't just that they help working moms find solutions to problems on the home front. They can have very practical effects on your career, by broadening your network in the office and exposing you to new opportunities. If you play a founding role in a parenting or women's support group at work, it might raise your profile, demonstrate your talents for organization and leadership, and lead to new recognition and new responsibilities.

Companies should take note: parenting support groups are a huge opportunity to increase employee morale and productivity with relatively little cost. Only 6 percent of moms in the <u>What Moms Want</u> survey said their companies currently offer parent support groups. And 62 percent said they'd highly value those groups if they were offered. That's a huge opportunity for companies. If your company doesn't already have a parenting support group, it's easy to start one. Here's how:

- **Do lunch.** You might not have time or energy to organize a formal group at work, but it's easy to drop an e-mail to a few other working moms and have lunch once a month. That might grow into a more formal support group later.
- **Measure interest.** Try lining up one speaker and holding a "lunch and learn" session for parents on a topic like discipline, balance, or homework. Hospitals, schools, family therapy practices, or other community facilities may be willing to send speakers for free. At the seminar, pass around a sign-up sheet to see who'd be interested in a regular parenting support group.
- **Enlist HR.** When social worker Gina Weaver, the mother of Sam, three, wanted to start a parenting group at her company, Chase Brexton Health Services in Baltimore, she persuaded her HR director to mention the group in the company newsletter.[6] HR can also be helpful in finding speakers and arranging regular meeting spots.

Casting a Wider Net: Associations, Affinity and Industry Groups

Careers are made on the strength of our relationships, and the more people you know, the more your work life will flourish. Believe me, I know. My own contact file includes about thirty-five hundred people—but I'm always trying to expand it. Inevitably, I find that someone I met last week or two months ago can help me achieve something important or offer me helpful advice.

As part of the deal we struck to buy *Working Mother*, we also acquired the National Association for Female Executives (NAFE), a networking group for high-achieving corporate women, business owners, and high-potential women striving to get ahead. As I got to know the organization, I was struck by the ardor of the sixty thousand NAFE members, who actively support each other's businesses. They seek each other out for subcontracting, they refer each other to new business, and they form brainstorming groups to help each other move ahead. To foster this ardent networking, we launched a series called the NAFE Breakfast Club in 2003. At every breakfast club, dozens of members get together to hear speakers, build their skills, and meet each other. We also invite our members to post their stories on our Web site, www.nafe.com. With all the pictures and stories these fabulous women post, the directory looks like a dating service.

Dr. Betty Spence, the president of NAFE, is the world's most ardent advocate for women and for networking. "Women need to stand for each other. Reach behind you or to the side and offer support to the women who need you," she told a group of four hundred women at our annual NAFE conference last year. And they will: NAFE members are fiercely loyal to each other— supporting each other's businesses, sharing advice, and offering loads of emotional support.

Women in general—and busy working mothers in particular— need to do much more networking like this if we want to advance our careers. In a survey of high-level corporate leaders (women and men), Catalyst, a nonprofit group working to advance women in the workplace, found that women consistently named "exclusion from informal networks" as a key barrier to advancement: 46 percent of women cited exclusion from networks as a barrier, compared with only 18 percent of men.[7]

When I visit companies around the country, I frequently speak to their parenting groups, which are a great place for moms to start networking. They're part of a bigger movement to connect like-minded employees through employee networks or "affinity groups," which are offering new opportunities for women to connect with and help each other. Among the 100 Best Companies, 70 percent had support groups for women. That's up from 43 percent in 1995.

"We've seen the power of networking firsthand," says Maria Ferris, IBM's director of global workforce diversity programs. IBM's 146 networks and initiatives for women, including La Red (Spanish for "the Network") for Latinas, have helped show younger women that executives can have a successful career and happy family.

"There's sometimes a perception by younger women that the women executives here somehow don't have children and are not married and had to give everything up," she says. "But sixty-five percent of IBM women executives are working mothers." Networking groups, as well as mentoring programs, help bust the myth that women need to make a choice between career and family. By building our own "new girls' networks," we can help advance our careers—and those of the women around us.

Networks for Women of Color

When Ameeta Gosain, the mother of Rahul, nine, and a managing director of JPMorgan Chase, moved from Bombay to New York in 1989, she missed the support of family and friends back home. So she helped found the company's Women of Color Connection, one of twenty-three employee networking groups. "Despite our varied heritages and backgrounds, women of color face a lot of common challenges," she told us. The group has helped women of color find mentors and connect with professional development resources. "The major issue all groups have championed is the need for professional development resources to accelerate our careers," she says.

Ameeta's not the only woman of color to note the need for mentoring and development. We hear the same thing over and over again at the annual Best Companies for Women of Color Town Halls that we host around the country. Multicultural women tell us that the number-one barrier they face in corporate America is a lack of mentors and role models. Company-sponsored networking groups for women of color are one step toward filling that gap.

"I don't play golf," says Miriam Vializ-Briggs, a Puerto Rican–born vice president of marketing grid computing at IBM. As the mother of thirteen-year-old Lucy, she doesn't have time for that kind of traditional male networking. Instead, she grows her contacts through La Red, which holds regular conference calls for Latinas on the executive track. The group also offers "one-to-many" mentoring, where a senior executive will meet regularly via a conference call or Webcast with fifty or more Latinas.

Groups like these can make a big difference to a company's culture. The number of IBM executives who are women of color has grown from seventeen in 1995 to seventy-four in 2003—a 335 percent boost. At Procter & Gamble, an affinity group called the Black Advertising & Marketing Leadership Team (BALT) helped increase the number of African-American brand managers and marketing directors at the company.

"I can't imagine that happening without our affinity groups," Dawn Williams-Thompson, the director of advertising development and BALT's staffing advisor, told us.[8]

And what's in it for the company? Profits and productivity. "Diversity absolutely makes us more effective. I see it every day," says Vializ-Briggs. "When we look at problems differently and challenge each other, we get better answers."

Getting Out and About: Industry Groups

Networking in your own company is great, but making more connections in your industry can lead to better jobs and greater opportunities down the line. It's not enough to join a group, though: to really make your time worthwhile, you need to become an active participant by volunteering for a committee, inviting speakers, or heading an event—anything that allows you to work closely with other women in the group. Business is all about the connections between people, and nothing builds connections faster than working side by side with someone on a project.

That's something I learned when I joined Advertising Women of New York (AWNY), a women's group dedicated to helping women advance in the advertising business. I was still young in the business when I joined back in 1983, and I didn't know any of the high-powered women in New York. I volunteered for a committee that brought the winning ads from the Cannes Film Festival to a screening in New York, even though I didn't know anything about the Cannes festival, or the international advertising that we screened. I soon found myself going to meetings at the homes of some of the top women in advertising, and meeting with heads of agencies and big clients who were involved with Cannes. Most important, participating on that committee gave me the chance to see how senior businesswomen ran meetings, behaved at cocktail parties, and conducted business with each other. Twenty-one years after I first joined AWNY, I became president of its board of directors, where I can help other women find the early career connections we all need.

If you don't believe me about the power of networking with other women, ask one of my idols, Madeleine Albright. I was privileged to meet the former Secretary of State at the Office Depot Success Strategies for Businesswomen conference in 2002. Secretary Albright was already a role model for me, trotting the globe as the first female Secretary of State and as U.S. ambassador to the United Nations. But many people don't realize that she was a young working mother when she launched her career, and she became a single working mother very early on. In her book *Madam Secretary*, she describes a women's network she created—at no less a workplace than the United Nations.

When she was ambassador, there were only 6 other countries, out of 180 member nations, that had women as their permanent representatives. Secretary Albright invited them to lunch, and they formed a group called G-7, which met once a month and worked together to help women at the UN and around the globe. They pushed for the UN to include women judges on the international war crimes tribunal. They met with the secretary-general of the UN to encourage the appointment of more women to high-level positions. But my favorite detail was this:

"[I] suggested that we pledge always to take each other's phone calls. The agreement on instant access upset some male representatives, who didn't think it logical that the ambassador of Liechtenstein could get through to the U.S. ambassador more readily than they could. I told them the solution was for them to give up their posts to women, which stopped them cold."[9]

Secretary Albright's network should be an inspiration to all of us. We can band together, create new kinds of networks, and promise to be there—whether it's to share parenting advice or to take each other's business calls right away!

Our Numbers Give Us Strength

Whether it's a bunch of working mothers playing in a garage band, an online forum where moms find out about the best pediatrician on the company health plan, or a ballroom full of professional moms listening to a keynote speech, the rise of these groups shows that women can help each other at home and at the workplace. There's no reason to feel isolated in a world where the vast majority of mothers work—not when all we need to do is reach out and help each other.

Chapter Eight

We Forget It Can All Fall Apart . . . Until It Does

When Julia was fourteen, she began complaining about headaches a lot. At first, the headaches weren't severe, just annoying. After a while, they became constant. Every once in a while, they were so bad she had to stay home from school and lie in bed.

I wanted to think she was just having trouble adjusting to her freshman year in high school. Bob, who's an EMT, took her complaints more seriously and insisted she see her pediatrician.

Julia's doctor shared Bob's concern, and sent her to a pediatric neurologist for a CAT scan. I thought this was a bit extreme for a headache, but I kept my Pollyanna opinions to myself as we waited over the weekend for the results. On Monday, the pediatrician called to say the scan had turned up a surprising diagnosis: a congenital condition of the brain called Chiari-1 malformation. The condition was creating a formation called a syrinx—a collection of brain fluid dripping into the spinal cord and pressing on Julia's nervous system. Brain surgery, it seemed, was the only option.

We set up a meeting with a noted pediatric neurosurgeon for the following Tuesday at New York–Presbyterian Children's Hospital's brand-new Morgan Stanley Pavilion. I felt my whole world quake, and I prepared myself for a very difficult meeting. But Dr. Feldstein disarmed us with his friendly manner and his Bugs Bunny tie. He didn't seem like he was about to tell us terrible news. He looked confident and relaxed. And he had cute animal stickers for his patients that Julia loved.

"Mommy, get me an extra frog sticker for Connor," she whispered, too polite to take more than one. I was glad to see her so interested in getting a sticker for her boyfriend. Perhaps her buoyant personality would be an asset here, I thought as I grabbed a frog for Connor and a giraffe for myself.

Dr. Feldstein described the condition carefully, complete with 3-D computer images of Julia's neck and brain stem that he manipulated and rotated to give us an extra-vivid view. The syrinx looked like a long thin bubble floating in her spinal cord.

I had looked up Julia's condition online at WebMD and was alarmed to read that some patients developed difficulty in walking and others needed multiple surgeries. But Dr. Feldstein told us that we'd already avoided the biggest danger—that of misdiagnosis. In the days before CAT scans, it was easy for parents to dismiss these mild but continuous headaches (like I almost had!). Ignoring the headaches can lead to disastrous consequences. Eventually, the syrinx begins pressing on the magnificent nervous system, interrupting the flow of information and ultimately leading to a loss of motor control. Julia needed brain surgery, and a delay could cause permanent damage, speeding up her reflexes and making it difficult to walk.

I had assumed that we might be looking at surgery in the summer, after Julia completed her first year of high school, but instead we found ourselves booking a date with Dr. Feldstein less than two weeks down the road. I canceled a week of meetings, a trip to Boston, and a board meeting for the Advertising Women of New York as I started making other plans: how to tell my aging parents about this; how to sleep on those fold-down chairs at the hospital; and how to get Julia's messy bedroom ready for a convalescent. As I became comfortable with the idea that this surgery was relatively safe (for brain surgery), I began to look forward to helping Julia through this very big event.

Julia, meanwhile, was light and breezy about the whole thing. She had never had anything serious happen to her. A sprained wrist, a twisted ankle, an allergic reaction to a beauty mask.

Robert, her older brother, had had all sorts of health problems, beginning but not ending with his early birth. Seizures, surgery at age one, a broken arm, a cyst that destroyed some of his permanent teeth, a bike accident. . . . Early and often to the hospital, that was our life with Robert. Julia, who couldn't really imagine the pain of recovering from major surgery, seemed to be enjoying the drama of the situation. "Finally," she said, "something is happening in my life that I don't have to make up."

Julia negotiated with the doctor like a pro. Her big concern was stitches, which she claimed to hate, even though she'd never had any. Dr. Feldstein said he would use a kind of derma-bond that wouldn't be like traditional stitches, if she preferred. Her hair was the next big thing. They'd only have to shave a strip about three inches by two inches at the base of her neck—which was acceptable to Julia. Finally, the big hurdle. Her birthday and her favorite holiday—Christmas—were coming up fast. Dr. Feldstein said that if we scheduled it as early as he'd like, she could be feeling pretty good by December 19—her fifteenth birthday. Completely satisfied, Julia began calling her friends to tell them the exciting news.

Inspired by Julia's infectious goodwill and positive spin, I put aside my fears and tears and began to plan her birthday party and my family's visit at Christmas. I felt hope and that heavy kind of happiness that a mother feels when she can come to the aid of her children—especially older ones who rarely seem to need her anymore.

Good Health Holds Our Lives Together

Julia's illness was a powerful reminder to me about the crucial role that health plays in the lives of working mothers. Of course, all mothers want our children to be healthy, and we're willing to fight tooth and nail to get our children the best possible care. But for working mothers, good health—for our children, our spouses, our parents, and ourselves—is the invisible duct tape that holds our lives together. When anyone in our family is ill, all the arrangements we've worked so hard to put in place suddenly fall apart completely. A major health crisis like Julia's surgery can mean weeks out of the office, unpaid for most employees. Even a minor flu can throw our lives into upheaval as we scramble for child-care arrangements or cancel our work schedule for the day or the week. To hold our complex lives together, working mothers have to play the role of health-care specialist for our families, which can feel like a second, very demanding job.

Almost all moms play a central health-care role for our families: a survey of four thousand mothers by the Henry J. Kaiser Family Foundation in 2001 found that 80 percent of all mothers are responsible for selecting their children's doctors, taking the kids to doctors' appointments, and providing follow-up care.[1] And 58 percent of mothers are primarily responsible for decisions about health insurance.

While most mothers, working or not, play this health-care manager role, working mothers face added challenges. Not only do we have to contend with illness itself and our anxiety about a sick child or husband, but we also have to schedule our work on this second job carefully, making sure that we don't give the appearance of being out of control, inaccessible, or overly burdened at our "day" job. We feel guilty when we're away from our sick family members, and we feel guilty about letting down our coworkers when we don't show up at work. And yet, this second job of keeping our families healthy is far more important than our paid employment.

Some companies realize just how important this health-care manager role is, and they realize that if they don't support us, we'll miss more work and be less focused. The Working Mother 100 Best Companies, especially, see the value of supporting our second, sometimes very demanding job as family health manager. Many of our 100 Best Companies allow parents to use sick leave either for their own illness or when a family member is ill. About half offer a single pool of paid time off (called PTO) to be used for vacation or illness of anyone in the family, so it doesn't matter whether it's the parent or child who's sick. And 25 percent of the 100 Best fund either backup or sick child care, with some even arranging for a babysitter to come to your house when your child is sick. (For more about sick and backup child care, see chapter 3.)

At the same time, many of the 100 Best are taking wellness one step further and offering on-site support for employee and family health. The insurance company Aflac, for instance, offers free mammograms near its Columbus, Georgia, headquarters; Lincoln Financial supports a huge gym at its Fort Wayne, Indiana, site; Bon Secours Richmond Health System in Virginia rewards employees who lose weight with a check of up to $600.

This kind of company support makes our jobs as family health managers easier and helps us stay productive in the office. Over time, I believe more and more companies will realize it's in their best interests to provide paid sick leave and other benefits that help us. Meanwhile, working moms have developed a set of health management strategies to make our second job a little easier.

Moving to Plan B (or Plan C or Plan D)

I certainly couldn't have foreseen that Julia would need brain surgery in December and that I would miss nearly three weeks of work time. But as working moms, we do know we can count on some kind of health problems cropping up ... at completely unpredictable times.

That's why the career coach Robin Ryan recommends creating a plan *before* health problems arise. "Sit down with your boss, partner, or colleagues and figure out how to proceed if your child is sick," she says.[2] "Can you catch up on weekends? Can you draw on vacation or comp time? Or take unpaid time off?" It's easier, less stressful, and more professional to set up some guidelines and ground rules when you're not yet coping with the reality of a family illness.

She also advises having a variety of sick-day solutions in your back pocket, based on how sick your kids are. Maybe you should plan on staying home whenever the kids have a fever, but can call a sitter when they don't. And, she says, don't assume that Mom's the one to stay home. If your partner has a more flexible workplace, or a more flexible schedule that day, he should be on sick duty, too. If you or he can't take the whole day, try splitting shifts, she says. "You might take the morning shift at home, and then go to work from three thirty to seven or eight p.m.," she suggests.

How Sick Is Too Sick?

When our kids are sick, it's usually the working mom, not the working dad, who stays home from the office. According to the Kaiser Foundation study, 50 percent of mothers miss work when kids are sick, compared with only 30 percent of fathers. Often, that's unpaid time we're taking. Fully half of working mothers don't get paid when they miss work to care for a sick child. Even if we do get paid, we worry that we'll look bad or let down our coworkers by taking time off. In the Kaiser Foundation study, 30 percent of all working moms feared their bosses or coworkers wouldn't understand if they stayed home with their sick children; 35 percent worried their work performance would suffer; and 30 percent worried their job evaluations would suffer.

Of course we want to be home when our children need us. So a key part of our strategy as health-care managers is understanding when they *really do* need us—just how sick is sick enough to stay home? Part of that strategy is developing a shared understanding with our day-care providers and our schools about how sick is sick and when we're needed at home.

To help advance that understanding, the American Academy of Pediatrics and the American Public Health Association jointly published guidelines in 1992 (revised in 2002) outlining when kids should be sent home from day care . . . and when it's okay for them to stay. Unfortunately, day-care providers (and even pediatricians) aren't always familiar with the guidelines, so they don't always make the right call.[3]

For instance, some day-care providers are under the misperception that kids must be sent home from day care if they throw up. Actually, the national guidelines suggest that children don't need to stay home unless they've vomited twice in twenty-four hours. Similarly, rashes without a fever, and ringworm, if it's being treated, aren't reason enough to banish kids from day care. On the other hand, sometimes kids are kept at day care when they really should be home, for instance, if they're uncomfortable due to eczema.

But most day-care providers, parents, and even physicians don't understand or know about these guidelines. As a result, working moms use our precious sick time when it's not essential.

"Child-care providers tend to overexclude, sending home too many children," says Kristen Copeland, MD, a physician at Cincinnati Children's Hospital Medical Center, who studied six hundred day-care providers, doctors, and parents in Maryland. Copeland and other researchers described various scenarios and asked the providers, doctors, and parents whether children in those scenarios should be sent home.

Depending on the illness, day-care providers answered correctly only 21 to 74 percent of the time. Pediatricians did much better, answering correctly 64 to 81 percent of the time. Parents got it right just a bit more often than day-care providers: 37 to 74 percent.

Of course, as mothers, we want to know when our children are sick and make good decisions about what they need. But we can do a better job at that if everyone on our Home Team understands and agrees what good health decisions look like.

To review the national guidelines, visit the National Resource Center for Health and Safety in Childcare at http://nrc.urhsc.edu/ and search for "exclusion standards."

The High-tech House Call

Some day-care centers and schools around the country are taking a more active role in keeping our kids healthy and determining when they need to be sent home. One brilliant solution: high-tech house calls, like the ones paid by Dr. Ken McConnochie of Golisano Children's Hospital at the University of Rochester Medical Center.[4]

When four-year-old Alexys Trott felt feverish after her nap, for instance, her day-care teachers at a YMCA in Rochester, New York, made a video call to Dr. McConnochie. The teachers used a computer equipped with a camera, stethoscope, and other devices to help Dr. McConnochie check Alexys's vital signs and listen to e-mailed sound files of her heart and lungs. Her illness wasn't serious, he said—just a cold. He prescribed Motrin, which the center gave her after phoning her mother, Christine Nobles, for permission. Christine received a written report about the exam—and the reassurance of knowing that her daughter had already seen a doctor and that there was nothing to worry about.

The Rochester telemedicine project, called Health e-Access, was launched in 2001 and now includes seven child-care centers and ten public schools, serving some eighty-five hundred kids. The results have been phenomenal. Child absences due to illness plummeted by an average of 63 percent at participating child-care centers; 92 percent of parents said the program let them stay at work; 94 percent said the telemedicine visits helped them avoid a trip to the doctor's office or emergency room.

While telemedicine visits are still a new idea, I expect them to spread. The idea has already caught on not just in Rochester, where the e-health program has received several major expansion grants, but as far away as Kansas, where students at dozens of elementary and middle schools can make virtual visits to the doctor via the school nurse's office. These are exactly the kinds of smart solutions that moms should keep an eye out for and advocate for as we strive to keep our children healthy.

Fight for Your Time Off

I was very lucky to be able to take the time I needed for Julia's surgery without worrying about my job or my paycheck. But most moms don't have that luxury. Nearly half of all employees in private industry have no paid sick leave at all, even for themselves, let alone for their children. Some lawmakers are trying to change that. One bill introduced in Congress, the Healthy Families Act, would guarantee at least seven paid sick days a year for full-time employees at companies with at least fifteen people. To learn what you can do to support this and other measures, visit the National Partnership for Women and Families at www.nationalpartnership.org. Meanwhile, if you work at a company with fifty employees or more, you do have the right to take up to twelve weeks of unpaid leave through the 1993 Family and Medical Leave Act (FMLA).

It's important to understand your rights, as well as your employers' policies about leaves, in case you need to use FMLA. The law lets workers take time off without losing their jobs or benefits to care for family members who have a "serious illness." Most people don't realize that workers can take FMLA in very small, intermittent blocks of just a few days, or even a few hours. (About 30 percent of all FMLA leaves last five days or less.[5]) Many also don't realize that a "serious illness" is often defined as an illness lasting three days or more, which could include many childhood maladies and even a bad cold or the flu.

Being able to take small chunks of FMLA time is great news for working moms, who often need the flexibility of a day or two when kids are sick. And it's essential for working moms like Wendy Kagan, a director of human resources at Citizen's Bank in Providence, Rhode Island. She was diagnosed with breast cancer when her son Zachary was four. To keep her routine and Zachary's as normal as possible, she scheduled her appointments at the beginning and end of the workday. Being able to take short amounts of time for recurring appointments helped prevent her treatments from intruding on her precious time with her family.

Unfortunately, cancer patients like Wendy and other parents who need short amounts of time off to care for themselves or their ill family members may not enjoy job-protected time off in the future. In 2005, the Department of Labor proposed changes to FMLA so workers could no longer take "intermittent leave" of a few hours or days. The changes would also redefine "serious illness," to make it more difficult for workers to take job-protected leave. This would be a serious blow to parents. Working moms need to make sure FMLA remains intact and ready to protect our families. To follow the proposed changes, visit the National Partnership for Women and Families' Web site. The site can help you contact your legislators and urge them to support FMLA.

Elephants and Chirping Birds

"Mommy, an elephant sat on my chest and then he got up and I heard a whole lot of birds singing to me," Julia told me as she woke from her surgery. "The walls were full of purple colors and I couldn't remember how to get out of bed!!" She went on and on for thirty minutes about the wonders of her subconscious experiences as her brain slowly woke up from the anesthesia. I was so glad to be there with her to hear her tales from beyond.

I had made some pretty ambitious plans about what I would do while I was in the hospital with her. I brought books and papers and yellow pads, even a laptop computer. I never opened my briefcase. Instead, Julia and I just talked and talked and talked. I don't think we had talked so much since she was ten or so. She slept in between conversations, and I did, too. I negotiated with the nurses for her: Can she have some ice cream? She needs to go to the bathroom. And so on. Julia healed quickly and was allowed to leave the hospital after four days. I took her home to her perfectly clean room (courtesy of me) and spent the next few days arranging visits from friends and watching TV with her.

Julia stayed out of school for four weeks, including her Christmas break. She later told me, "Mommy, that was the best month of my life! I didn't have to go to school or do homework. I got cards and flowers and presents from so many people, and everyone was so nice to me!" Talk about a silver lining! On a very sweet note, she didn't really feel up to having a birthday party, so her boyfriend, Connor Styles, and her best friends, Victoria Migdal and Joe Breen, came over on her birthday and read her favorite children's stories out loud while she rested and enjoyed their company.

When Mom Is Sick

It's terrifying when our children get sick. But when Mom is the one who's seriously ill, we carry the double burden of coping with our own symptoms and treatments at the same time that we worry about sheltering our kids and keeping their lives as normal and happy as possible. We need special strategies for coping with this most difficult of situations.

Wendy Kagan, the Rhode Island mom diagnosed with breast cancer, held it together for nearly a year of treatment, including chemotherapy, a lumpectomy, and radiation, by clinging to her routine and four-year-old Zachary's. She planned her chemotherapy sessions for Fridays, so she could recover over the weekend. And she stuck stubbornly to her work schedule, missing just eleven days in ten months.

"Something in me prevented me from taking too many days off," she says. "I felt if I started giving in, I'd fall apart."

She approached her appointments and treatments like any other work-family issue. She informed her colleagues about her appointments and made sure they knew when she would be available and how to reach her. At home, her husband, Andy, took over many of the household duties. Wendy says there were many days when she felt frightened and exhausted. "It felt like there was no light at the end of the tunnel," she recalls.

Several key strategies help working mothers like Wendy cope

with their own illnesses, according to Kristine Breese, the author of *Cereal for Dinner: Strategies, Shortcuts, and Sanity for Moms Battling Illness.*

- **Separate obligations and options.** Sometimes, things that seem like unavoidable responsibilities at work simply aren't. List the things that must get done at home and work . . . and distinguish which of them really must get done (by you personally), and which can be dropped or delegated.
- **Make a work plan.** Realistically evaluate how much work you can do—and are willing to do—while you recover. Make it clear to your boss and coworkers what you will and won't be responsible for, and how long you expect the situation to continue.
- **Make a health to-do list.** Realize that you have more to do now that you're ill. You have to make time for doctors' appointments, treatments, and—most important—rest. It's easy to forget to add these to your to-do list, and to overestimate your own ability to perform through illness.

Eventually, Wendy made it through—and so did her family. Her cancer went into remission and life returned to almost-normal. "I do look back and think, 'How did I do it?' But that's what women do," she says.

Our Parents Need Us, Too

Just as we were getting over the crisis of Julia's brain surgery, my mother's health reached a crisis of its own. She had been diagnosed with multiple myeloma, cancer of the bone marrow, two and a half years earlier, when she was eighty-two. I struggled to understand the disease and its possible treatments, getting my best advice and information from Doreen Semel, a fellow working mother in Chappaqua who is a case worker for multiple myeloma patients.

She explained to me the stages of the illness, and my ebullient mother courageously endured the hemodialysis, chemotherapy, pain, and weight loss that Doreen warned me would come.

We had spent a low-key but grateful Christmas together after Julia's surgery. Just three weeks later I got a call from my dad that my mother was in a terrible state. I ran from a photo shoot in my office to catch a plane to Chicago, where I arrived in time to spend one last day with her. I held my mother's hand and touched her face and spoke to her as if she could understand me. I told her I loved her more than I had ever managed to convey. She died on Saturday afternoon, January 22, 2005, as a beautiful snowfall slowly swirled outside her hospital window, leaving a void in our lives that will never be filled.

Dealing with the loss of my mother has been much harder than I ever imagined it would be. I found myself challenged in my effectiveness and capability in the office at a time when I desperately needed to catch up on all the work I had put aside to take care of Julia. At the same time, knowing how much my mother cared about my career, and how proud she was of my work at *Working Mother* magazine, helped me to push ahead, even when I felt like I couldn't.

Moms in the Middle

As working mothers, we often find ourselves managing the health care of our aging parents and our children at the same time. In fact, more than two out of five moms ages forty-five to fifty-five find themselves sandwiched between kids and aging parents who need care, according to the U.S. Administration on Aging. Many moms live far away from their parents, like I do, complicating the task of taking an active, decision-making role in their health care. To do this, we need to become elder-care specialists, learning about our parents' needs at the same time that we take care of our own emotions about the aging, possible disability, and eventual death of our parents.

That's what Patricia Sprague, a mother of two and a tax attorney in New York City, did when her elderly father became ill—and then her mother couldn't get out of bed one day. "All of a sudden, they couldn't take care of themselves," she told us. "I just hadn't realized how bad things had become."[6]

Patricia and moms like her find that elder care doesn't just mean looking out for the health of aging relatives. They often need legal assistance to arrange their estates and financial planning help as well. Fortunately, these moms are finding more and more strategies and resources to draw on as the population ages and the dilemma of the so-called sandwich generation becomes increasingly clear. Among them is the national elder-care locator, at www.elder care.gov (or 1-800-677-1116), run by the U.S. Department of Health and Human Services Administration on Aging. The service can refer you to organizations serving older adults in any zip code.

You can also find support for your parents' day-to-day needs through some colleges, like Temple University in Philadelphia, which runs the Time Out Respite Program. For just $7 an hour, students spend time with and run errands for senior citizens. Local organizations, like the Family Caregiver Alliance in San Francisco, will provide free consultations with elder-care experts. And some moms turn to elder-care professionals, who can coach you on the health-care, legal, and other support services your aging parents may need. You can find aging experts through the National Association of Professional Geriatric Care managers at www.careman ager.org.

The Fastest-Growing Benefit

Fortunately, many companies are starting to realize how many of their workers face elder-care problems.

"One of the most important benefits companies will be adding in the next few years will be elder care," says Michelle Thomas, the chief diversity officer at Wrigley Gum. "Because of the aging of the population and our workforce, and because our parents are living longer, that's going to be a top priority for every company."

No wonder it's becoming a top priority: U.S. employers lose up to $29 billion in reduced productivity due to the amount of time that employees take off to care for aging relatives, according to a study by the National Alliance for Caregiving and AARP.[7] Companies are realizing that they need to help us if they want to keep us. Nationwide, about 21 percent of companies offer elder-care referral services, where employees can access expert advice and referrals to care facilities near them or their parents. But the Working Mother 100 Best Companies do much better: 99 percent offer elder-care resource and referral services. These programs are spreading quickly—ten years ago, just 75 percent of our Best Companies offered elder care.

When Patricia Sprague faced her unexpected elder-care dilemma, she found that her employer, Pfizer, offered elder-care support, including a resource and referral service connecting employees with experts in senior living arrangements, caregiving, medical help, insurance, and legal issues. The company also offered a support group for employees dealing with elder care. Thanks to all this practical and emotional support, Pfizer has found that employees who use their elder-care resources experience less stress and are better able to focus at work.

Crises and Clarity

Whether it's our parents, our kids, or ourselves, when someone in our family faces a health crisis, it becomes clear that as the family health managers, we can and will handle whatever we need to handle. The work we do outside the home may be important and exciting, or difficult and frustrating, but it is in a large sense only a backdrop for the work we do every day when we hold our daughter's hand or kiss our son good night, or tiptoe into their rooms before we leave on a business trip just for that last little glance at their sleeping beauty. Or when we help our daughter prepare for brain surgery. Making sure our loved ones are healthy and well cared for is our first and most important job.

During times of crisis, it's clearer than ever that we're mothers first. In fact, sometimes health crises can help clarify our priorities and lead us to find more supportive companies, jobs, or careers—and those adjustments can be a blessing in disguise. For instance, when Eugenia Kim's son Van was born three months early, she used all her banked vacation time, maternity leave, and unpaid leave to take time off to care for him when he came home from the hospital. Although she loved her job as a graphic designer with the Public Broadcasting Service in Alexandria, Virginia, Van's continuing health issues forced her to reevaluate and make a change to a more flexible career path. She left the organization and started her own freelance graphic design business. Since she's a night owl married to an early bird, she took her son to doctors' appointments and therapy during the day, and worked at night while her husband watched the baby.

"I remember most vividly the hours I spent designing a brochure on the computer, while behind my home-office wall, I could hear Jeff rocking Van to sleep . . . the creak, creak of the chair, the click of the crib latch," she says.

Today, Van is a teenager and Eugenia still works for herself. "Our plan worked," she says. "I have more business than I can handle. A surprise payoff has been that attention given to Van has allowed me to give attention to my own needs, and I've become creative in ways I wouldn't ever have envisioned. I've not only learned how to limit the business so it doesn't demand too much of me, but I've found other ways to fulfill my creative urges."

Eugenia learned one of the best secrets of the family health manager: despite the hardship and stress of dealing with serious family illness, our roles as family health managers and as advocates for our children's well-being can transform our lives in ways that are deeply fulfilling, both at home and at work.

Chapter Nine

We Tinker with the Venus/Mars Equation

When I first met Bob, he was a thirty-seven-year-old confirmed bachelor, a former tennis teacher with sparkling eyes and a high-spirited sense of fun who usually dated two or three women at the same time—until he met me.

After Bob realized he couldn't teach tennis eight hours a day for the rest of his life, he went into the insurance business and later sold mutual funds. Although he did well, and was rewarded with annual trips to the "President's Club" meetings held in beautiful resorts, he never really loved his work. I, on the other hand, was madly passionate about my career in publishing and my job at *Working Mother* magazine. Thanks to this fundamental difference, Bob and I ended up making choices that neither of us could have imagined. Gradually, he downsized his career, eventually working part-time and becoming the first "at-home dad" we knew . . . but not the last.

The idea of Bob staying home with the kids would have seemed completely ridiculous to both of us early in our relationship. After all, I almost ended our relationship because he didn't seem to want to have children in the first place.

I always knew I wanted kids, and I assumed everyone else did, too, including Bob . . . until we attended the christening of Lauren Knight, the first baby to be born to our circle of friends. As I held the tiny bundle of baby in my arms, agog at her newborn beauty, I looked up at Bob with love in my eyes and said, in front of all of our friends, "Oh, Bob, wouldn't it be great to have one of these?"

Bob looked right back into my eyes and said flatly, "One of what?"

That's when I knew I had to get serious about my future. I was thirty-one years old, and although I loved being with Bob, I was *not* going to marry him if he didn't want kids. So a few months later I gave him the Ultimatum. I told him that he had six months to decide if he wanted the whole nine yards—wife, kids, home, responsibilities. I told him I wouldn't nag him about it or point to the precious toes sticking out of baby backpacks anymore. He simply had until December 1, and if he didn't decide by then, I'd be on my way. Or rather, he'd be on his way, since we had been living in *my* loft in Greenwich Village for two years.

He never did actually propose. He just stood up before a group of thirty-five friends gathered at a restaurant in West Hampton Beach and said that we were "talking about getting married." He must have been having a deep conversation with himself—the *M* word had not crossed my lips since the Ultimatum. But it was wonderful anyway—and it was November 1—a whole month before the deadline.

After he skipped the proposal, we never got back on the traditional wedding path again. First, I picked out and bought my own engagement/wedding ring while I was on a business trip in Minneapolis. My clients at the Campbell Mithun ad agency saw the ring before Bob did. Then Bob picked out my wedding dress when we wandered into a shop in Greenwich Village called the Gallery of Wearable Art. It was a one-of-a-kind dress made in France (and on sale!) with alternating panels of white satin and pink sequins, with appliqué flowers waltzing down the pink panels. What a dress! Before I could say how much I loved it, Bob had whipped out his credit card and was paying for it. Then Bob turned into Mr. Wedding Planner and made all the arrangements for our wedding himself, down to the asparagus wrapped in grape leaves and Bill (nephew of Guy) Lombardo's Swing Band. Bob and I decided to foot the bill for our wedding and reception in Greenwich Village ourselves, so we wouldn't have to negotiate with my parents. (They held a lovely reception for us in Illinois a month or so later.)

I never legally changed my name, explaining to Bob's mother that I was not willing to spell the unpronounceable C-o-u-l-o-m-b-e a dozen times a day in my business, especially when I didn't think women should have to take their husbands' names anyway. And E-v-a-n-s had always worked so well for me!

These may not seem like revolutionary changes, but our lack of convention prepared us for choices we would make later, when our own baby bundles were finally in our arms.

When we moved to Chappaqua after Robert's second birthday, I had an easy commute, but Bob faced a long trek down to Wall Street. Within a year, Bob decided he couldn't take the commute anymore and moved his base of operations to an agency in downtown Chappaqua, with a window looking over the local branch of Citibank instead of the towering skyscrapers of Wall Street. Several years later, he moved his office into a tiny corner of our house. As his value around the house grew, he devoted less time to his business. Over time, his commitment to volunteering in the community—first with the fire department and then with the ambulance corps—became his passion. Slowly but steadily, Bob turned into a work-at-home dad with a part-time business and an important role in the town we had adopted. And he became a trailblazer of sorts, exercising the new choices that working mothers have created for our partners as well as ourselves.

We Give Men New Choices

Over the last twenty-five years, working mothers have given men a huge opportunity to change *their* lifestyles. For the first time since the industrial revolution drove men off the farm and into the modern workplace, men have some freedom to venture outside the traditional forty-hours-a-week, forty-years-in-a-row model. Yes, the number of true stay-at-home dads (those with no paid job) is tiny—less than 1 percent of fathers, or about 98,000 dads, in 2003. But many men are starting to use flextime, to work at home, and to downsize their careers like Bob did. Others launch their own companies or take bigger career risks than they could otherwise afford to chance, while their working wives provide a steady paycheck and benefits.

At first, Bob was the only work-at-home dad that we knew. People called him Mr. Mom, and he took a lot of flack from colleagues. Larry Moss, his mentor and friend, warned him repeatedly that he needed to pay more attention to his career, and that he was missing big opportunities. But over time, we noticed that other dads we knew were making new choices as well. Two of our friends veered off the traditional path: Frank Knight decided to go back to school and get a teaching degree after he took early retirement from NYNEX. John Sloan was downsized from a corporate technology job and started consulting from home. John soon found that being home after school with his teenage son was a great bonus. He used his freedom from the nine-to-five grind to take his son fishing during the long days of summer, and to get involved in his community. He successfully ran for councilman for the town of Cortlandt, New York, and has been able to spend time on the daily chores of town government for the last eight years.

Frank was able to try his hand at teaching because his wife, Luci, worked full-time as Working Mother Media's conference director. John was able to work for himself and sit on the Town Council because his wife, Rita, worked full-time in the controller's department at AXA-Equitable. Bob was able to scale back a career he didn't love because I wanted to go full steam ahead at *Working Mother*. Our careers gave our partners new choices—and they became more involved fathers because they had more time and more flexibility.

Today, I see many examples of moms and dads rejecting the conventional gender roles. In the magazine, we write about stay-at-home dads, flextime dads, and dads who proudly announce they're leaving the office to go to a ball game or a dance recital. Our readers write to us about husbands who do much more than "help out" around the house. We hear more and more examples of men who are taking paternity leave. And I sometimes meet young dads like Warren Hart, a member of the Chappaqua Ambulance Corps who works at IBM. He told me that he was at a lacrosse game at 3:30 on a Friday afternoon when he ran into a fellow IBMer watching his daughter's soccer game on the adjoining field. "Our dads would never have had that experience!" he said with a laugh, proud of his involved fatherhood.

Bruce Tulgan, the founder of RainmakerThinking, a management training group that studies the changing workplace, summed up the difference between dads twenty years ago and today's Generation X and Y fathers. "For boomer dads, if you were really involved with your kids you were 'cool.' For Gen X dads, if you're not involved, you're just lame."[1]

Today, men are spending much more time with their kids than fathers did twenty years ago—on average a full hour more per day than fathers spent with their children in 1977.[2] They also spend forty-two minutes more per day doing household chores than fathers did in 1977. Hooray for that!

Building Better Fathers

This new and improved parenting doesn't happen automatically or overnight. Many, many moms tell me their partners are not pulling their fair share. In our What Moms Want survey, only one out of three of the working moms said their partner takes an equal role in parenting. Another third said they spend "somewhat more time" parenting than Dad, while one out of four spend "much more time."

Not surprisingly, the moms who had equal partners were happier. They were more likely to call themselves "fulfilled" (34 percent) than moms who spent much more time caring for the kids (24 percent). But these moms weren't just blessed with perfect, involved husbands. I e-mailed a group of readers to find out what the secret ingredients were to insuring a more equal partnership, and I found the same three strategies kept coming up again and again—passing the baton, leaving Dad in charge, and nixing the nagging.

Dad Strategy 1: Passing the Baton

Many of our working mom readers arrange their schedules so they're home when the kids come back from school in the afternoon or in time to pick the kids up from day care. For some of them, that means starting work very early . . . and that simple adjustment of their schedule often pressures Dad to adjust his schedule, too—in a way that gets him more involved.

"I arranged to go in early at seven or seven thirty a.m. and leave by three thirty p.m.," says Pauline Rockwell, who works at Salem Radio Group in Boston. As a result, her husband, Rick, a vice president of a real estate company, handled "the early morning get-the-baby-ready-fed-packed-and-off-to-day-care routine," because his work allowed him to come in a little later. The staggered hours made her husband a more equal dad—and made Pauline a happier mother to Madison, now age thirteen.

"It's an awesome arrangement," she says. "I probably would have been a psycho stressed woman if I had to handle the morning ritual on top of everything else!"

We also heard from many readers who work different shifts from their partners. Research analyst Laura Cleary of Milwaukee, for instance, works on days when her husband, Joe, is off: he works two twelve-hour days in a row, then has two days off. He's fully in charge of the kids on those days.

"It has not been an easy road, honestly," Laura says. "But working out the logistics has been worthwhile." Laura says their staggered schedule and equal contributions have made them both fully equal parents.

Recently, I had a bout of dizziness, and I dropped into DOCS, a twenty-four-hour medical clinic in town, to check out the problem. The technician who took my blood work told me she had purposely studied to become a lab technician because she wanted to work weekends—and knew there was a high demand for health professionals to work on Saturdays and Sundays. Her weekend schedule meant that she and her husband didn't need *any* child care: she took care of the kids Monday through Friday, while her husband worked a traditional schedule. Then he took over as full-time parent on Saturday and Sunday. This passing-the-baton strategy let her husband become an equally responsible parent. It also let them both work without having to find child care—a big money saver.

Dad Strategy 2: Leave Dad in Charge

My jobs have always required a lot of travel. That's meant that Bob is the primary caregiver whenever I'm gone. And painful as it is to spend time away from the kids, it's often the fastest way to get dads fully involved and up to speed as parents . . . and the fastest way to train ourselves to trust them, too.

"My husband does more than half the work. This was inadvertent on my part, but I happen to have a job with pretty heavy travel," wrote reader Rosanne Petros, a clinical research specialist in Laurel, Maryland, and the mother of Alina, twelve, Brennan, seven, and Connor, three. "When Alina was born we needed my income, and so I went back to work and needed to take periodic trips (about four times a month)—even overnight trips." By leaving Alina in the charge of her husband, Kevin, a contract specialist with the Department of Defense, she discovered just how good he could be with the kids, and that everyone survived just fine when she was gone.

Leaving dads in charge—even though we may be tempted to correct their parenting styles—gives them the experience of day-to-day parenting. "Last summer, Laurel was almost three months old when I returned to work full-time," wrote reader Sarah Lingenfelter, a media relations coordinator at Houghton College and the mother of Laurel, now two, and Maddie, four. Her husband, Ben, a teacher, had the summer off and served as primary caretaker. "I think it helped him see what a mother really has to do daily. I wish more husbands would take some time off and fill the role as primary caretaker—even if for just one week."

When reader Catherine Parsons's husband, John, took six weeks off from his job as a branch manager at Citibank after their first child, Sabrina, was born, it proved to be an eye-opening experience. "He thought he was going to build a shed," says Catherine, who works with the school system in Dutchess County, New York. Needless to say, the shed never got built, and John got a real feel for the demands of parenthood. As a result, he's much closer than he would have been to Sabrina, now six, and Donald, three. "I heard him talking to someone a year later on the phone," Catherine told me. "He said, 'I wouldn't trade that time for anything.' "

Dad Strategy 3: Nix the Nagging

When I e-mailed our readers and asked how they encourage their husbands or partners to be equal parents, many told me they bite their tongues and do whatever else it takes to stop themselves from nagging. Not only does nagging annoy the dads, they told me, but it makes moms feel like they have one more child.

I have personally had a very hard time following this advice. The theme of my relationship with Bob is summed up nicely in the Off-Broadway smash hit *I Love You, You're Perfect, Now Change*. I have asked Bob to change his parenting style, his eating habits, the amount of time he spends sleeping. . . . I nag him on a million subjects, all for the good of the family or his health or the house. . . .

The no-nag idea is a powerful one, and I'm going to see if it can settle into my brain and replace the behavior modification program I have been working on for twenty years—to very little avail!

One of my favorite ideas that I want to try came from a reader I'll call Jane (she didn't want her real name used, in case her husband figured out her secret). Jane's no-nagging tactic was actually inspired by a book on toddler behavior.

"Instead of coming out and asking your husband to do this or that, you say something like, 'Honey, do you want to set the table while I get this load of laundry folded, or do you want me to set the table while you fold laundry?' "

Jane says this approach works much better than saying, "Get your lazy butt off the sofa and help me out here," since it gives him a choice.

"The caveat," she says, "is that it doesn't usually work more than twice in one evening, so choose your chores carefully!"

For other moms, the secret to involving Dad without nagging came down to dividing tasks according to natural talents and how much time each parent has available. The more both partners like the tasks they're assigned, the more likely they are to get them done.

"When our youngest child was born, I wanted to go back to work and my husband agreed, but with three children, I said I can't do everything," reader Susan Gradishar told us. "Since he likes to cook and I definitely do not, having him do all the cooking seemed the perfect solution."

For Lorraine Scheller, a manager of bioanalytical chemistry at Southwest Research Institute in San Antonio, dividing labor means she dusts and cleans the kitchen, but her husband, Tom, an engineering manager who has every other Friday off, does the heavy labor—bathrooms, vacuuming, and laundry. As a result, all the housecleaning gets done during the week, leaving more free weekend time to spend with their kids, Austin, twelve, and Sarah, nine. "We'd rather do fun things together than housework," she says.

Research analyst Laura Cleary calls her husband, Joe, a "totally equal co-parent" to Melyssa, eight, and Sean, seven, and says the secret to making it work is letting him do things his way—not hers. "I have encouraged [equal parenting] by not complaining about the way he does things—where he puts things away, shrinking my shirts in the dryer, the not-so-clean pots and pans, the mismatched kids' outfits for that day, and letting him completely handle kid problems when he is the 'first on the scene.' "

Helping Out and Other Irritating Myths

At the same time that we nix the nagging, we also need to stop acting as if our husbands are being especially generous when they take care of their own kids, or that they are "helping us out" when they keep their own house clean.

"I find it difficult to listen to friends asking their husbands if they can 'watch the kids' so that they can go get their nails done. Their husbands never ask for the same level of permission," says Catherine Parsons, the schools specialist from Dutchess County. She also finds it irksome when colleagues at conferences ask who's taking care of Sabrina and Donald. When she says Dad is in charge, they typically reply, "That's nice of him."

"It is not 'nice of him,' " she fumes. "It's his God-given duty, not a favor he is giving me. He's the daddy." She assumes that John is equally responsible, so he's not "babysitting" for them—he's just taking care of his own children. To make their shared responsibility work, they use a family calendar showing who's available when.

"I make my nail appointments and put it on the family calendar, and he knows to work around it," she says. "I go to a conference, it goes on the family calendar, and he knows the carpooling is his while I am gone."

Challenging our own gender stereotypes can be the toughest part of building a new relationship with men, but when we treat our husbands like equals, and stop assuming that all child-rearing and household responsibilities default to us, they become better parents and better people—and so do we.

For Men, It's a Diaper Ceiling

When Robert was a baby, I had to teach Bob a lot of things about him. It wasn't the physical stuff that required remedial training so much as the psychological stuff. When Robert repeatedly woke up crying just as Bob was crawling into bed, Bob believed that the baby was purposefully trying to get under his skin. I had to explain to Bob several times that at three or four or five months, Robert didn't even know that Bob existed. He hadn't developed an awareness of others yet, and he certainly wasn't trying to get Bob's goat!

"How could he be trying to push your buttons when he doesn't even know you exist yet?" I asked. And I felt a giant chasm between us—an expertise gap between what I knew about Robert and what Bob knew about Robert. This expertise gap carried over into every aspect of raising Robert, as I studied all the books, and made all the decisions about Robert's care mostly on my own, always pushing Bob to do things my way.

My intention was to provide Robert with the best of care, but now I see that I contributed to a phenomenon I call the Diaper Ceiling—a compulsion moms feel to be the expert in their children's well-being and to constantly correct and educate dads. Like the Glass Ceiling that excludes women from the corner office, the Diaper Ceiling excludes dads from the inner sanctum of parenthood.

What causes the Diaper Ceiling? Some people would simply point to the biological bond between mother and child that tends to exclude Dad. But I think there are other reasons.

Many new parents start out more or less equally clueless about a new baby, but moms start to zoom ahead as they devour baby magazines and books during their pregnancies. And then if Dad doesn't take paternity leave (68 percent didn't in our <u>What Moms Want</u> survey), he doesn't learn as much about the baby because he's not there. He doesn't take part in establishing a routine with the new baby, or change a dozen diapers a day until he can do it with his eyes closed. So moms get a head start that some dads never make up, and the new family starts out with habits leading to the Diaper Ceiling.

One clear solution to help fathers feel closer to their babies— and mothers to feel more confident about Dad's parenting—is for companies to offer and encourage the use of paternity leave. We need to see more companies like Microsoft, which offers twelve weeks of paid paternity leave, or Republic Bancorp, which offers six. Even just two weeks of paid paternity leave can make a difference, if dads will take it.

"When my son was born in December, not only did my management allow me to take advantage of the firm-offered parental leave, they *mandated* it," Booz Allen associate Jim Turner told us. "I was able to stay with my wife and baby through the hospital stay and into the first week at home. After that, I was able to sprinkle parental leave days into my first week back at work, making it much easier for us to learn how to be a family."

Unfortunately, while FMLA guarantees dads the same twelve unpaid weeks of family leave that moms get, hardly any companies ease the financial burden by offering *paid* paternity leave. Only 15 percent of companies surveyed by the Society for Human Resource Management offered paid leave for dads. And even among our 100 Best Companies, only 47 percent of companies offered paid paternity leave. It's important for companies to start offering paid leave for dads, not only because it helps families financially, but because it shows that companies believe paternity leave is important— which helps take away any stigma fathers might feel for taking time off with new babies.

Let Dads Be Dads

Meanwhile, whether dads take paternity leave or not, we moms need to make sure we're not contributing to the Diaper Ceiling.

We need to give husbands time and space to learn, and we need to let them develop their own parenting styles. Sometimes that might mean learning to tolerate—even to laugh at—minor meltdowns, as physician Suzy Human of Bemidji, Minnesota, learned. When her husband set out for an afternoon of fishing with two-month-old Tommy in tow, she resisted the urge to pack the diaper bag herself. "I decided to back off and let him figure out this stuff on his own," she told us.

Five hours later, her husband burst in with a naked Tommy held at arm's length, peeing everywhere. He hadn't packed enough diapers. He never made that mistake again. In fact, soon after their third child was born, Suzy was the one who forgot the diaper bag. Fortunately, her husband had learned to keep a stash of diapers under the front seat of his car.[3]

When we leave men in charge of the kids and stop ourselves from second-guessing their decisions and choices—even when we have to bite our tongues!—we help dads develop confidence and expertise. In the end, that helps us by creating equality at home—and helps our kids by bringing them closer to their fathers and providing great role models for their future.

Changing the Diaper Ceiling: How Companies Are Helping

Companies are also helping dads beat the Diaper Ceiling by offering fathering seminars and support. Microsoft, for instance, offers a "Dads at Microsoft" support group and a parenting seminar called "Men Have Babies, Too." And in 2003, Colgate offered its first "Work and Family Balance for Dads" seminar.

The good news is that despite the Diaper Ceiling, men are proud of being evolved fathers. Dads are reading to their kids at night, playing games, changing diapers, and giving bottles. They're going to parent-teacher conferences, sporting events, and father-daughter scout nights. And it's paying off: studies show that babies with fathers who are very involved in their care are more social than infants with "traditional" fathers,[4] and that kids with involved dads are more likely to do well in school.[5]

Men Need Balance, Too

Whether your partner (if you have one) is naturally enlightened, or you've had to work him into shape, involved dads have one thing in common: the more involved they are, the more they realize they need work-family balance too. And the younger they are, the more they want it. My friend Ellen Galinsky, the president of the Families and Work Institute, did a study comparing the attitudes of baby boomer dads in 1977 to those of Gen X and Gen Y dads in 2002. Ellen found that fathers today are much more likely to feel that their job and family interfere with each other (45 percent in 2002 versus 34 percent in 1977).[6]

Other studies have shown that younger workers—both men and women—value work-life balance more than baby boomers did. Generation X and Y workers were more likely to call themselves "family-centric" or "dual-centric" and less likely to be "work-centric" than baby boomers.[7] And workers under thirty-five were more likely to rate work-life balance as "very important" than workers fifty-six and older in a study by the Society for Human Resource Management.

Clearly, work-life balance isn't just a women's issue anymore—and yet, you'd never know it when you examine how many men actually use work-life programs offered by their companies. Men are far less likely to use flex options or work part-time, according to the Bureau of Labor Statistics.

So why are only a small minority of dads taking paternity leave, cutting back their hours, or using other work-life benefits when they are offered? Dave, a dad from Boston, summed it up when he wrote to us recently:

"I'm often at a greater disadvantage in the workplace because people don't expect that I have family issues to deal with. Common concessions made for working mothers aren't extended willingly to working fathers. It's obvious from the looks I get when I need to leave early to go to school meetings or to take my child to the doctor or the dentist."

Many working moms I speak to would disagree with this assessment—feeling that it's easier for men to slip out of the office for their kids' games than for women. Either way, Dave accurately captures the oppressive feeling that there's a stigma attached to actually using work-life benefits.

Whether it's true or not, there's a perception that using family-friendly benefits will hurt your career. "In our research, we've seen that a steady thirty-nine percent of employees feel their job will be jeopardized if they use the flexibility they have. Even though companies have gotten more flexible, the level of 'perceived jeopardy' has stayed absolutely steady over the last ten years," says Ellen Galinsky.

This "perception of jeopardy" may be even higher among upper-level management, according to Ilene Lang, the president of Catalyst, a research organization focused on women's advancement. "Very few people on the fast track feel they can take advantage of those types of programs," she says. According to one Catalyst study, "eighty to eighty-five percent of people who are successful and have ambitious goals feel they will take a career hit if they use these benefits," Lang says.

James Levine, the founder of the Fatherhood Project, a national research project focusing on dads, thinks perception weighs heavily on dads' minds. "Women are sometimes reluctant to bring up family issues at work, because they feel they'll be thought of as less committed," he says. "But women feel more of a sense of permission to bring up the issues than men do. It's part of the allowable discussion at the workplace. Men, on the other hand, often feel it's simply not allowable for them to bring up work-family problems. They feel they'll be violating some unspoken norm or rule."

At a recent seminar at Viacom, one father told Jim he wanted to be more involved, but his job wouldn't let him. Levine asked him a simple question: Did you talk about the problem with your boss? It turned out he had never asked his boss for flexibility. He just *assumed* he was too valuable to be out of the office at all during the day.

"In most cases, when guys are willing to put the family on the table and recognize that family is a business issue, they find their boss has the same concerns," Levine says.

Here's Jim's advice to help men broach the work-family balance issue. Share these with your partner and try them yourself. (They work for women, too!)

1. **Know your office policies . . . and use them.** "Most people treat the office manual the way they treat a software manual . . . nobody ever looks at it," Levine says. As a result, he often encounters men at very progressive companies who have no idea that their company has official flextime policies for *all* employees . . . not just women. "You've got this paradox. A good number of companies are working to be responsive to family needs, but their employees don't realize this applies to them." Understanding what flexibility policies are already on the books makes it easier to ask for what you need—because you can point to the precedent.

2. **State the business case.** Even if policies aren't on the books, men should talk to their supervisors about their need for work-life balance. "If you don't ask, you don't get," Levine says. When talking to the boss, it's important to present the business case. "Put it on the table in a mature, healthy way that says, 'I have to get this work done and I can, but I have issues on the family side that are going to make it difficult for me to stay here.'"

3. **If the boss says no.** If the boss seems reluctant to grant flextime or other measures, Levine suggests two responses. "Number one, you can say, 'I wonder if others are facing the

same problem.' " A little research around the office will certainly show that other dads are facing the same problem,
and that more flexibility could help boost employee morale
on a large scale. Or you can suggest a short-term experiment. "Say, 'Let's try this for a week or two and then evaluate it,' " Levine suggests. That gives managers a low-risk
opportunity to try something new.

Our Own Worst Enemy

Sometime it's our own assumptions that prevent change from
happening. Many women assume that their husbands' jobs are
more important than their own, or will be less flexible than their
own. That creates a cycle: Mom doesn't ask Dad to take on more
parenting responsibilities, so Dad doesn't ask for more flexibility,
so companies don't realize fathers need more help. "The feedback that gets back to the business world is when, say, a child is
sick, Mom stays home," says Levine. Of course, there are jobs—
held by both women and men—where it's more difficult to find
flexibility, and there are bosses who just don't get it and never
will. "But in general," says Levine, "there's really more latitude
for fathers to be involved than men or women realize. Parents
need to take some responsibility for that and not just blame it on
the company."

Revolution at the Top

Rapid change in corporate attitudes toward dads will only come
when senior-level managers—especially men—start taking work-
family balance seriously. Evolution can come from below, but revolution needs to come from the top.

Jim Sandman, the managing director of the law firm Arnold &
Porter, summed it up in a keynote address at our WorkLife Congress

in 2003. "Ultimately, senior management needs to not only encourage, but to do it themselves," he said. Jim really knows what he's talking about: he took an *eight-month* paternity leave from his job as partner in the law firm to care for his newborn son while his wife returned to work.

Figuring he'd have plenty of time on his hands since he was giving up a sixty-plus-hour workweek, Jim decided that his paternity leave would be a great time to reconnect with an old love that his busy career didn't allow—playing the piano. He scheduled a series of piano lessons and put together a daily practice schedule, with plenty of flexibility built in to accommodate the baby's needs. Like many new parents, he had no idea that babies—especially newborns—have no respect for *our* needs, *our* time schedules, or *our* interests. The lure of the piano was no match for the insistent cries of the baby. Jim's stories sent the five hundred women in the conference audience into a wicked combination of laughter and tears: to hear the familiar tales of new motherhood coming from a man, and a very buttoned-up lawyer at that, reminded us both how far we've come, and how far we haven't.

Jim was deeply affected by his time with his son, and when he returned after paternity leave, he fought to make Arnold & Porter worthy of the Working Mother 100 Best list. Today, it's one of only a few law firms to ever have achieved that honor. Twelve years later, Jim is certain that his paternity leave has had a lasting effect on his relationship with his son.

In order for working mothers to find balance in our lives, we need senior-level men like Jim Sandman to step up to the plate and start using work-life balance policies themselves.

Many younger CEOs are breaking the mold and becoming more involved fathers—and learning firsthand about the struggles moms face. Steve Sanger is a favorite example of mine. Right after he became CEO of General Mills, he traveled to New York City for his first big meeting with Wall Street analysts—and took his wife, Karen, who's a lawyer, and his daughters (then nine and two) on the trip. Minutes before he was slated to go down to the packed ballroom and speak, his toddler locked herself in the hotel bathroom.

"I was in a suit on my knees talking to a two-year-old through a keyhole," he told us.[8] "It's funny how your priorities shift when you become a parent." Steve got his daughter out of the bathroom and made it to the podium in the nick of time.

Steve should be named an honorary mom for that "working mother moment." Experiences like these, by the leaders of America's biggest companies, help change the way business treats family.

The Paycheck Factor

I have been outearning Bob since the day I met him, usually by a healthy margin. That was so remarkable in the 1980s that we were invited to appear on the *Oprah Winfrey Show* to talk to Oprah about what life was like when a wife outearned her husband. We talked about it with a lot of bravado on TV, but in the privacy of our home, we came to realize we were defining a new kind of husband-wife relationship that held dangers for both of us. I noticed that I was "managing" Bob a lot, practicing at home what I did all day at my job. Constantly making decisions based on the demanding aspects of *my* job accelerated Bob's gradual disconnect from *his* career. But when he made less money as the years went forward, I often complained that we didn't have enough money coming into the house. I never lost the feeling that I could have done a better job at parenting than he was doing, and when the kids hit troubled patches, it was easy to blame him.

Couples around the country are facing new marital issues as the traditional models of family crumble in the face of so many changes in our family lives. Today, about 24 percent of wives earn more than their husbands—up from just 16 percent in 1981.[9] It seems like bigger paychecks can be a double-edged sword. On the one hand, many moms tell us that earning more gives them more negotiating power in the relationship.

"I have always earned about twice my husband's salary," reader Rosanne Petros, the research consultant from Laurel, Maryland, told us. "I think having a good income leads to equality at home and with child-rearing tasks."

On the other hand, more negotiating power can lead to more tension and resentment.

"You can't imagine how many times people say, 'Well, you don't need to work,'" Maria Bailey, the founder of BlueSuit Mom.com in Ft. Lauderdale, told us.[10] She's married to a lawyer in private practice—but she's the major breadwinner. "I generally don't speak about it because I don't want to hurt my husband's business. I don't want it to appear that he is not successful as an attorney."

The best strategy to cope with these tensions, our readers tell us, is to value each partner for the contributions they make to the family and to the workplace, regardless of how much cash they bring in. "I don't care if he makes any money at all," one working mom, a real estate developer married to a teacher, told us. "But I care enormously that he makes a contribution to society."

Of Men and Marriage

Perhaps the most jarring issue working mothers face regarding the man in their lives is whether he is an asset or a liability to her in her effort to be a self-actualized person. Women often talk among themselves about their husbands in somewhat condescending ways, noting how clueless they are about some aspect of the large load that women bear. And then sometimes women feel that their husbands are a burden to them—a second or third child, but without the cuteness. The men are from Mars, women are from Venus equation that John Gray discusses in his famous book has huge implications for working moms as we challenge old paradigms of male-female relationships, but cling to the oldest and most basic one of all—being parents together.

Before our babies are born, women operate under a set of assumptions that will be bent or broken by the tsunami of motherhood's gigantic feelings. We assume we will still be able to watch our favorite TV show: one Thursday night Bob and I looked at each other and laughed as we realized that simply watching *Hill Street Blues* together, our Thursday night ritual that we kept for years, was just not possible with Robert running around being the terrible toddler that we loved so much. We also assume that we will be able to share in the rearing of the baby in ways that we may not want to after the baby is born.

A simple truth: mommies do not want to be daddies, and they don't want their husbands to be mommies. So we are left to create a new order where husbands get closer to their Venus side without taking over, and wives take some Mars roles without giving up the primacy of their central position as mommy. What a tall order that all is! And yet, it's being done in millions of households around America.

Who Needs That Hairy Man Anyway?

Motherhood does indeed change everything—even the way we feel about men. I was much more interested in men before I had my babies than after. Before I became a mother, I wanted to be with men, I wanted to know men, and I found it difficult to live without a man in my life.

This urgent sense of need changed after Robert was born. Before we were married, Bob went on a business trip to Arizona and met up with a college buddy to play golf. A snowstorm blew into New York, giving him the perfect excuse to stay a few days longer than he'd planned. I was distraught and wanted him to come home anyway, which he did, much to my delight and his friend's dismay. If that happened post-baby, I would have encouraged him to be safe and stay in the nice weather until the storm blew over . . . not because I'd gotten more rational, but because I had Robert to be with, and because Bob had moved out of the position at the center in my universe. Robert had moved into that center spot.

I can almost hear a chorus of women saying, "Who needs that hairy beast of a man when we have our beautiful babies snuggling in a way that no man ever has, gazing into our eyes for hours on end, grabbing us back to them after a moment's separation and completing us in a way that we never knew possible?"

For some of us, that gorgeous man who was so fascinating, who strode down the aisle next to us, who danced into the night with us, can suddenly look like an unnecessary third wheel after the birth of a baby. With our intense new bond and the stress that both working moms and dads feel as we adjust to life as parents, it's no wonder marital satisfaction often hits a low after our babies are born, and stays there for a few years.

I'll admit there have been times, post-baby, when I have felt like Bob was part of the problem, not the solution. And even more extreme, I've spoken with many working mothers who have felt their husbands were a burden—a second or third child whining and bellyaching instead of stepping up to the plate.

Some single moms have told me their lives seem easier without men. With their Home Team in place, they can focus on their work, give all their after-work attention to the child—and feel happy with their choices.

Of course, many single moms feel overwhelmed and undersupported, especially if they're not receiving financial support from fathers. But some also feel a sense of satisfaction at being on their own. Certainly, being able to walk away from a bad husband because of the financial independence that work allows is a source of strength for many women. In fact, many mothers keep working because they don't want to be financially dependent on their husbands.

For me, those moments of looking at Bob as an alien in my cozy motherhood world wore off after a while. As my babies turned into children, into preteens and then into teens, Bob began to move back toward center position, and I began to think of what my life with Bob was going to be like without the kids in the middle. And as I read back over my journal, I see how many times he played a key role in parenting our kids that I just could not fill. And how many times he suddenly looked like a savior to me, a hugely needed confidant and partner.

Strategies for a Long Relationship

Bob and I do not have a perfect marriage—but we do work hard to keep it intact. As my children start spreading their wings to fly the coop, I feel more and more grateful that we've been able to weather our particular marital storms.

"I think having children forces you to work at your marriage because the stakes are so high for the kids," says Rosanne Petros. "Yes, there's more strain, but there are definitely more reasons to hold it together." "I have to remember that the focus of the family really should be on the marriage, because after the children go off to school, it will be just us," adds reader Kim Rapp, an executive secretary who lives in Downey, California.

My own marriage may be a model only in that we have worked very hard to preserve it through twenty years of ups and downs. Here are a few strategies that have helped us over the years.

- **The Sex Date.** Marriage without sex is a cruel joke. You have the intimacy of living together without the intimacy of the bond that defies all rational thought—sex. My solution: sex once a week whether we want to or not. The trick to a sex date is to either schedule it at the same time every week, or have a deadline by which time if it hasn't happened you have an automatic, firm date. Once a week, I remember what a loving and fun man I married—and sometimes that may be the only time in a week that I remember!

- **The Movie or Dinner Date.** Notice I say movie *or* dinner, not movie *and* dinner. It's easier to take the time to be a couple if you don't set your expectations too high: a few hours out for either dinner or a movie—just the two of you—can be enough of a challenge without setting ourselves up for the disappointment of trying for both! And the irony is that a simple movie or dinner date is much more difficult to schedule than the impossible-to-schedule sex date! Babysitters may need to be hired and reservations made. If you have gone more than a month without a movie or dinner—get the babysitter on the phone now. Some companies are letting employees keep their kids in the day-care center late once a month so Mom and Dad can go out.

If you don't have time for a weekly date, you might be able to set some other special time aside, as do Becka Yturregui and Che Eagle of Newton, Massachusetts, the parents of Harris, age three.

"We're both thirtysomething children of divorced parents, so we're *always* thinking about how we can solidify our relationship," Becka told us. Even though their jobs keep them very busy—she's director of marketing publications for Simmons College in Boston, and he works at Brandeis University as director of employee relations, employment, and training—they make a point to have alone-time every single day.

"We try to spend at least twenty minutes talking to one another—uninterrupted—each evening. And nothing is off-limits—our son, our days, our sex life, whatever we need to talk about, we do. That helps. We do try date nights, but they're harder to coordinate, and the twenty-minute talk time is easier (and cheaper!)."

- **Marriage Mentoring.** When Bob and I were married in the Episcopal Church, the minister, who was a woman, asked all the married couples in the church to commit themselves to helping the marriage of Carol and Bob to be a good one. And many of them have helped, sometimes without knowing it. Our friends who married before we did have been great examples to us and we have looked to them for marriage mentoring. John and Rita Sloan, Doug and Chris Blair, and Frank and Luci Knight have shown us how to deal with in-laws, elderly parents, troubled teens, lost jobs, changing health, unhappy news, and more by modeling behavior that has worked and held them together.

I also keep a close eye on other married couples for behavior I want to avoid. Out to dinner with other couples or at family gatherings, I've seen bossy, domineering, and condescending behavior, and examined my own heart, asking if I've behaved the same way.

- **Professional Help.** When Bob and I ran into problems that were too big or too personal for our mentors to help us with, we opted for a marriage counselor. Even though this was one of the most painful experiences of our lives, and even though it didn't seem to be working at the time, it did work. Just making the commitment to go, to invest the time, money, mental energy, and emotional risk, somehow reminded us that we did care about our partnership—and that we could make it work. If you're considering marriage counseling (and I recommend it), find out if your company has an Employee Assistance Program. These confidential programs can direct you to professionals who can help, and might even pay for some of your counseling.

Our Twentieth Anniversary

On September 15, 2005, Bob and I were trying to celebrate our twentieth anniversary with a dinner with the kids, and everything was going wrong. Robert had to go to court at 7:30 p.m. for a traffic violation; my 4:30 appointment ran long and I didn't get home on time; Julia forgot to make a cake for us and now it was too late. But we raced to our favorite restaurant, La Cremelier, where we hadn't been in years, and managed to have a lovely dinner—just the two of us. Back at the house, Robert and Julia had set up a surprise: candles, dessert, and coffee served by our two big teenagers. Julia put my wedding dress, in all its sequined glory, on display in the dining room, and Bob gave me an anniversary ring (that Julia had picked out) and asked if I would marry him. Twenty-one years after the Ultimatum he was back on track with a proposal.

I said yes.

Chapter Ten

We Ask for What We Need— and Get It

Julia is a master negotiator. She has a lawyerly approach, often proposing a contract of some sort, which she writes out and signs with great fanfare. Recently, she wanted an iPod, and came up with the following proposal:

I, Julia Rose Coulombe, hereby announce the following; in order to earn the iPod of my dreams I promise to:

- *Discontinue asking, begging, or hinting toward the owning of a Chihuahua (or rodent, as Dad says), a guinea pig (hairy or non), or anything else with four legs.*
- *To work this summer as an intern for one to two days a week for Mother—at her disposal, including the occasional conference.*
- *To work harder on my grades.*
- *Mostly—to shop less! It's hard, but I will try.*

Thank you for the opportunity to own and hold my dreams, enhance my musicular interest and my intellectuality.

Julia Rose Coulombe

Having negotiated with Julia since she could only grunt her wishes (but grunt them very clearly!), I knew her crafty nature all too well. I saw a crack in the contract and insisted that she add a ban on two-legged, as well as four-legged, pets. (She's been known to ask for ducks, chickens, and geese—and I've been known to give in.) "You caught me!" was her admiring response to my counterdemand.

Robert, on the other hand, has few desires. He wants only select things, but these he wants deeply. He often waits patiently for Christmas or his birthday in January, gives me a list with only those things he really wants, and clearly indicates the most important thing on his list so I won't make a mistake. New video game equipment is usually on top, and he's happy to explain why he needs a new system or game. He doesn't try to manipulate, but lets me know this is all he wants and that he'll be quite satisfied and happy if he gets what he has asked for.

If it's not his birthday, he will ask for what he wants in a very straightforward way—no fancy contracts or bargaining. He explains the need and he accepts a no if that's what he gets. He often does get what he wants on the first round because he asks for so little (compared with his sister) and because we know that if we say no, he won't be back to ask again—but he'll be sad for a while.

We Get What We Ask For

Like Robert and Julia, many working moms have mastered the art of asking for what we need—and getting it. In our <u>What Moms Want</u> survey, we found that more than two out of three had asked their companies to make family-friendly changes. And the vast majority got what they wanted!—74 percent of the moms who asked for a change in their jobs or their company policies succeeded in their requests.

The most common changes these working mothers asked for were to work at home at least occasionally, to work flexible hours or compressed workweeks, and to work reduced hours, either for a limited period or permanently.

How do we get what we need? These four tactics are very effective for working moms: the Ironclad Proposal, Straight Talk, Behavior Modification for Managers, and the Yardstick Strategy.

Not every tactic is effective in every situation: we need to know them all, so we can choose the right option for the right situation. Working hard for change is well worth it—when we *do* succeed, we make life better for *our* family and for many other families at our workplace too.

The Ironclad Proposal

Julia's no-begging-for-pets contract is a junior version of the highly effective Ironclad Proposal strategy. The Ironclad Proposal is a written document that describes what you want, anticipates and answers all the objections that management might raise, and uses facts and figures to make a business case for whatever it is you're requesting.

One of the most effective Ironclad Proposals I've ever seen was put together by Jaime Duffy, an advertising salesperson for *USA Today*. Jaime was assigned to me as part of a mentoring program run by Advertising Women of New York.

When I first met Jaime, she was a young go-getter doing great things in her career. Jaime was a planner. She'd recently been promoted, and our first few mentoring breakfasts focused on her desire to plot a course that would help her become a top-notch manager. I noticed that she had lots of energy and enthusiasm, but often wasted both by overanalyzing office politics.

At our breakfast meetings, I reminded her that in sales, the proof is in the numbers. Office politics matter, of course, but I encouraged Jaime to clear her mind of these daily details and focus on growing her numbers day after day, quarter after quarter. She took my advice and ran with it. Her numbers kept climbing as she gained strength and confidence as a salesperson and manager.

Our mentoring relationship changed dramatically when Jaime

found out she was pregnant with her first child. She was exhilarated and scared, just like she had felt about her position in the office. We now focused our breakfast talks on issues of motherhood and working. She wanted to know what it had been like for me, what I regretted and what I embraced about my life as a working mother.

After her maternity leave, Jaime went back to work full-time, but soon realized she needed a change.

"I gave it three months so I could see how I felt," she told me. "It just wasn't going to work. I have an extremely stressful job, and a long commute, and it was weighing on me that I wasn't spending the time I wanted to with my daughter, Shelby."

Being a planner, Jaime plunged deeply into the body of knowledge on other arrangements she could make. She concluded that a job share would be the perfect solution and decided to write a proposal for her supervisor's consideration.

As an experienced salesperson, Jaime knew exactly how to pull together a persuasive presentation. First, she plunged into the research. She read magazines and books on the topic, used the Internet extensively, and picked many brains, including my own, to gather statistics and case studies. She discovered a great online resource, a Web site called WorkOptions.com, where work-life expert Pat Katepoo offers proposal templates for a variety of flexible work arrangements. Using Pat's templates as a guide, Jaime tackled her proposal with the energy and detail she would put into any important sales presentation.

"I was nervous because I felt like this was something I really needed and if I didn't get it, I might have to explore other opportunities," she said.

Armed with her research, she wrote a five-page proposal where she marshaled all her arguments and data. Her proposal is a fantastic model for any working mother who wants change. It included five sections.

1. **Introduction.** Jaime started out by explaining the purpose of the document—to request a change in her job from full-time

to a job share. She talked about other companies that used job shares, pulling data from the Working Mother 100 Best Companies list. She also highlighted the fact that many of her company's clients offered job sharing to their own employees and would therefore easily understand and adapt to her own new situation.

2. **The Plan.** According to Pat Katepoo, the developer of the job-sharing proposal template Jaime used, the plan section is the core of any proposal. "It should succinctly address how you plan to handle your schedule, job responsibilities, communication with other people in the office, and the physical setup you'll need if you plan to telecommute," Pat says. In Jaime's proposal, she described exactly how her job share would work, down to the specific days each partner would be in the office. Jaime proposed working Monday through Wednesday, with a partner who worked Wednesday through Friday. She planned to overlap the jobs on Wednesdays so the partners would have a whole day to communicate and work together every week. She outlined how job responsibilities would be jointly handled and made it clear she'd attend occasional meetings on her days off if clients needed her. "I tried to address any objections up front so they wouldn't have a valid reason for saying no," she told me.

   Pat Katepoo says this section should also outline your compensation if you'll be working fewer hours—how much you'll be paid and whether you'll get benefits. You may also want to include an evaluation paragraph, setting a time frame for periodic reviews of your work and the flexible arrangement.

3. **Benefits to the Employer.** In this section, Jaime explained that the job share would help the company. "I pointed out some big benefits, including continuity of workflow," she told me. "If one person leaves the company or has to take time off, there would be continuity because the other person

would understand the job and be able to step right in." Presenting the company benefits and business case helps managers feel less defensive—and gives them arguments they may need to sell the idea to *their* bosses.

4. **Benefits to the Employee.** Jaime also devoted a section to showing how the arrangement would help her. "I felt like they needed to know that I wanted this and how important work-life balance was to me. I wrote that this would enable me to continue a career I want and love, but would also let me spend time with my family." Because Jaime had proven she was a top performer, she knew the company would want to make her happy if they could—and understanding her needs was an important step toward that goal.

5. **Success Stories and Statistics.** Jaime provided ample evidence of the benefits that other companies had reaped from job sharing and other work-life programs. "I talked about the different studies I'd found showing how work-life benefits have proven to be invaluable. I talked about how flexible work arrangements in general make for more productive employees," she said. "And I mentioned that when employees get what they want, they work very hard to protect that arrangement. If the company works hard for us, we're going to work even harder for the company."

Jaime's hard work and research paid off. She'd drawn up an offer her company couldn't refuse. Today, the job share she created with her partner is the envy of many other working moms in her office. Her advice to them: "This will only work if you've proven yourself to be a low-maintenance, top performer. With that comes trust. Your employer has to trust that the two people sharing the job are going to make this work for their clients and for the company."

Recently, Jaime came to a dinner at Pace University in New York

City, where a student group had named me their Woman of the Year. I was so happy to introduce my mentee Jaime to my daughter, Julia, and as I looked at them chatting together, I realized my daughter's iPod contract is a sign of what's to come when she reaches Jaime's age. She'll be a natural at writing the ironclad, no-point-in-refusing contract that can serve working mothers so well.

Straight Talk

Powerful as it is, the Ironclad Proposal isn't always the right negotiating tool. If your company or manager has a more informal style, or you're bringing up an idea for the first time, you might want to use a simple, up-front style like Robert's straight talk strategy.

My longtime assistant, Barbara Rosenthal, taught me the pure and simple power of Straight Talk in the office. In 1991, when Barbara and I were at *Stagebill*, Barbara was feeling tremendous pressure because her three children needed homework help every night—and lots of it. She wasn't there to help them because she worked crazy hours keeping up with my own workload. Her work suffered as she became more and more distracted by her worries.

Finally, Barbara came to me to have a straightforward discussion of the issues. She hadn't been complaining, so I had no idea she was having a problem at home. I'd noticed she was having trouble keeping everything organized on the job, but I thought we were just giving her too much to do. Barbara is a very talented woman, so we often pile more and more tasks on her because we know they'll be done well.

Barbara is not a salesperson and never will be. She didn't come to me with a written proposal or even a concrete plan. She had no eloquent words about her talent and our needs. She simply explained the problem and offered a solution.

"Carol," she said, "my kids need me to help them with their homework, and when I get home late I'm too tired and have too many other things to do to help them. Could I come in early and leave early?"

For the next three years, Barbara worked for me from 8:00 a.m. to 4:00 p.m. It worked out just fine. If I really needed her to stay late she would, but as a general course of business, she was out the door at 4:00. We rarely had a problem, and her level of work soared. She became a mainstay of our company, taking on jobs that no one else wanted and using every working minute like it was a precious resource—which, of course, it was.

When I left *Stagebill* to go to *Chief Executive*, I tried to take Barbara with me, but she wasn't ready to make the risky leap to a new company. Six years later, I acquired *Working Mother* and needed an administrative assistant. I almost lost the chance to hire Barbara because I'd forgotten the lesson of Straight Talk! I knew Barbara had left *Stagebill* and was looking for a new job, but I just didn't see how her early schedule would work for us this time around. As CEO and owner, my responsibilities were more complex than ever, and I couldn't imagine a system that would cover us for those later afternoon hours. Fortunately, our CFO, Bruce Appel, suggested the obvious.

"Why don't you just call her and ask if she can work nine to five?"

Ah, yes. Straight Talk.

I called Barbara, asked if she was interested, and said I couldn't accommodate an early-in, early-out schedule. She laughed and said she hadn't been able to work that flexible arrangement since I left *Stagebill*. And anyway, her kids were now six years older and didn't want her homework help anymore.

I almost lost a golden opportunity to hire an excellent right-hand person because I forgot about Straight Talk! Whether it's a flexible schedule like Barbara's, or an Xbox like Robert's, sometimes simply asking is the way to get your heart's desire.

Behavior Modification for Difficult Bosses

Unfortunately, some managers just aren't going to respond to well-reasoned proposals or a simple ask-for-what-you-need strategy.

"I asked for a more flexible work schedule of compressed workweek and work-from-home options," wrote Sharie Hyder of Seattle, Washington, one of the women who responded to our survey. "While it is stated in our HR literature that these are offered, it's up to the manager to decide if they want to let their employees use them. My manager said no."

I've heard many complaints like this over the years. Nothing makes working mothers more angry, and more susceptible to leaving their current jobs, than to be denied options that are supposed to be available. The problem is, no matter what your employee handbook says, it's often your individual manager who decides whether you can use a flexibility policy.

When you know in advance that your boss just isn't going to give you what you want, it sometimes makes sense not to ask for permission at all, but simply to make changes gradually, over time. I call this Behavior Modification for Managers. It's a technique that many moms know well from Richard Ferber's book *Solve Your Child's Sleep Problems*. His behavior modification approach tells us to accustom the baby gradually to solving her own sleep issues by withdrawing from the baby's room for increasingly long periods each night. Little by little, as you adjust *your* behavior, the baby adjusts *her* sleep habits as well. Ferber's method was only moderately successful for me because I'm a big softie when it comes to crying babies. But I had much more success when I applied his methodology to an insensitive boss.

When I joined Chief Executive Group, my boss, the CEO, had been running the company for years with little regard for the needs of his working parent employees, even though his management team was a youngish crew: his three most senior managers had seven young children between us. One of my boss's core management

tools had been a Monday night dinner meeting with his management team that often lasted until 11:30 at night.

When I joined the company, I knew this was not going to work
for me. I already had to travel extensively and wasn't about to miss
every Monday night of Robert and Julia's lives (they were then
nine and six). I didn't believe it was necessary or appropriate for
the management team to meet regularly into the wee hours . . . and
I found it especially annoying that my boss was often late to his
own dinners! Once the wine was ordered, the business conversation inevitably drifted to more general talk, so the business we'd
gathered to discuss often had to be taken up in the office the next
day anyway. I had never seen such a colossal waste of time, money,
and energy!

The other members of the team felt the same way I did. They
were dedicated dads who also worked long hours and traveled a
lot. But they had become accustomed to the dinner system and
didn't believe it was possible to change it, even though they all
complained about it endlessly. So I decided to apply Ferber's behavior modification method, one step at a time.

Right after the first dinner, which ran on and on, I said to my
boss, "Arnie, I'll need to leave these dinners by nine p.m. so I can
catch the nine nineteen train home so I can get back in the morning
for my sales calls." Note: no mention or complaint about the babies. My reasons—at least the ones I gave him—were strictly business. At the next meeting, I reminded him of my timetable before
the dinner started, and left promptly at nine p.m. Because I'd
drawn a line in the sand, he began to arrive at our six p.m. dinners
on time, since he knew I'd be leaving three hours later.

Next, I launched Phase 2. I suggested we move the dinner meetings to the office once in a while, ordering in food from restaurants
we liked instead of eating out. I showed him how much money this
would save the company and how much more we could actually
get done. He agreed to try it. Once this habit was established, I
suggested moving some of our meetings to lunchtime, so we could
bring people into the meetings to report or confer—employees

who usually left by five or six p.m. This, I argued, would make us more productive. And it did.

Eventually, most of the meetings were held in the conference room at the noontime slot. They became very efficient and everyone was delighted, including my boss, who could see how our productivity skyrocketed. Morale improved and the camaraderie he hoped to foster became real instead of forced. Occasionally, we'd schedule a dinner meeting so we could enjoy bonding over a bottle of wine. These dinner meetings became something special, rather than a dreaded weekly assignment.

The rest of the management team was ecstatic, of course. They had believed it would be absolutely impossible to change our boss's long-standing bad habit. But by using behavior modification to make small changes over time, and by arguing the business case, not the family reasons, for each little change, we gained the advantage. It wasn't easy and it required a long-term strategy and delicate execution. But in the end, everybody—the managers, our families, and the business—ended up winning.

This strategy of gradually training our managers has worked for many other moms, too. One of our readers wrote us to tell us exactly what she was doing to coax gradual change from her old-fashioned boss, who didn't want her to work from home a few mornings a week—even though her employer, a city government, did have a telecommuting policy. Since she was still Ferberizing her unsuspecting boss, she asked us not to use her name or job title.

My strategy for the past year has been to "train" my boss by doing my office work from other, off-site city workplaces (with preapproval), and heading out in the morning without coming into the office first (always with a phone call to let him know what I am doing). I acquired a laptop that allows me to access my office files via intranet, as though I am sitting at my office desk. I taught the clerical staff how to handle e-mail attachments, so I can sign off on final proofs when I come through the office. I forward my desk phone calls to my cell phone. I keep my boss informed of potential headaches so he is not blindsided. I probably communicate with him more as an off-site employee than those who spend most of the day with him.

So far, it has worked. I have established a high credibility, shown that my work is getting done and the public is well served, even though I am not right there in front of him. I am doing everything now that I want to do except for the "at home" part. The last step is to be able to do office work from home at specific times in the morning and afternoon.

This gradual approach takes patience and commitment, but sometime it's the only way to make progress.

Manager Training: Building the Perfect Boss

Some companies are giving working moms a head start in the behavior modification department by providing special training to managers in work-life issues. These companies realize that just adding a policy to the employee handbook won't improve morale or retention. Good training shows managers the bottom-line benefits of work-life programs, so they're more likely to say yes when we ask to use them.

When Mary Dean Lee, a professor at McGill University, studied part-time workers and flexibility over seven years, she found that training programs for managers made all the difference.

"One company I studied was scared to death about flexibility seven years ago. But now, programs are spreading like wildfire," she says. When she asked why, managers pointed to a training workshop they'd attended.

"The workshop was very powerful in getting managers to think about what people face in terms of health issues, family issues, and the unexpected stuff that comes up," she says. "One manager I spoke with had worked full-time after having three children, and she said, 'Quite frankly, I was impatient with these women under me who wanted more accommodations. But after that workshop, I developed a whole new understanding.' "

When we pick the Working Mother 100 Best Companies, we ask whether companies train their managers in the benefits and practicalities of flexibility programs. In 2004, 88 percent of our Best Companies offered training. At General Mills, managers analyze case studies about employees asking for flexible work arrangements: they discuss the issues, identify barriers and solutions, and provide a recommendation. At Prudential, managers take a combination of classes and online training that includes role-playing and case studies.

Programs like this can make a substantial difference in manager acceptance of flexibility. After JPMorgan trained some five thousand managers in managing work-life programs, the company's annual employee survey showed a huge jump in the number of men—particularly officers and senior managers—who said they understood the business case for work-life programs.

Managers seem to be getting better at other companies, too. In surveys by the Families and Work Institute, "we've seen people say their managers are more supportive in the last five or ten years," says Ellen Galinsky, president of the institute. "It's become more legitimate to bring up a personal or family issue in the workplace."

But training alone isn't enough. It has to happen within a culture that truly supports work-life balance. Some companies—including many of the 100 Best—encourage a family-friendly culture by grading their managers on work-life satisfaction in their departments. At IBM, for instance, managers have to define and meet goals in a variety of areas, including people management. "Unless you are a top performer in people management—and that includes work-life—you can't get the highest rating," says Maria Ferris, IBM's director of global workforce diversity programs.

When managers are evaluated and rewarded for promoting work-life satisfaction, that's a gigantic step toward real change. Maybe someday we won't need Richard Ferber in the office!

The Yardstick Method

In the early years of *Working Mother*, we didn't have any maternity leave policy. Women were expected back in the office six weeks after giving birth, and they had to use their vacation time in order to get any pay during those weeks. That was status quo for businesses at the time—but I knew some magazine companies were giving more leave, because I asked around. I decided to use that yardstick with Ray Eyes, the president of our parent company. "This is embarrassing," I told him. "*Working Mother* needs to be a role model in the publishing industry. No magazine should offer more maternity leave than a magazine created just for working mothers! If we don't get a better leave policy, I won't be able to hold my head up in the industry," I said.

Ray agreed and instituted a new policy for the entire company—not just for *Working Mother* magazine—providing three weeks of paid leave and up to three months of unpaid job protected leave. Today, that sounds like peanuts compared to what the 100 Best Companies offer, but in those days before FMLA, any maternity leave was a welcome support.

Offering proof that other companies are providing better work-life support is one way to get your company to take action on behalf of working mothers. That's the beauty behind the Working Mother 100 Best Companies yardstick. Many CEOs and senior managers don't want to be left behind in the war for talent. The 100 Best list provides millions of mothers with specifics and comparisons of what different companies are doing to support their working parent employees year after year. I frequently hear from readers who tell me how the facts and figures in the list have helped them argue for change. Here's a letter that Shannon Barker, a forecaster with the U.S. Air Force, wrote me last year:

I am on active duty with the U.S. Air Force and have been trying to get the military's leave policy changed for almost three years. Your list has provided me with documentation of the benefits that civilian companies are giving to attract and keep quality employees, as well as proof that "family leave" is not just being offered by a dozen or so big name corporations.

—*Shannon E. Barker*

For me, it's been thrilling to see how many companies have started measuring their family-friendly programs since the Working Mother Best Companies list debuted twenty years ago. And once they started measuring, they started to change.

"We've gotten the following benefits approved because of the way we can benchmark against the Working Mother 100 Best Companies," says Michelle Thomas, the former director of corporate diversity, inclusion, and work-life at Abbott Laboratories. "Increased adoption assistance, percent tuition reimbursement, lactation programs, including a consultant, and paternity leave. With all these, we took the Working Mother data, built the business case, and went to the CEO."

When I came back to *Working Mother* in 2001, I was so inspired by the success of the Working Mother 100 Best Companies in creating change that I set about launching other initiatives based on its model. Today, Working Mother Media proudly publishes the Best Companies for Women of Color, the Best Small Companies, and the NAFE Top 30 Companies for Executive Women. All of these competitive rankings of companies give women facts and figures that you can use to help drive change in your own companies.

The easiest way to use the Working Mother 100 Best Companies list is to check out the chart that's published in the magazine every October, or visit our Web site at www.workingmother.com and click on the 100 Best Companies section. Look for competitors in your industry or for companies of similar employee size and work type—manufacturing or health care, say. Make a list of what they have that you don't, and start a discussion with other employees about what might be really helpful to you and your coworkers. Every level of employee can benefit from this strategy—from top executive moms to moms who earn an hourly wage. The power is in the group—whether it's one hundred moms who network together or two mothers talking over coffee.

Making a formal request to add a program can be done at the HR level or with your immediate boss. If you *are* the boss, don't be afraid to ask your employees what would really help them. Exploring needs is not the same as making promises.

You can use all of our lists to examine how your company stacks up: the Best Companies for Women of Color comes out in *Working Mother*'s June issue, and Best Small Companies is published in the April issue. Both are online at www.working mother.com. The NAFE Top 30 Companies for Executive Women is a competition among the country's largest companies, which must have at least two women sitting on the board of directors just to apply. This list is published in the spring issue of NAFE magazine. You can find it at www.nafe.com.

If your company doesn't already apply for the *Working Mother* or NAFE lists, you can encourage your HR department to apply by giving them this Ironclad Proposal: apply for these lists so that we will learn how we stack up against other companies in critical areas that lead to employee satisfaction, improved productivity, and reduced turnover. Focusing on the company's return on investment in these programs (in addition to your needs) will get their attention. It's not just good for you—it's smart for your company.

Other yardsticks can help as well. Internal company measurements can wake managers up to the importance of work-life balance. At JPMorgan Chase, an internal survey found that 23 percent of their employees worked flexible arrangements, but an additional 35 percent *wanted* flexibility, but couldn't use it due to the nature of their jobs. From other surveys, the company already knew that flexibility increased commitment and productivity, but management hadn't realized so many people wanted flex and couldn't use it. Thanks to this measurement, JPMorgan Chase has launched efforts to improve manager sensitivity to work-life balance.

If your company does an annual employee survey, and it doesn't include work-life questions, ask your human resource department to add a few questions about balance and family-friendly programs. It's an easy, low-cost way for you and the company to learn more about what employees really want.

Build Your Own Yardstick

Of course, many companies don't do annual employee surveys. But you can do your own research to find out how many other working moms in your company have the same needs and problems that you do. The growth of moms' groups and women's affinity groups in the office (see chapter 7) make it easy to e-mail other working moms in your company with a few questions. You can launch your own survey about problems, solutions, or specific measures working mothers would like, or encourage an affinity group to probe more deeply into existing statistics or issues.

It worked at Hewlett-Packard. In 2003, a women's mentoring circle became concerned about a career and development program called the Technical Career Path, which helped employees advance to the vice president level. The women's circle studied the program statistics and found too few women in the program's upper levels. Armed with the facts, the group persuaded senior leadership to create a task force to improve the recruitment, retention, and development of women.

Voting with Our Feet

There's one more highly effective strategy that working moms are using to get the work-life balance they need: we vote with our feet. When our best efforts at asking for change just don't produce results, we leave—for another division, another employer, or to start our own businesses. The more that working moms refuse to settle for jobs and employers who don't give us what we need, the more pressure companies everywhere will feel to become more flexible, more compassionate, and, ultimately, more productive workplaces.

Chapter Eleven

We Have an Escape Hatch . . .
and We're Not Afraid to Use It

In May 2001, I heard that *Working Mother* magazine was going to be put up for sale. The owner, the third man to own the magazine since we launched it in 1979, had made a huge Internet investment that had nearly bankrupted the company. With advertising in a downturn, he would have to sell the magazines he owned—and no one knew what would happen to *Working Mother*. It might be closed, or folded into another magazine, or left with no investment funds to carry it through the downturn.

The news sent a jolt of maternal protectiveness through my body. The magazine I had helped to birth was in danger, and my deepest motherly instincts were telling me to throw myself in front of the oncoming train to save it.

At the time, I was working at *Chief Executive* magazine, where I regularly rubbed shoulders with CEOs and founders of companies of all sizes. As I hosted dozens of CEO round tables, dinners, and conferences with these mostly male captains of industry, I started asking myself, "What do they have that I don't have?" The answer was . . . nothing. Except their power, influence, and money, of course. And their gender.

After meeting and getting to know thousands of CEOs over a five-year period, I realized that I was not any less intelligent, capable, or experienced than many of these top dogs. I noticed that they came from all kinds of economic backgrounds, not just privileged ones—and had gone to all kinds of schools, not just Harvard and Yale—and that some were talented at sales, others at finance, others at managing people. They all had their strengths and weaknesses, and their raw talent varied widely. I came to believe that if they could succeed at the top, I could too. And I began to visualize myself owning and running my own business, if I just had the right opportunity—if I had a business idea I could throw my heart and soul into. And then suddenly, there was *Working Mother*, my pride and joy, on the auction block.

Before I could even think about the obstacles I would face, I sat down and wrote a business plan to revitalize *Working Mother* and to build a new company around this valuable property. Then, I began calling possible investors.

The funny thing about buying a company is that if you haven't bought one before, you're not in the club . . . and the club seems designed to keep people out. The fact that I knew exactly how we had built this magazine years ago into a profitable entity; the fact that I was a working mother and understood everything about this lifestyle and what working moms need; the fact that I had successfully run two other publishing companies—none of this seemed to matter. All that mattered was that I had not played this acquisition game before.

And that I was a woman.

I am not a knee-jerk feminist. A feminist, yes. But one who believes in the cooperation of the sexes. One who believes that men and women are stronger when they work together. One who had worked, until that point, almost exclusively for men. But when I set out to acquire *Working Mother*, I saw a prejudice against women entrepreneurs that seemed completely out of place at the beginning of a new century. Later, I learned that only a miniscule percentage of venture capital money (less than 5 percent!) goes to women-owned businesses.

So, finding investors to help me save *Working Mother* was an uphill battle. I started by calling a famous women's investment fund, only to be told they wanted to invest in "sure bets." I was astonished at how quickly they turned me down. The magazine was twenty-two years old in 2001 and they were acting as if it were a start-up.

Next, I turned to women I respect for advice. I gave Gloria Steinem a call because she had acquired *Ms.* magazine, finally making it a women-owned business again after years of male ownership.

"Does *Working Mother* rely on advertising?" she asked me. "If so, I would run screaming from it. Advertising is a game you cannot win. Don't do it," she counseled.

I knew the pain she had experienced as she tried to make *Ms.* a success in the face of vociferous advertiser opposition. I respected her opinion, but I'd worked in advertising my entire career and knew *Working Mother* wouldn't face the same problems *Ms.* had.

One of Bob's ambulance corps volunteers, Marsha Veit, told her husband, David, a well-known Wall Streeter, about my quest, and he very kindly put me in touch with a top magazine investor I'd hoped to meet—Peter Ezersky of Quadrangle Group.

Peter met me in Quadrangle's beautiful teak-paneled offices near Rockefeller Center and listened to my plan. He was in the middle of a busy day and closing a big deal, but he gave me his full attention.

"Carol," he said, "*Working Mother* has a lot of problems and I don't think you're going to find too much support in the investment community. We see this as a high-risk investment. Don't be surprised if you find a lot of doors closing on you. I see your passion and your ideas, but the property is what the property is."

I was grateful for his honest assessment, but felt determined to keep going, despite the pessimistic review.

Next, I stepped down a level and started to call entrepreneurs who had bought at least one company. But everyone in the smaller sphere felt that *Working Mother* was too big to get involved with: the investment was too high for the smaller players. My dream was starting to look like a pipe dream.

By July, I had called, met, or spoken to thirty-six different potential investors, and I was getting nowhere fast. I feared I was headed for disappointment when my phone rang one day in late July.

"Carol, this is Jon Slabaugh from MCG Capital. We understand you're interested in buying *Working Mother* magazine and we'd like to speak to you."

I nearly dropped the phone, but with hope in my heart I set a date for a meeting. I flew to Arlington, Virginia, where I met the principals of MCG Capital, a large fund run by Steve Tunney and two other financial whizzes. They had a substantial investment in *Working Mother*, and did not want to lose their money. They were ready to take over the business, and believed that partnering with a woman made good financial sense for a magazine devoted to . . . women. A few days after our first meeting, we struck a deal to acquire the assets of the bankrupt owner, and on August 17, 2001, we took possession of the company.

My dream had come true and my journey as an entrepreneur had begun.

Taking the Escape Hatch

My journey to becoming a business owner was not intentional. But all along, I was driven by a deep, subconscious desire to be my own boss. At every major turning point, I chose the more independent option. When I left *Working Mother* for *Stagebill*, some of my most respected colleagues and friends told me I was crazy to take the job. "It's too small for you," they said. That was discouraging, but I didn't let it stop me. I wanted to be part of the inner circle of decision makers and owners, even if that meant going to a smaller company. And I was excited by the 5 percent ownership stake I'd been offered.

After we sold *Stagebill* to Primedia, I continued on my path toward owning my own business by taking the chief operating officer job at *Chief Executive* magazine. There, I fought hard to launch a new publication aimed at the high-testosterone world of dot-com CEOs, and learned how to create funding for a new venture. At every stop along my career path, I was learning the skills that would help me run my own business.

My adventures as an entrepreneur aren't so different from the journey that thousands of other working moms take every year as they launch their own companies. Women are launching businesses at twice the rate of men: between 1997 and 2004, the estimated number of women-owned businesses grew twice as fast as the number of all start-ups. Women-owned firms employ 19.1 million people and generate $2.5 trillion in sales, according to the Center for Women's Business Research.[1] Some 3.8 million women were self-employed in 2003—that's almost 10 percent of all working women.[2]

Why are women outpacing men when it comes to starting our own businesses? Some of us are seeking more control over our lives. Some are angry and frustrated with corporations for not giving us the tools to combine work and family effectively and efficiently. And some of us are tired of waiting for the top jobs, or get discouraged when we see top positions offered to less talented men—so we decide to create them for ourselves. Many, many companies are still failing women and working mothers—and they're losing some of their most talented, most dedicated workers. While the Working Mother 100 Best Companies have steadily moved ahead with progressive programs and supportive cultures, many companies have not.

Too many companies still value face time over actual work contribution. Too many companies allow individual managers to undermine good corporate intentions by discouraging employees from using work-life programs. And far too many companies have paid lip service to work-life balance without really embracing the cultural shifts that have proven to help both employees and the bottom line.

So, working mothers are voting with their feet. When all our other strategies fail to win us the changes we need within companies, we know we have an escape hatch—we can create our own businesses. Because we value our children, our families, and our careers, we're not afraid to take risks to find a better balance for all three.

Hey, Lady in the Lime Green Wig!

If you've ever thought seriously about voting with your feet, you've already pondered some of the same frightening questions I asked myself as I moved into more and more entrepreneurial jobs. Will I be able to support my end of the finances for my family? Will it take more time than I'm putting into my current job? Do I have the skills this will require? What are the long-term risks if it doesn't work out? These are wise and necessary questions to confront before taking the escape hatch. But at the same time, it's important not to let our fear of risk keep us from making a leap.

My boss at *Stagebill*, Arthur Levitt Jr., made a leap when he promoted me to president of the company. Many people thought he'd choose his very experienced male CFO instead of me, the publisher with less financial background. But Arthur told me, "When I make business decisions about people, I say to myself, 'Who would I wish I had at my side if I were walking down a dark alley?' You are that person."

It was an excellent analogy, because running any company means fighting your way out of many dark alleys, from recessions to loss of customers to the rapid shifts and changes of the marketplace. Risks are everywhere, but so are rewards.

Whether you're on the brink of leaving your job or still in the "wouldn't it be great if" stage, you can prepare to use your escape hatch by training yourself to take small risks every day. The more comfortable you are with risk, the easier it will be for you to strike out on your own one day and face those dark alleys.

I've always taken risks in my career, but I have a yearly ritual that helps remind me of how hard—and rewarding—risks can be. Every Halloween, I wear a long, fluorescent, lime green wig to work. I put it on in the morning and wear it on the train into Manhattan, and keep it on all day long.

It sounds fun and wacky, but it's not as easy as you'd think. Year after year, I'm the only one on the commuter train wearing anything unusual. The one day of the year we're all given permission to be weird—and it's completely status quo for the commuters on my train line. My, how predictable adults are!

The first time I wore it, the guy who runs the ticket booth at the station in Chappaqua was so excited he called out to me across the tracks, "Hey, lady in the lime green wig! You look terrific!"

I *did* look terrific . . . but I felt ridiculous! Once on the train, I felt a dozen pairs of eyes furtively glance my way, checking me out. Maybe they were jealous, or repulsed, or supportive. I wouldn't know. Commuters are silent judges. I kept thinking I should just pull the wig off and conform to the norm. But I kept it on, and felt a sense of triumph come over me as I challenged the usual order of commuting and the mundane expectations of everyday life. Once I got to the office, the fun really began. The lime green wig encouraged everyone to laugh and enjoy the day—a great way to prepare for the trick-or-treaters at home!

Nearly every year since, I've worn my lime green wig to work on Halloween as a test of my ability to take a small risk. It might sound silly, but when I took the major risk of acquiring *Working Mother*, I found some measure of comfort in my familiarity with small risks—even those as inconsequential as being the lady in the lime green wig.

For working mothers who think they might leave their secure jobs someday, it's important to practice taking risks. You don't have to wear a green wig to work. You can start by asking for changes on your job or in your office. Approach someone you respect and ask her to mentor you. Ask for a raise. Propose one of the changes that you long for, like flextime or job sharing. All these smaller risks can help prep you to take bigger risks later on.

The Least Risky Risk

A great strategy to increase your comfort with risk is to take them within your own company, before—or instead of—striking out on your own. Debra O'Shea, a mother of two, took a big risk when she approached her boss and admitted she was bored with her job as vice president of investor relations at Focal Communications, a Chicago phone company.[3] She realized she'd hit a plateau and that her current job wouldn't give her the experience necessary to move into the very top ranks of management. So she suggested a daring idea: she asked to move into a financial planning role, even if it meant taking a lower-ranking title. Her boss resisted at first, but a few months later, he offered her the job of director of corporate planning. It meant giving up her vice president title, and she feared it would look like a demotion to her peers. But she decided to take the risk, knowing that the new job would put her on a path toward senior management. She hasn't regretted it—in fact, she feels invigorated and challenged in her new job, which offers great opportunities ahead.

Proposing an original idea, business, or venture within your own company is another way to take a risk, without completely opening the escape hatch. This "intrapreneurial" approach can give you the satisfaction of launching and controlling your own idea without the risk of going solo. That's what I did when I launched the magazine for dot-com CEOs at Chief Executive. And that's how Laura Alber came to head the tremendously successful Pottery Barn Kids chain. As a vice president at Pottery Barn, she wrote the business plan for Pottery Barn Kids while she was pregnant with her first child, Samantha, now six—with help from a few other moms in the company. "We worked after hours and on weekends to put the plan together, present it to our board, and then get it done," Laura told us.[4] The business was a huge success; Laura became president of Pottery Barn Brands and went on to have a second child, Jackson, now four.

Another way to go it alone without *really* being alone is to do what Carol Chin did. I met Carol when I was part of a panel of entrepreneurs last year. Carol, mom of Karen, twenty-five, Jennifer, twenty-one, and Andrew, thirteen, and operator of seven very successful McDonald's restaurants, figured franchising was the perfect way to be in charge while still enjoying the support of a major corporation. Carol is so enthusiastic about her work—she loves combining motherhood with running her own business, and feels that having the resources of the national McDonald's organization has made all the difference. Many other women agree: some 30 percent of the country's 300,000 franchises are owned by women. The International Franchise Association (www.franc hise.org) has a Women's Franchise Committee that holds an annual conference and provides rich resources to help women get started.

Entrepreneur Moms

Shifting your current employer to the role of client is a very creative way of becoming an entrepreneur mom without leaving everything you've built in a corporate career behind. As you may remember from Chapter Four, that's exactly what Barbara Bella did. Barbara had a glorious career at *Working Mother* magazine, serving as West Coast sales director and then ad director in New York. When she married, she moved back to California to take on the West Coast management job, but as soon as she found out she was pregnant with her daughter, Bree, she felt an urgent need to have more control of her hours, her work-life balance, and her future. Barbara wanted to find a new path as a working mother without leaving the company she loved behind, so she created an Ironclad Proposal for going out on her own, building a business in the territory she knew so well, with *Working Mother* as her first and most important client.

By taking this brave step, Barbara got what she was looking

for. She built her business into the most successful magazine rep firm on the West Coast, giving *Working Mother* and many other magazines an unprecedented level of service and success. And she got what she wanted as a working mother. Her business became a family affair, with husband, John, managing the books, and daughter, Bree, becoming an integral part of the team. From the time she could walk, Bree had her own office at Barbara Bella and Associates, first contributing artwork for the walls, and then becoming a part of the unique persona that every entrepreneurial company creates. Whenever I came to town, visits with Bree were a highlight of my trip—giving me back a little family life when I was so far from my own.

Work with Your Strengths

My advice to escape-hatch moms who hope to start their own businesses is to follow Barbara's example: start with your strengths and look for a market need you can fill. That doesn't mean that if you're an accountant you can't launch a career as a freelance writer . . . but it does mean that you'll use your expertise in accounting to position yourself as an expert and start writing for publications that specialize in accounting-related topics. The key is to find new ways to use the skills you've already developed. You need to understand your weaknesses, too—if you're not a self-starter, or don't enjoy selling yourself and your business, or find yourself tempted to watch Oprah while working at home, self-employment may not be a perfect fit for you!

At the same time, don't overlook all the skills you possess that you *don't* use on the job—including your expertise as a mom. These great businesses were spurred by moms who spotted a niche that only a mother could love:[6]

- Julie Aigner-Clark started Baby Einstein in her home in Lone Tree, Colorado, in 1997. A teacher who had taken three years off with her newborn, she wanted a part-time job she could do from home, so she started making videos for babies. Two years later, she had a line of fifteen videos, CDs, and flashcards. When she found the job was interfering with the work-life balance she wanted, she sold the company to Disney. She continued to work for the company on her own terms to keep herself balanced.

- Cherie Serota, a mother of three, and Jody Kozlow Gardner, a mother of two, launched their Belly Basics line of maternity wear when Cherie was pregnant and couldn't find a thing to wear.

- Doris Christopher, a former home economics teacher, launched the Pampered Chef line of kitchen gadgets so she could be at home when her daughters, then eight and five, returned from school. The company now employs thousands of independent salespeople around the world. In 2002, the investor Warren Buffett bought the company—but left Doris in charge.

- Addie Swartz founded B*Tween Productions to produce books and merchandise for girls ages nine to thirteen because she found so few books to help her own daughters through their awkward tween years. B*Tween publishes the wonderful Beacon Street Girls series, about the adventures of five preteen friends.

These moms all launched companies in search of work-life balance . . . and found great success at both!

Do Your Homework

The more you know about your new field of business, the greater your chances of success are. I recently gave a speech to a working mothers' networking group and met a mother named Margie Shumel, who had worked at Pfizer for years and seemed well established on the gold-watch career path . . . until she read a *Working Mother* cover story about a Seattle business called Dream Dinners, Inc. At Dream Dinners, busy working moms get together at a commercial kitchen to make a week's worth of dinners in one night, take them home to their freezers, and make the week ahead a little easier. The Dream Dinners owners—working moms themselves—do all the shopping, cutting, and chopping, not to mention the cleanup.[7]

The story inspired Margie to combine her own passion for cooking with her great organizational and business skills. She envisioned a similar business that would let her take more control of her time, express herself, and eliminate her commute, so she could spend more time with her six-year-old twins, Hannah and Malcolm.

I was very impressed by the amount of time and research Margie put into her plan. She didn't just quit her job and jump into it. She spent the better part of a year researching the market, finding a place for her business, and writing her business plan. She traveled around the country visiting similar businesses. She developed beautiful marketing materials. When she felt ready to launch, she doubled her workload for two months, working her regular job and her entrepreneurial job at the same time to see if she really wanted to go through with it. The day before I met her, she'd quit her job and launched One . . . Two . . . Three . . . Dinner.

We all know that the business world can be cruel, even to the most prepared of entrepreneurs, but Margie's careful research and preparation have certainly reduced the risk involved in her new venture. Any working mom considering her own business would be wise to start out like Margie—spending at least several months, if not an entire year, researching the market. The United States Small Business Administration (www.sba.gov) offers excellent resources for would-be business owners, including guidelines for writing a business plan, advice on funding your business, and local training and mentoring programs.

Another wise way to research the market and prepare yourself to launch your own business is to network with moms who have already done it.

"Talk to other self-employed moms about what to expect. If you still think you'll be able to balance everything perfectly, talk to some more," Gale Kaufman, the president of Kaufman Campaign Consultants of Sacramento, California, told us.[8] When Gale launched her business, she assumed balancing work and family would get much easier. Instead, she discovered that her clients expected her to be available 24/7. Initially, Gale brought her nine-year-old son with her to meetings and events, but soon realized she needed to factor the costs of a nanny into her business planning. "I'm always talking about my experience to other mothers who are considering self-employment so they'll know to anticipate some of these stresses," she says.

Women's business organizations like the National Association for Female Executives offer great opportunities for networking with other women who own companies. NAFE has twenty thousand members who are entrepreneurs—and eager to share their advice and experience with other women.

Just Say No

Many entrepreneurial moms I've spoken with over the years share a common problem. Sometimes, they start businesses to find better work-life balance ... and then that business starts taking over their lives! Julie Aigner-Clark of Baby Einstein knew she was off balance when she noticed her employees were routinely walking through her kitchen in the morning while she was in her bathrobe making pancakes for her daughters. Doris Christopher stored the inventory for the Pampered Chef in her basement ... until the boxes started creeping up the stairs and into the dining room. And many self-employed moms find themselves taking every possible job and agreeing to every client request.

"I was so afraid the work was going to dry up, I would do whatever clients asked," says Barb Shepard, a self-employed marketing consultant and stepmother of two in Toronto. "I would write the marketing plan, deliver layouts to the printer, and even order food for events. And when clients would cut the budget in half, I'd still do the same amount of work, which set a very dangerous precedent."[9]

If you made your mark in the corporate world by being the perfect team player who always said yes, you'll need to retrain yourself for working on your own. Barb eventually started taking only client assignments that really excited her. It felt risky, but once she started saying no, she felt less physically and emotionally exhausted.

If you don't say no, you need to at least be sure you're charging what you're worth. Unfortunately, women aren't always comfortable negotiating for the money they deserve. A Los Angeles pension consultant, Marcy Elkind, dreaded calling clients to collect fees . . . until she started picturing her ten-year-old daughter when she picked up the phone.

"I learned early on that if I wanted to put a meal on the table for her, I had to open my mouth about money," she told us.

Jane Banser, a mother of two, ages ten and six, in Oak Brook, Illinois, owns an executive search firm. She found herself consistently undercharging her clients. "If you respond too quickly to a request for a fee, you could throw out a number you'll regret later," she told us. "Luckily for me, a client came right out and told me I wasn't charging enough." She started taking more time to analyze her costs before naming a fee.

Three Weeks Later . . .

Entrepreneurial dreams are easily dashed, and I did not think that our new company would survive in the terrible days after 9/11. We had signed our deal and taken control of *Working*

Mother just three weeks before the terrorist attacks shook New York City, Washington, D.C., and the world. As I looked straight down Fifth Avenue on my way to work and saw black smoke billowing out of the Twin Towers, I felt a huge responsibility to make sure our employees were okay. I had this odd thought: even though I didn't know everyone's name yet, I might now be responsible for making sure they made it home alive.

In the days that followed, we witnessed the darkest time New York City has ever seen, with posters on every lamppost calling out for news of lost relatives, with anthrax found two blocks from our offices, with funerals down the street at St. Patrick's Cathedral every day. Business ground to a halt, and the advertising industry disappeared for months and months. Our 100 Best Companies WorkLife Congress had been scheduled for September 26. We moved it to October 10, making it the first conference to be held in New York City post-9/11. We rewrote the program and retitled it "Employees in Crisis: Well-Being and Recovery in the Age of Terrorism."

Everyone in the publishing industry assumed *Working Mother* would go out of business at this point. How could an independent publisher survive the worst possible economic conditions—just after an acquisition? We had too many strikes against us, and as magazine after magazine failed, I began to lose faith too. But my investors had an iron will, and we just kept doing our best, running as fast as we could to stay alive.

We didn't have a chance to work on anything as lofty as our mission statement until well into November, but when we did, we found our rudder. After hours of wrangling over what our mission might be, Erica Gruen, a friend and consultant to the company, said, "You know, sometimes it just takes a few words to express your vision." We stopped wrangling and took a deep breath. Our mission, and our mission statement, is "To Serve Women Boldly." That clear sense of purpose and direction has kept us going ever since, and allowed us to survive where others have not. That, and our good friends at MCG Capital.

Another Escape Hatch: Plan B

At a recent reader breakfast, we asked, "Do you ever feel like leaving your job to stay home?" This ambitious group of go-getters, who had just been telling us about their dreams for bigger, better, higher-paying jobs, instantly turned into a group of quitters.

"Every minute," one woman answered. "I think about quitting every minute."

Of course, she was exaggerating, but the idea was clearly top of mind for many of the participants.

"I wonder if my kids would be better behaved if I stayed home," one reader pondered. "I know in my heart they wouldn't be, but I can't help thinking about it."

For many working mothers, ambition and quitting are two sides of a very thin coin. We are proud of our work and we want to get ahead and be recognized and move up, but many of us hear a voice in our heads telling us, "This is not going to work. How can I possibly make this work?"

So some of us shift to Plan B . . . we quit our jobs. Or we switch off the fast track, downsizing our hours and our ambition. In our <u>What Moms Want</u> survey, we found that 49 percent said they would quit their jobs in an ideal world.

And yet, those mothers we surveyed who *had* dropped out of the workforce often found that staying home was no cure-all. Of the 28 percent of mothers in our survey who actually left the workforce for a period of time, only 31 percent said they loved staying home; 16 percent said they felt bored or lost, and 18 percent worried about the lack of money. Most (58 percent) returned to the workforce within a year; another 32 percent were out from one to three years. Plan B, it seems, isn't always about staying home forever. As Helen Raczkowski of Hillsborough, New Jersey, wrote to us, "I used to lament that I had to work. I longed to be home with my kids. Then I lost my job and got what I had always dreamed of. And guess what? I hated it! Bliss, being at home with two preschoolers? I don't think so." Working, she told us, "makes me a better mom."[10]

Bob and I talked about Plan B all the time. Our Plan B wasn't about me quitting and staying home—it was about scaling back so I could work less. The Coulombe/Evans Plan B went like this: I quit my job, we sell the house, we move to a less expensive area of the country, and use the money from the sale of our house to support a less expensive lifestyle somewhere where Bob becomes a paid EMT and I find a less intense career.

All kinds of bumps in the road made us contemplate Plan B: fear of losing my job when the inevitable advertising recessions hit, unhappiness with a dopey male boss, financial strain from sending Robert to a private school for dyslexic kids, and the stress, stress, stress of overwork. The most compelling motivation for Plan B, though, was my fear that I wasn't spending enough time with the kids. When I felt that heavy guilt that comes from not being there enough, or when they were weepy as I dashed off for a business trip, my heart would break. I would start working on Plan B in earnest, finding out what the current value of our house was and researching other possible career paths.

We never did use our Plan B. In the end, I always persevered by rearranging the load when I felt out of balance and fighting for my kid time through all the strategies in this book . . . saying no, training my boss, fusing my work and home life, and devoting my weekends and vacations to Robert and Julia (and Bob, too). But somehow, having Plan B in our hip pocket gave Bob and me some comfort, and some room to breathe during difficult times. It made me feel like I had options and some control over my life.

Opting Out: Revolution or Evolution?

More and more moms are deciding to take Plan B. In 1998, 58 percent of moms who had babies less than a year old worked; in 2002, that number had dropped to 55 percent, according to the

U.S. Census Bureau.[11] While still a minority (77 percent of all married moms worked in 2003), the data caught our eye.

This shift, particularly strong among Gen X moms, caused us to make a major change in *Working Mother* magazine's editorial stance. In September 2002, when we launched a redesign of our magazine, we wrote our first feature about opting out, called "Chart Your Own Course." We talked to several moms who were taking time off or forging their own new family-friendly career paths. One mom, Jennifer Woodruff, was a twenty-nine-year-old principal of a highly regarded school in Montclair, New Jersey. When her daughter Dora was born, she decided to stay home for three or four years.[12] What riveted our editors' attention was that Jennifer thought of herself as a working mother, whether she was in the workforce or not. Taking three years off became part of her career plan, not a deviation from it.

We realized Jennifer represented many other mothers in their late twenties and thirties—women who had created a professional identity before they had children, and would continue to think of themselves as part of the workforce even if they stayed home for a period of time. Working motherhood, we realized, was a state of mind for many women. And that state of mind wasn't entirely related to whether they were employed at the moment or not. So at the magazine, we adopted a simple policy to identify our readers: if you think of yourself as a working mother, you *are* a working mother—even if you've opted to take Plan B for a while.

Two years after we published our story about charting your own course, the idea of Plan B, or opting out, suddenly captured a lot of media attention. Lisa Belkin, who writes a wonderful column for the *New York Times* on work-life balance, published a story in the *New York Times Magazine* called "The Opt-Out Revolution," which provoked an avalanche of e-mails and a firestorm of controversy. In this article, Lisa made the striking observation that women were dropping out of the power game. The women who graduated from Princeton with her in the 1970s and 1980s were supposed to be running the world twenty years later, she wrote, but instead, many had dropped out of the workforce to stay home, had shifted gears into less powerful careers, or were working part-time. The title of the piece and the media attention it received suggested that women were embracing the stay-at-home choice in a cultural shift of astronomical proportions and leaving the world of political and corporate power to men.

Lisa told me that she could tell the generation of her e-mailers within a few words. Boomers were appalled that she would write such a piece. Gen Xers were happy to have the issue aired. Many women faulted the article for having a very narrow focus on highly privileged white women who had married men rich enough to support an affluent lifestyle on one income. Other women complained about Lisa's conclusion that women weren't all that interested in the corner office—at least one study of senior executives proves men and women are equally interested in the CEO job.[13]

But to me, the controversy over this article missed the real point of the opt-out discussion, which is that all women, not just the privileged few, want to have choices that work for them. Choices that allow them to contribute to the world of work and still become the mothers they yearn to be. Much of corporate America still isn't giving us options that allow us to meet both our family goals and our professional goals—which makes Plan B ever so much more attractive.

Taking time out doesn't mean you've cashed in your ambition forever. As we discussed in chapter 2 ("We Alter the One-Size-Fits-All Career Track"), when companies really support our family and work goals, taking time off or gearing down for a while doesn't have to keep women from powerful positions. Just look at Karen Hughes, a key advisor to George Bush, who dropped out of the workforce to tend to the needs of her sixteen-year-old son—then rejoined the administration. Or Brenda Barnes, the former poster woman for opting out, who took nine years off, and then became CEO of the multibillion-dollar Sara Lee Corporation.

I suggest that what we have now is not an opt-out revolution, but an *opt-in evolution*, where increasingly women can create new and varied career paths that let them meet their own definitions of success. These paths may include periods of full-time work, periods of slowing down, and periods of time off. Opting in to a creative career path is a strategy available to millions of moms through tactics we share in this book: phase back from maternity leave, part-time professional work, flextime, working from home, job sharing, sabbaticals, controlling overwork, and extended time off with a plan to stay connected. Opting in is a sustainable evolution that can mean huge rewards for millions of mothers and the companies that value them.

Some companies are evolving faster than others, of course. But I strongly believe that if companies put their full support into creating family-friendly programs, training their managers, surveying their employees about work-life satisfaction, and making a real effort to retain working moms, far fewer of us would act on Plan B, and many more would opt in to a sustainable, whole life. Companies would start stemming the brain drain and stop losing some of their most talented employees to their competitors, self-employment, or staying at home. We know this is true because it's already working at the Working Mother 100 Best Companies. When companies create cultures that truly encourage family balance, they start winning the war for talented employees. And working mothers start winning the war for a happier balance between work and home.

Chapter Twelve

We Live Full Lives

One day three summers ago, Julia and I were lying in the hammock in the backyard. I was exhausted from a demanding week running a hugely successful conference that launched our Best Companies for Women of Color initiative. Julia was not exhausted. She was in high-energy mode and had a very specific goal in mind. Julia wanted a farm animal. Any farm animal. It had become an obsession with her, and her highly developed sales mind sensed that now, in that hammock, was the time to strike. Her prey was weak but happy, reveling in the presence of her offspring after three nights away from home, and particularly vulnerable to persuasion.

Julia had tried many times before. Her success rate for pets was very high and she felt it was only a matter of time before she had a win at the next level. Over the years, she had somehow talked us into owning guinea pigs (many generations), mice (who multiplied like crazy), rabbits (who need special outdoor care), hamsters (who all got lost), gerbils (so fast you can't hold them), cockatiels (which I adore), turtles (no comment), fish (we finally learned how to keep them alive), and the teacher's chinchillas (cute, but jumpy), which we babysat for the summer.

But all along, Julia's goal was a farm animal. Maybe because we live on Old Farm Road. Maybe because both her Welsh and French-Canadian ancestors were farmers. Maybe because there's

an old stone barn in our backyard. We use it as a surrogate basement, since our house doesn't have one, and it's filled to the rafters
with the flotsam and jetsam of life. But still, it *is* a stone barn.
Whatever the reason, she was determined.

Julia had investigated all kinds of farm animals. Thanks to this
quest, she became a master of Web research, and although she was
an average student, she got all As when it came to presenting the
case for her chosen species. She started trying for a horse, then
moved to smaller, more physically manageable animals, including
pigs, sheep, miniature donkeys, ducks, and her perennial favorite—
chickens. There were reasons, very sound reasons, for saying no to
each one, and the negatives always came out in the research. Saying
no hadn't been that hard—not even for a romantic like me—
although I admit I was tempted by the miniature donkeys for sale
on the Web. "Mom, look at this one. . . . His name is Charlie . . .
ooh, he's so beautiful! And only twenty-eight inches tall. We can
manage him, Mommy!"

So I really didn't see the goose thing coming. I was just swinging peacefully on the hammock, nonchalantly listening as she told
me about her latest idea—buying a goose from Medger Farms, a
commercial supplier to farmers. They ship the goose to you by
mail, and they're so cute, and please, please, please, Mommy . . .
and the next thing I knew, she was saying, "Oh, Mommy, thank
you so much! This is going to be so great! You won't regret it, I
promise. I'll take care of them so well. You won't need to worry
about a thing. This is going to be the best summer of my life!"

A week later, she told me that Medger Farms said they couldn't
ship just one goose, so she had ordered more than one, but that I
shouldn't worry, because they only cost $3.58 each. Julia was ter-
rified the geese would die in the Chappaqua post office, so we
called to make sure they knew we were expecting a shipment of
live geese. They called one day at six a.m. "Mrs. Coulombe, your
birds have arrived!"

I was shocked to find eight baby geese peeping through the
holes of their tiny cardboard container. But they were, individually

and collectively, the cutest creatures I had ever seen, outside of my own children and a puppy or two. We set them up in Julia's room, in a dry kiddy pool that sported a purple elephant head. Its trunk was a slide. The baby geese didn't mind the odd quarters. They settled in and began peeping loudly, demanding their meals with clockwork regularity and infantile insistence.

Geese grow very fast. And very big. But Julia and everyone else, including me, fell crazy in love with these geese. When they outgrew the purple swimming pool (in about three weeks) we made a special home for them in the barn, in a bigger dry pool without the elephant trunk slide.

Julia was in farm heaven, and ran around the yard with the eight goslings cackling and honking and following close on her heels. "Come *on*, geese!" she would shout. "Come on, Platypus, Dopples, and Sugarlump! Come on, Olive, Webster, Julie, Ernie, and SnipSnap-Gingertap!"

She had her moments of doubt. "Do you think they really love me, Mommy?" And she had her moments of joy, when she was able to hold one of the geese quietly on her lap. In between, it fell to me to make sure these creatures were well cared for.

Julia tried to keep her end of the care bargain going, but she has never been a morning person. Once the geese moved to the barn, I realized there was no point in trying to wake her up for their six a.m. breakfast. So feeding the geese became part of my routine. Take out the old food and water. Rinse the feed container with the hose. Rake out the hay the geese slept on. Fill the water contraption. Give them some fresh grass from the yard. All in a day's work—before my day's work had really begun. And this is how I became the only CEO that I know of who had to slop geese every morning before getting on the train to go into Manhattan to run a major women's magazine.

One night when Bob was out at a dinner, I got a desperate call at the office as I was about to leave. "Hurry, Mommy, hurry home. Platypus is sick!" Just when we needed the EMT to help us with our brood, he wasn't available. The goose was indeed sick and struggling to breathe. Julia convinced me, in a torrent of tears, to take Platypus to the twenty-four-hour pet hospital, where the veterinarian didn't even raise an eyebrow at the fact that we had an ailing goose. Instead, she rushed the goose to a fancy, superclean room and put her in an oxygen tent. Two hours later, she came back to the waiting room, where Julia and I were falling asleep, and told us that Platypus had a respiratory infection and needed to stay overnight.

I saw dollar signs and inquired politely what the charge would be for an overnight stay. She shuffled through her papers and did some calculations. "It will be about $635, unless she needs to stay longer," she said.

I explained that we could set up an oxygen tent at home, that Bob was an EMT, that I knew how to feed the medicine with a syringe, having raised baby cockatiels, and that we would prefer to take the goose home. Reluctantly, she released the goose to my care as I paid the $256 in charges we had already incurred. So much for the $3.58 goose!

Platypus made it through just fine in our homemade hospital tent, rigged up with the oxygen tank that Bob kept in the car for EMT emergencies. She was back with her friends in just three days, and Julia was so proud that she had saved her life.

By the time the eight geese were each the size of a tricycle, we all knew the gig was up—even Julia. I called Farmer Joe at nearby Muscoot Farms, a historically preserved working farm, and used my strongest selling techniques to get him to take the geese. He was extremely reluctant, saying that he got calls about unwanted animals all the time. "Not geese, I imagine." I said enthusiastically, "And they're five different breeds—not one of them is a plain old Canadian goose. It will be so educational for the children!" He paused for a very long minute and slowly said, "Well, we haven't had any geese for a while. . . ."

It was a sad day when we drove them up to their new home. We videotaped Platypus, Ernie, and the rest as they popped their heads up to peek over the edge of the blue plastic tubs where they rode in the back of the minivan. You can't really kiss geese good-bye, and they don't show a lot of emotion themselves, but Julia and I cried on the way home, even as we felt ourselves relaxing, as if some long-term burden had suddenly been lifted from our shoulders.

Bothering to Build Full Lives

Sometimes in my busy life, it can seem like the geese and the oxygen tent and all the other miscellaneous stuff that happens are just distractions from some bigger life I'm supposed to be living. But as the years roll on, I'm realizing that all the "stuff that happens" *is* my life and that the accumulation of my experiences would be so much less rich without all the ingredients I mix in. Without my workplace and its roster of characters, without my children and their enormous place in my psyche, without every piece that I mold together, my life would be smaller.

Maya Angelou once told me that we are the architects of our own lives and we have to take responsibility for what we build. What have I built? I have built a life that I love living. Not a "having it all" life, or a life free of conflict and anxiety or fear or pain, but a life full of energy and learning and hope and possibility and accomplishment and humor. A life with spirit. And much of that spirit comes from the small pieces that I allow myself to fit into the grand scheme—the geese, the house, the dogs, the garden—and not from the "grand scheme" itself.

Of course, it would be easier to say no to the geese, or a million things like them. But for me and many, many other working moms, "easier" is not the point. Taking the trouble to squeeze it all in—work, kids, pets, hobbies, exercise, church, volunteer work, or whatever it is that makes our lives feel whole—*that's* the point. In fact, even though people ask us over and over, "How do you do it all?," the more interesting question is, "*Why* do you do it all?" We do it all because we want to live full lives.

I see this in the stories of countless readers who let me know how important a full life is to them. Yes, we're all crunched for time. In our <u>What Moms Want</u> survey, the most common challenge working mothers shared was not having enough time—for themselves, for housework, for everything they have to do. But at the same time, when we asked if they had "hobbies," almost all said yes. The most popular were reading for pleasure (76 percent), socializing with friends (61 percent), going to the movies (49 percent), shopping for fun (48 percent), and traveling (43 percent). Others included music, cooking, fitness, crafts, and gardening. Many moms enjoy more than one of these passions. What a colorful group we are!

Some of these interests are pursued alone, to keep a part of ourselves from disappearing beneath the vast sea of our responsibilities. Some create joyful bonds with our kids, friends, or husbands. But these passions all give us enough pleasure and satisfaction and joy to justify the time they take and the effort they add to our lives. "The truth is, when something is really important to you, when it motivates you and stirs your innermost desires, you will find some time for it," wrote Laura Stack, the author of *Leave the Office Earlier*[1] and the mother of Meagan, ten, Johnny, five, and James, four.

Of course, we can't find time every day for reaching beyond the ordinary. Sometimes we can barely find time even once a year for our special passions. But over and over, our readers tell me how rewarding it is when they make the effort to create and live a full life.

No-Work Zone

Tucking the things we love to do into our very full and busy lives is part determination and part deliberate scheduling. I schedule *some* things carefully, setting aside specific time, but mostly I fit things in by putting some boundaries around my work life. My best strategy is that I don't work on the weekends (except to write this book!), and I do take every vacation day I have coming to me (unlike more than one-third of Americans, who take less than their full vacation time).[2] And when I walk in the door at the end of the day, I am truly home, not just halfheartedly home.

Protecting your home time is key to creating a full life.

"I section off family time," says Pegeen Reichert Powell, a professor at Duke University and the mother of Charlie, four, and Elizabeth, two.[3] Pegeen won our Raising a Ruckus Award for organizing a parents' group at Duke that successfully lobbied for more family-friendly policies. But her own best family policy is keeping certain hours sacred. "The hours between dinner and my kids' bedtime is for family only. I don't try to do three other things at once. When Charlie says, 'Let's play trains,' we play trains—without my giving a thought to what else I could be doing."

Of course, protecting your time is easier said than done in an era of overwork. "Jobs have become much more demanding and hectic, with longer and longer hours," says Ellen Galinsky, president of the Families and Work Institute, which completed a study of work hours in 2004. The study found that one in three workers are chronically overworked, and 54 percent of the one thousand employees surveyed felt overwhelmed by the amount of work they had to complete in the past month. "The culture of overwork is very much alive and well," Galinsky says.

Some companies are trying to remedy the ill effects of overwork. The consumer products company S. C. Johnson in Racine, Wisconsin, organizes social events and clubs for its workers—they have a wine-tasting club, a scrapbooking club, and archery, bowling, volleyball, and golf teams. Ford Motor Company offers classes in genealogy, cooking, and time management to its employees. JFK Medical Center in Atlantis, Florida, and several other Best Companies offer "date nights," keeping child-care centers open late on Friday night so parents can enjoy a night out. These companies realize that employees with full lives and less stress are more productive and creative workers.

I also fit things in by cutting other things *out*. I try to keep my house from becoming unruly, but it's certainly less than perfectly clean. Bob and I divide housework and have a housekeeper come in two mornings a week (the kids are pretty unreliable as household help). We pay for services like dry cleaning and takeout that will save us time. I don't entertain very often because it's too hard. I don't watch much TV unless I can find something to watch with the kids. I gave up on tennis years ago because of the time commitment, and I play golf only once a year, just to amuse my husband.

Lower Your Standards to Build a Full Life

I never thought I would call myself a gardener. It seemed like such an old-lady activity. It makes me think of my Danish great-grandmother, Cecelia Petersen, with her babushka covering her head, hunched over her rake in the garden by the side of her little house in Iowa. She grew potatoes and lettuce and bountiful flowers. She didn't speak much English and I didn't know any Danish, but she knew I loved her garden and she talked to me about it in words I only guessed at.

Decades later, the compulsion to garden came upon me quite unexpectedly when we bought our house in Chappaqua. It had been a farmhouse and had some wonderful ancient beds just waiting for someone to take out the weeds and put in the flowers. I succumbed to their siren call soon after we moved in.

At first, I saw gardening as a way to spend time with Robert on those wonderful summer weekends. Bob and I planted vegetables that first year, and Robert was proud as punch of the big, red, juicy tomatoes he could pick all by himself. There was a small round pond by the side of the house where the silo had once stood. We filled it in with dirt when I couldn't stop worrying that Robert would fall in as he toddled round and round the bricks that formed its base. This became the "roundy garden," where I would plant concentric rings of annuals every year. We knew spring was really here when Robert, and later Julia, and I prepared the roundy garden to accept the year's chosen varieties.

Year after year, I added to the gardens. One year I created a perennial garden in the old stone ruins back by the stone barn, and another year I built a tiny herb garden with a little brick path I laid myself. Then I discovered the world of native plants and shade gardens, buying wild ginger, ferns, may apples, and yellow rocket and planting them under the hemlocks.

By the time the kids grew old enough to do anything really useful in the garden, they immediately lost interest, and I found myself without any excuse to be out with my plants. Gardening became a guilty pleasure, just for me, and a race against time. I would get up hours before anyone else in the house and quietly slip out to my garden, weeding and planting until Robert called from the kitchen, "Mommy! Are you in the garden? Want to watch cartoons with me?" Of course I did, and that was it for gardening for the day.

Most of what I know about gardening I learned at the Millwood Garden Center by reading the plastic tags that come with the plants, and asking the owner a few questions on each shopping trip. I don't really plan my gardens—I put plants in the ground, and if they do well, I add more. The perennials often surprise me by growing taller or shorter than I expect, so the garden often looks like a crazy quilt of sizes and shapes.

One year, I had a company picnic at my house, and was proudly showing my garden to a bigwig at Primedia, the conglomerate that bought *Stagebill*. Her husband, a brilliant financial analyst, had a bemused look on his face. He turned to me and said, ever so gently, "You know, Carol, the tall flowers are supposed to be in the middle and the short flowers are supposed to be around the edge."

Once he pointed it out, I saw that indeed, the tall plants were gracing the outer edge and the shorter ones were happily peeking out of the middle, as if protected by a phalanx of powerful guards.

I imagine that one day when I'm retired, or the kids are out of the house, I will actually learn to garden. In the meantime, I set my standards low. If my garden is beautiful, it's a thrill—if not, there's always next year. My low standards keep me going: if my garden had to be perfect, that would be the end of my gardening, period.

As adults, we sometimes set our standards too high for everything we do, and forget about sheer playfulness. By setting our expectations low, we can have so much more fun. Low expectations for my beloved garden make it the perfect refuge. No words are spoken in my garden now that the kids don't join me there. No one has to be cajoled or sold to or listened to or promoted or nagged. The plants and I know each other, respect each other, and grow together.

Girlfriends Are Essential for a Full Life

One night when I was in tenth grade, my best friend Jan came over for a sleepover. We should have called them wakeovers because our goal was always to stay awake as long as possible. We would think up ever more ridiculous things to do to keep ourselves awake until sunrise, but we would usually fail, falling asleep hours short of our objective. (I have no idea now why this was such a thrilling goal for us, but I do remember that its allure lasted a long time and that one of Bob's great charms was his ability to stay awake every Saturday night to hear the birds chirping for our first summer together.)

On this particular night in 1968, Jan and I played monopoly until we'd completely sated our capitalistic instincts. My parents went to bed, allowing us to stay up watching TV in the living room. We left the TV on and snuck into the kitchen to see what we could do for fun. First, we made vanilla pudding. (We must have been out of chocolate pudding mix; we never would have chosen vanilla over chocolate.) Then we decided to check out my dad's liquor cabinet, on the top shelf way in the corner of the kitchen cupboards. Jan, who was (and still is) eight inches taller than me, stood on the counter to reach. There she found several unappealing bottles of liquor with names like Old Grandad and Beefeaters. Yuck. But toward the back she came up with a tall sophisticated can that said Brandy Alexander.

The exotic-looking can held a bottle of brandy, a powdered mix of flavors, and a recipe for Brandy Alexander that sounded tempting: brandy, the powdered flavorings, and several scoops of ice cream! Who couldn't drink that? That was our first experiment with alcohol, and our last for a long while.

The Brandy Alexander we shared probably had a very low alcohol content, but the excitement of doing something so daring and out of the ordinary was exhilarating. We not only saw the sun rise the next morning, but we also snuck our bikes off the front porch and toured the town wearing our nightgowns and our ear-to-ear grins.

Jan and I have been joined at the hip since seventh grade. My dad called her "Tall Daughter," and my mother considered her the blonde, blue-eyed child her Danish lineage deserved but never produced.

Over the next thirty-seven years, Jan and I concocted many adventures, and lived through many ups and downs together. We are very different from each other. She is tall where I am short. She is blonde where I am brunette. She wears size twelve (!) shoes to my size six (but I shouldn't tell everyone that because she thinks her feet are too big—she used to be just a size eleven!). She never had kids, but married a widower with five and ten-year-old daughters, and thus became a stay-at-home mom quite suddenly one summer. Although she has worked at many jobs, she never found a career path that suited her.

Her husband, Phil, is even the opposite of Bob: he can fix or build anything, whereas Bob can't even hang a picture on the wall. However, Phil can't deliver a baby or resuscitate a heart attack victim.

We may be opposites, but we've nurtured, supported, and amused each other since the seventh grade. It didn't just happen: Jan and I have worked at our friendship all these years, sometimes talking on the phone every week, sometimes only once in a while. We have rarely lived in the same city since our high school days, but have used that distance as an opportunity to spend more concentrated time at one home base or the other.

Bob is happy when Jan and I call and travel to see each other.

"You always laugh a lot when you're talking to Jan," he says. And indeed that is the fundamental characteristic of our friendship: we laugh together.

I believe that Jan and I will live longer because of our friendship. Studies have shown that friendships provide a different kind of sustenance than family, and that people who build friendships reap rewards in health, mental stability, focus, and longevity.

Readers also tell us how important their friendships are to them. When we asked working mothers about their most popular pastimes, spending time with friends was second only to reading for pleasure, with 61 percent saying they made time for friends.

A full life requires a close friend or two, outside of work, outside of family, outside of any obligation. The only way to ensure friendship is to be deliberate. Scheduling phone calls, celebrating birthdays and milestones together, keeping track of when you last spent real time together so you don't go too long without seeing each other—the same strategies you would employ to keep an important client in your circle need to be applied to friendships. And the rewards are much greater than any client can bestow.

One tried-and-true working mother strategy is scheduling dates and getaways with our friends. Jan and I are living proof that it works. When we both lived in New York, our lives moved in different directions—me, the career mom, she, the single girl. Since she married Phil and moved to Boulder, Jan and I have actually become closer in many ways. We schedule trips to see each other, which means we have special, dedicated time together that creates a much richer experience than a luncheon here or there.

On her last visit to see me in New York, we went to Pier 54 to see "Ashes and Snow," a photography exhibit of extraordinary beauty and emotion. Jan was asking the security guard at the gift shop about the photographs (she's very friendly), when the guard said, "The artist just came in and is standing over there—why don't you ask him?" The photographer, Gregory Colbert, spoke to us for fifteen minutes. It was thrilling to hear him talk about spending twelve years in quest of these ethereal photographs of elephants, leopards, whales, and birds—and I know I would have missed the whole thing if Jan hadn't been there to make New York special for me again.

Scheduling getaways with friends has helped many other working moms preserve friendships through some of the most challenging times of motherhood.

Working moms Cathy Fenimore and Lillian Morrow have also been best friends since the seventh grade. But even though they work for the same company in the same building in Seattle, they rarely get to see each other during the week. So they went away together to FriendFest, a weekend retreat for women friends at a lodge on Washington's Columbia River.

Founded by Lynn Edwards, a mom from University Place, Washington, FriendFest has held retreats in the Pacific Northwest, Georgia, and Massachusetts. Edwards started the company after years of organizing retreats with her old college buddies. "It's amazing how a weekend with my girlfriends recharges me," she told us. She wanted to share the experience with other moms, and she knew the secret to making it work. "You need somebody to say, 'Here's the date. Here are the details. You're going.' "[4]

But you don't have to plan a weekend getaway to schedule in friend dates.

"I signed up for a dance class with my best friend," Sandy Smolenski of Mount Prospect, Illinois, told us. While grandma babysits the kids, Sandy and her friend spend one night a week imagining they're on Broadway. "It's a blast," she says.[5]

Writer and teacher Anndee Hochman has been meeting weekly with a group of friends for Monday night dinners for years. The group has made some adjustments over time—dinner used to start at seven, but now starts at six to accommodate the growing number of kids. One couple split, one friendship imploded, but somehow the group has survived. "We've learned a few things in ten years," she told us. "Friendship is a tricky, time-intensive brew. You can't rush it."[6]

When a weekly or monthly or even yearly date just won't work, some moms find a regularly scheduled call can make all the difference. Janet McNaughton and Mary Portlock have a standing phone date every Friday at four p.m. Even though it's just fifteen minutes, it gives them the chance to check in with each other and share good news and bad.

Whether it's a lifelong friend like Jan or a Mommy and Me classmate, friendships give working mothers a refuge from the extraordinarily crowded lives we lead. Without Jan in my life, how lonely I would be some days—even with all the characters who crowd into my day and week and month.

Making Compromises for a Full Life

When I was young, I wanted to read every great novel ever written. I despaired over the fact that even if I read a book a week for the rest of my life, I'd never read them all.

Sometime after I moved to New York, I stopped reading the great novels of the world, but books stayed in my life in other ways. I started reading business books and trade magazines— something I could never have foreseen. As soon as I got pregnant, business books gave way to every book I could find on the care and feeding of babies. Soon my reading habits changed again as Robert, Julia, and I followed the antics of Curious George making trouble at the firehouse, baseball game, construction site, and circus. I read *Goodnight Moon* until my eyes clamped shut with exhaustion. I read *Aunt Ippy's Museum of Junk* and *Hazel's Amazing Mother* so many times that the pages got all raggedy. And on some special nights, I sat in the big chair and read *Winnie-the-Pooh* like my father did to me, and tried to mimic his Pooh and Piglet voices as near as I could remember.

When Robert was diagnosed with a serious reading disability, reading out loud to him became one of my missions. I wanted him to love books the way I do. As he got older, his book selection turned from the magnificent "Chronicles of Narnia" to the latest hits of R. L. Stine—scary tales that reminded me of the *Twilight Zone* on speed. Then came Animorphs, a series of books where children fight an alien invasion of the ugliest order. I finally turned

Robert's book reading over to Bob, who has a much stronger stomach than me.

But then, for a few brief shining years, my children's tastes in books straddled my own. Julia and I spent one delicious summer reading the "Anne of Green Gables" books. And that same year Robert discovered Orson Scott Card's fascinating science fiction trilogy *Speaker for the Dead*. Robert and I read out in the hammock in the yard for hours. Julia preferred me to read to her in her room, where she liked to doodle on a pad while I made the voices that she insisted on for each character.

Now we're all reading on our own and I'm back to business books, an occasional contemporary author, and writing a book of my own. It's been years since I dreamed of working my way through the world's great novels. But I know there are ten thousand books out there waiting for me to read . . . and they are very, very patient.

As working moms, we know our time is very limited for several years of our lives . . . but that our hobbies and passions will wait for us if we keep in touch with them, however tenuously. While almost all of the working moms in our survey had a hobby of some kind, few found much time for it—more than half spent five hours or less per month on their hobby. But even an hour here and there doing something we love helps us stay connected to the person we were before our kids—and the person we hope to be after they leave the house. With passions and hobbies we love, even a little goes a long way to maintaining our sense of self.

Sharing Interests for a Full Life

We all need "me time." But sometimes "we time" can have the same restorative effect, if you find a shared passion that brings you closer to your kids. That's what Donna Dayton, a lab manager from Bloomington, Indiana, learned when she and her thirteen-year-old daughter Kelsey started volunteering for a local pet shelter. "It was amazing to have this time with my daughter away from the TV, the phone, and all the other interruptions that so often take up the life of a typical teenager," Donna told us.[7]

Julia and I also found a new bond that's brought us closer together: she has become my personal shopper.

As Julia matured, we lost one activity after another that kept us close. Snuggling in front of the TV became forbidden. Playing Little Mermaid in the tub? Don't even think about it. Reading aloud—no! Swimming, biking, dancing in the living room . . . all outlawed. Play Taboo? Sure . . . next week we'll play Taboo. We held on to painting with acrylics for a while longer, but that too became an embarrassment and joined the blacklisted activities.

But shopping. Ah, yes, shopping. One of my least favorite activities in the whole world gradually developed into the thread that held my precious Julia and me together during the long winter of her teenage years.

I've never really liked shopping. I'm a penny pincher. Faced with a store full of choices, I become paralyzed. If I finally do make a choice, I'm often plagued by buyer's remorse for weeks. Bob, on the other hand, has great skill as a spender and never suffers from buyer's remorse. For years, Bob helped me shop for my clothes. Julia inherited his shopping gene—and turbocharged it to boot. Sometime around her thirteenth birthday, she took over from Bob and asserted herself as my personal shopper.

It started out as shopping for *her*. I had the credit card and she had the insatiable appetite for clothes. I put her on a clothing budget to keep her under control and she soon hit her limit. She learned, gradually, to shop in less expensive stores to stretch her dollars. But her shopping desire still wasn't fulfilled, so she started to shop for me. And she definitely wasn't looking for my usual wardrobe staples. "Black, brown, navy, and, oooh, maybe a gray suit once in a while" was her summation of my standard palette. "Mom, you need a little color in your life!"

The first outfit she bought me was a lavender skirted suit with ladies' faces imprinted on the fabric in a soft pattern. The jacket was tightly cut with elegant bows at the side. I would never have tried it on in a million years, but once I did, I could see the tight cut of the jacket was very flattering to my middle-aged shape . . . which didn't have that much shape on its own. I wore the suit to an industry function and everyone oohed and ahhed over it. Hmmm, I thought. Maybe she's on to something.

Next came the black-and-white polka-dot suit with fringy edging and a tight-cut jacket. I wore it for the first time to give a speech about work-life balance in Chicago, where I confessed to the audience that I didn't usually wear polka dots, but that my daughter had taken control of my clothes shopping. Again, the audience loved her choice. Some women even asked if they could hire Julia to spruce up their wardrobes.

Julia's ultimate victory came on Mother's Day, when she bought me a bright red suit straight from the Victoria's Secret catalogue that fit like a glove right out of the box. I wore that suit when I was on the *Today* show and needed the most powerful support that Julia's bold imagination could offer. When we shot the cover for this book, I dragged in much of my wardrobe to give Laureen Rowland, my publisher, some choices—but that powerhouse red suit was her first and final choice.

Julia is now officially in charge of my wardrobe. On each trip to the mall, we shop a little for her and then a little for me, and it is pure joy.

Looking Forward by Looking Back: Finding the Joy in Our Everyday, Full Lives

Through all the ups and downs of working motherhood, there's one thing that has helped me savor the joy of my full life: keeping a journal. It's something I recommend for every mom.

I've been journaling on and off since my early twenties, when I wrote impassioned entries full of the turbulence of a life transitioning to adulthood. Once Robert was born, my journals changed dramatically, reflecting the simple truth that having a baby changes everything, as our friends at Johnson & Johnson say so beautifully in their ads. When the babies were little I wrote about Robert's, and then Julia's, cute moments, their development, needs and joys, their habits and achievements, their words and explorations. The tiniest details are the most precious:

February 13, 1991 [Robert is four years old]
Robert is an incredibly wonderful boy. Tonight he washed his hair by himself!! He also baked Ninja Turtle cookies (I helped) and decorated them. Yesterday he came home with a valentine and I said, "Is that for me?" He said, "Oh, Mommy," (with great scorn) "you big silly, of course it's for you!"

April 12, 1991 [Julia is sixteen months old]
Julia is an outdoor girl. All she wants is to go outside. She cries by the door to be taken outside even when its dark and raining. She wants to look out the window in her bedroom all the time.

In between baby entries, I wrote about my own successes and failures at work, and the conflicts that arose where work and motherhood did not neatly go together.

February 27, 1995 [Robert is eight years old, Julia is five]
I'm flying to California for a trip with too few appointments! Robert cried this morning. He woke up and hugged me and was sad and he told me I had to wake up Julia—"You promised!"—and then she cried and they kept hugging and crying and then they stood in the picture window and waved.

Over the years, I've kept all kinds of journals: lined notebooks, a reproduction of a 1914 baby's journal, plain old blank books. In 1999 I discovered the Five Year Journal in the Levenger catalog. Each of its 365 pages has space to write about that date each year for five years. When it's complete, you can look at a single day and see what you did on that day over a five-year span. It's the perfect journal for a busy working mom, because we may not consistently have time to write long entries—but even a few jotted notes make a big difference in threading the details of our lives together.

I asked Bob to give me the Levenger journal for my Christmas present in 1999. It arrived in black leather binding with CJE embossed in silver lettering on the front. I wrote my first entry a few days later:

January 1, 1999
Snowstorm! Hurray! Pond is frozen. Yea! Hangover from Frank and Luci's New Year's Eve party-Boo! Robert playing video games. Brunch at the Rosens' next door, then the best— ice skating on the big pond. Julia and I were awesome together. It was sunny and beautiful.

The first five years went by in a flash, it now seems. But when I read over the entries I see that so much happened, that we did so much together as a family, that my life as a mother was incredibly rich. In those 365 pages are a record of nearly everything we did, and wonderful tidbits of what I was feeling and thinking. When I was living through those days, I thought I would never forget the tender moments with Robert and Julia that filled my heart, or the powerful feelings that came with my career successes and failures, but I am often astonished to read an incident that I have completely forgotten, a sentiment that I no longer knew I had, a conversation that took place and then left my memory bank. Aided by my journal entries, I can revel in those memories, cherishing the positive, and learning from the painful.

May 5, 2001 [Robert is fourteen]
Robert is so sweet. He still likes to hug and give kisses. He always says, "You're the best mommy in the whole world!"

January 14, 2002 [Julia is thirteen years old]
　　Julia wrote a beautiful poem about me and Dad. Then she wrote a very loving note—just when I thought she was too old to write loving notes anymore.

Besides reminding me of the details of my motherhood, a quick read reconstructs the details of our life as a family: visits with my parents and in-laws, the pets duly recorded as they are purchased, get sick, or die, sleepovers, promotions, vacations, hirings, books, gardening, the ambulance corps, our marriage, ideas, dreams, plans, and of course the occasional hilarious story.

December 4, 1997 [Julia is nine years old]
　　The new cleaning lady threw Blue Bear away! We found him in the garbage!!
　　How horrible!

These few sentences conjure up the story of Blue Bear that threads through all the years of Julia's life. The big fluffy blue bear was given to Robert by his favorite aunt (Ma Tante Joyce) and adopted by Julia when she was a baby. She rubbed his tag off and never stopped that tactile relationship. She still sleeps with him today, at age fifteen. When we left him at my parents' house in Florida, he had to be FedEx'ed back; when he was left behind at McDonald's, we made Lost Bear posters and got him back; when Maria threw him in the garbage because he looked like a pathetic rag, we discovered her mistake in the nick of time. From time to time Memere sewed Blue Bear's arms back on, until eventually she performed major surgery, re-covering him in new blue fur, but leaving Julia's favorite touching spots exposed. These adventures are all there in my journal—and if they weren't, who would remember so many stories about a blue bear?

　　The negatives are there too. Fights, bad behavior (from each of us in our turn), doubts, fluctuations in weight, missed opportunities, failures—all recorded in a few words . . .

March 30, 1995

Julia must have heard us talking about my worries at work. She said, "Mommy, if you get fired, will our house burn down?"

During Christmas vacation in 2004 my mother noticed my diary and immediately wanted one for herself. She had been diagnosed with bone marrow cancer two years earlier, and was putting up a great fight with chemotherapy and dialysis marked by her usual high-voltage optimism. But when she asked me if I would order her a five-year diary, even I was awed by her sense of possibility. I didn't say what I was thinking, that she would not live long enough to fill in the years. She talked about the idea with such excitement that I put aside my negative thoughts and ordered a navy blue leather diary with "2005–2009" embossed in gold on the front.

My mother slipped into a coma just days before the diary arrived three weeks later, and I wept over its empty pages that could have been filled with her amazing life force. But as I read back over my own, I find her strong presence again and again throughout the years.

March 26, 2003 [Visiting their Florida home]

Boating Day. Saw four baby otter and one adult in Dora Canal. Home at 4:00 to get Mom ready for her play. She was Mr. Svetlanka in one skit and one of the Four Old Broads in another. She was great!

At the age of eighty-three my mom was learning a whole new skill: acting. Role modeling for me yet again.

The power of journaling comes from the firm grip you have on the present as you write it, which allows you to use your journal to both remember the details of the past and chart a course for the future. When I reread my journals in search of guidance, I discover that I have been a very loving and guiding force in my kids' lives, that I am proud of the work I do, that my marriage has great rewards, and that my life as a working mother, while crazy full, is full of joy. I wish that discovery for each of you.

The Last Word

Whatever your passions are, being a working mother doesn't mean giving up on yourself and your own needs. Making a place for those needs on that long to-do list is the key to leading a full life—which, when you think about it, is the whole reason many of us wanted to have kids in the first place. To create a fuller, richer, more complete life for ourselves.

The more that we working mothers can hold on to the thread of joy in our lives, by asking our companies, our communities, and our families to respect and support our efforts to be great mothers and great workers, the more joyful life will be for everyone—most important, for our children.

The last word on the joy of working motherhood comes from the many mothers I have spoken of in this manifesto: the lab technician at the DOCS clinic, the moms at Second Shift, the president of Pottery Barn Kids, and so many others. Their voices speak of their love for their children and their pride in their work. By allowing themselves to be mothers first, but believing they can also be dedicated and productive workers, by asking for the flexibility and support they need at work and by bothering to build full lives at home, they're uncovering the joy of working motherhood every day.

Notes

Chapter One

1. Bureau of Labor Statistics, 2005.
2. "Why Do You Work?" Jennifer Gill, *Working Mother*, October 2002.
3. "Why Do You Work?," *Working Mother*, October 2003.
4. "The Way We Are," Ellen Galinsky and Susan Lapinski, *Working Mother*, November 2004.
5. MRI Doublebase, 2005.

Chapter Two

1. "Ambitious and Proud of It," Dawn Jefferson and Rosanne Welch, *Working Mother*, March 2005.
2. "2004 Benefits Survey Report," Society for Human Resource Management, 2004.
3. "All the Right Moves," Mary Quigley, *Working Mother*, January 2005.
4. "Fertility of American Women: June 2002," U.S. Census Bureau, October 2003.
5. "The Hidden Brain Drain: Off-Ramps and On-Ramps in Women's Careers," Sylvia Ann Hewlett et al., *Harvard Business Review*, March 2005.
6. "Crafting Lives That Work: A Six-Year Retrospective on Reduced-Load Work in the Careers and Lives of Professionals and Managers," M. D. Lee and E. E. Kossek, 2005. Faculty of Management, McGill University.

Chapter Three

1. "Raising a Ruckus," Claire Whitcomb, *Working Mother*, April/May 2005.
2. "Subcontract Your Sitter," Jennifer Gill, *Working Mother*, March 2004.
3. "Babysitter Love," Patti Jones, *Working Mother*, February 2004.
4. Ibid.

5. "They Bring Their Babies to Work," *Working Mother*, October 2004.

6. "Investment Impact Study," Bright Horizons, 2005.

7. "How to Assess the Value of Work-Life Programs," Leah Carlson, *Employee Benefit News*, December 2004.

Chapter Four

1. "Life at the Top," Michael Marmot, *New York Times*, February 27, 2005.

2. "Got a Mentor?," *Working Mother*, June 2005.

3. "You, Only Better," Cheryl Dahle, *Working Mother*, August 2003.

4. "It Is All About You," Jennifer Gill, *Working Mother*, September 2003.

5. "Ready for Departure," Alison Overholt, *Working Mother*, December 2002/January 2003.

Chapter Five

1. "Working Families and Afterschool: A Household Survey," Afterschool Alliance, May 2004.

2. "It's 3 PM: Why Can't You Find Afterschool Care?," *Working Mother*, September 2001.

3. "Working Families and Afterschool: A Special Report from America After 3 PM," Afterschool Alliance, May 2004.

4. "It's 3 PM: Why Can't You Find Afterschool Care?," *Working Mother*, September 2001.

5. Ibid.

6. Ibid.

7. "You've Made It Through the Diapers, Playdates and Field Trips—Now What?," Maggie Jackson, *Working Mother*, October 2003.

8. "Patricia Hajduk-Condon Masters the Art of Balancing Work and Family," Sharon Reuben, *Nursing Times Newsletter*, JFK Medical Center, 2003.

9. "The Downtown School Community Report," Kelly Lacey and Jan Holmes Drees, Downtown School, 2000.

10. "Working Class Moms," Maria Padian, *Working Mother*, May 2001.

11. Ibid.

12. "Building Bridges," Brian Hanson-Harding, *Working Mother*, September 2000.

13. Ibid.

14. "Overwork in America," Ellen Galinsky et al., Families and Work Institute, 2001.

15. "Family Matters," *Working Mother*, May 2000.

16. "Building Bridges," Brian Hanson-Harding, *Working Mother*, September 2000.

17. Ibid.

Chapter Six

1. "Workplace," *Working Mother*, November 2001.
2. "The Ultimate Guide to Flexibility," Maggie Jackson, *Working Mother*, September 2004.
3. "One Flex-Timer's Story," *Working Mother*, December/January 2000.
4. "The Ultimate Guide to Flexibility," Maggie Jackson, *Working Mother*, September 2004.
5. "Flexibility in Corporate America: The Business Case for Expansion," Corporate Voices for Working Families, 2005.
6. "Fair Shares," Abby Margolis-Newman, *Working Mother*, February 2002.
7. "Designing Women," Helene Stapinski, *Working Mother*, October 2003.
8. "Flexibility in Corporate America: The Business Case for Expansion," Corporate Voices for Working Families, 2005.
9. Ibid.
10. Ibid.
11. "Balancing Act Spotlight," *Working Mother*, April 2000.
12. "Flex Is Not Enough," Hilary Davidson, *Working Mother*, March 2002.
13. "Making Telecommuting Work," Susan Wells, *HR Magazine*, October 2001.
14. Ibid.
15. 2004 Benefits Survey, Society for Human Resource Management.
16. "You've Made It Through the Diapers, Playdates and Field Trips—Now What?," Maggie Jackson, *Working Mother*, October 2003.
17. Ibid.
18. "Why Do You Work?," Jennifer Gill, *Working Mother*, June/July 2003.

Chapter Seven

1. "Welcome to the Clubhouse," Jennifer Gill, *Working Mother*, April 2003.
2. "Dallas Moms Really Know How to Rock," *Working Mother*, December/January 2005.
3. "Philly Artists Cooperate and Create," *Working Mother*, October 2004.
4. "What's for Dinner?," Victoria Scanlan Stefanakos, *Working Mother*, May 2004.
5. "Moms on a Mission," Julia Lawlor, *Working Mother*, February 2004.
6. "Widen Your Circle of Friends," Jennifer Gill, *Working Mother*, February 2004.
7. "Women and Men in Corporate Leadership," Catalyst, 2004.

8. "Affinity Groups Can Make a Difference," *Working Mother*, October 2004.

9. *Madam Secretary*, Madeleine Albright, Miramax Books, 2003.

Chapter Eight

1. "Women, Work and Family: A Balancing Act," Issue Brief: An Update on Women's Health Policy, The Henry J. Kaiser Family Foundation, April 2003.

2. "Sick Day Solutions," Claire Whitcomb, *Working Mother*, November 2004.

3. "Childcare Illness Evaluation Guidelines Not Always Followed," Cincinnati Children's Hospital Medical Center, Press Release, 17 May 2005.

4. "Marcus Welby Goes to Day Care," Jennifer Gill, *Working Mother*, August 2003.

5. "The Cost and Characteristics of Family and Medical Leave," Issue Backgrounder: Contemporary Issues in Employment and Workplace Policy, Employment Policy Foundation, April 29, 2005.

6. "Caring for Your Aging Parents—and for Yourself," Sharman Stein, *Working Mother*, October 2004.

7. Ibid.

Chapter Nine

1. "Chart Your Own Course," Sarah Mahoney, *Working Mother*, August/September 2002.

2. "Generation and Gender in the Workplace," Families and Work Institute and American Business Collaboration, 2003.

3. "Trusting Dad," Lynnell Mickelsen, *Working Mother*, June 2004.

4. "Paternal Involvement in Child Caregiving and Infant Sociability," France Frascarolo, *Infant Mental Health Journal*, November/December 2004.

5. *Fathers' Involvement in Their Children's Schools*, U.S. Department of Education, National Center for Education Statistics, 1997.

6. "National Study of the Changing Workforce," Families and Work Institute, 2003.

7. "Generation and Gender in the Workplace," Families and Work Institute and American Business Collaboration, 2003.

8. Ibid.

9. U.S. Census Bureau, Current Population Survey, Annual Demographic Supplements, 2001.

10. "Bringing Home More Bacon Can Really Burn," Ellyn Spragins, *Working Mother*, October 2002.

Chapter Eleven

1. "Women-Owned Business in 2004: Trends in the U.S. and 50 States," Center for Women's Business Research, April 2004.

2. "Self-Employed Business Ownership Rates," Robert W. Fairlie, University of Santa Cruz, U.S. Small Business Administration, December 2004.

3. "Internal Combustion," Jennifer Gill, *Working Mother*, August/September 2002.

4. "Why Do You Work?," Jennifer Gill, *Working Mother*, June/July 2003.

5. "A Business of Her Own," as told to Heather Chaplin, *Working Mother*, October 2004.

6. "From Home Biz to Big Biz," Margaret Littman, *Working Mother*, April 2002.

7. "Can Cooking Really Make You This Happy?," Jennifer Gill, *Working Mother*, February 2003.

8. "You Inc.," Melinda Cross and Gretchen Effler, *Working Mother*, June 2001.

9. Ibid.

10. "Letters," *Working Mother*, November 2003.

11. "Parents and Children in Stay-at-Home Family Groups," U.S. Census Bureau, Fertility and Family Statistics Branch, 2002.

12. "Chart Your Own Course," Sarah Mahoney, and "Taking a Sabbatical," Marjorie Ingall, *Working Mother*, August/September 2002.

13. "Women and Men in U.S. Corporate Leadership," Catalyst, 2004.

Chapter Twelve

1. From *Leave the Office Earlier*, Laura Stack, in *Working Mother*, May 2004.

2. "Overwork in America: When the Way We Work Becomes Too Much," Families and Work Institute, 2005.

3. "Raising a Ruckus," Heather Chaplin, *Working Mother*, May 2004.

4. "Moms Get a Playdate," Jennifer Gill, *Working Mother*, March 2004.

5. "Factor in Some Fun," Victoria Scanlan Stefanakos, *Working Mother*, March 2004.

6. "Room at the Table," Anndee Hochman, *Working Mother*, December/January 2004.

7. "Newsbreak," *Working Mother*, December/January 2005.